THE SPLITS

*A Chronicle of
Conflicts in a Young Man's Life*

A MEMOIR

BORIS RUMNEY

The Splits

All rights reserved. This book contains material protected under International and Federal Copyright Laws and Treaties. Boris Rumney has asserted his right under the Copyright, Designs and Patents Act, 1988, to be identified as Author of this Work. Any unauthorized reprint or use of the original material written by Boris Rumney is prohibited: these sections of the book may not be reproduced or transmitted in any form or by any means, electronic or mechanical, including photocopying, recording, or by any information storage and retrieval system without express written permission from the author/publisher.
This edition first published in August 2016.

Copyright © 2016 Boris Rumney

ISBN-13:978-1535289214
ISBN-10:153528921X

Dedication

First and foremost to Rona
for her patience and for pricking my
propensity to pomposity and prolixity in the
writing of this book but also to Stephen, Tanya, Ben,
Fabio, Gabriel, Susannah and Esther for whom it was written.

Acknowledgments

Blake Morrison, Francis Spufford,
Michael Goldman, Jack Fox, Tony Denning,
Nadine Smith, Arnold Wesker, Janet Denny, Maggie Smith,
Greg Watts, Rebecca Milligan and Tom Thompson. My special thanks and gratitude to Stephen Rumney for his support, time and creativity in the design and production of this book.

CONTENTS

THE SPLITS 1

CONTENTS 3

PROLOGUE 6

1. FIRST LINES 7

2. THE GAME OF THE NAME 8

3. A DIVIDED HOUSE 11

4. A DIFFERENT KIND 15

5. PATRIARCH, PEDAGOGUE AND POET 16

6. ALBION ROAD STOKE NEWINGTON 19

7. THE OUTSIDE WORLD 22

8. MY FATHER – A CLEVER FOOL   PART 1 26

9. INTRODUCTION TO JUDAISM 30

10. CHARLTON ROAD BLACKHEATH 37

11. CONVALESCENT HOME 41

12. BACK TO CHARLTON ROAD 44

13. AND THEN BACK TO STOKE NEWINGTON 46

14. EVACUATION 50

15. LIVERPOOL 54

16. WEST KIRBY 61

17. CALDAY GRAMMAR SCHOOL 69

18. LETCHWORTH AND HITCHIN GRAMMAR SCHOOL 1942-43 75

19. LETCHWORTH 1943-45 80

20. MY FATHER – A CLEVER FOOL   PART 2 83

21. PASSIONS 1943-46 87

22. CONTEMPORANEOUS EVIDENCE: 1946 95

23. SIXTH FORM (1946-47) 105

24. NAOMI 113

25. SIXTH FORM (1947-8) 117

26. WAITING FOR CALL TO ARMS	123
27. OLD FRIEND	125
28. ARMY LIFE: TRAINING	130
29. KINMEL PARK	138
30. STRIFE AND STRIVING	149
31. MY FATHER – A CLEVER FOOL PART 3	157
32. LONDON SCHOOL OF ECONOMICS YEAR 1	159
33. LONDON SCHOOL OF ECONOMICS YEAR 2	173
34. LONDON SCHOOL OF ECONOMICS YEAR 3	179
35. MY FATHER – A CLEVER FOOL PART 4	183
36. GAP MONTHS	185
37. ARTICLES – PART 1	188
38. ARTICLES – PART 2	194
39. CONTEMPORANEOUS EVIDENCE: 1955	197
40. A VERY BAD THING	201
41. LAST LAP TO QUALIFICATION	205
42. PARIS 1956	207
43. FIRST JOB	211
44. MAIDA VALE	214
45. SOLE PRACTITIONER	217
46. BETTER LUCK NEXT TIME	224
EPILOGUE	225

PROLOGUE

Current thinking on the development of the male sex, puts twenty-eight as the age at which the man becomes a fully developed human being. By chance, twenty-eight is the age at which I bring my memoir to an end. It is a story of myself as an ordinary boy into man who had to negotiate his way between the numerous conflicting forces and influences, both external and internal, which burdened him from his earliest years. Anglo-Jew and the difficulties of integrating the Anglo and the Jew. A paternal family where intellectual and academic brilliance was the attribute most admired and celebrated and a maternal one, uneducated, where industry, reliability and earning a living were the paramount virtues. An unreliable, absent father both loved and resented and a parental couple whose relationship and separations impacted so adversely on me. Added to this were the usual pangs of adolescence, burgeoning sexuality and the yearning for love, the desire to succeed and be noticed in an uncaring and competitive world and hardest of all, the struggle to create an authentic identity.

But this is no misery memoir. I did not retreat into melancholy or depression. I believe that I had sufficient resilience to enable me to transcend setbacks and disappointments and throw myself into new activities and enthusiasms. I have tried to write an honest, unsparing, warts-and-all account of the first twenty-eight years of my life.

1. FIRST LINES

I was born on the 10th of February 1930 at the City of London Maternity Hospital within sound of Bow Bells. While my mother was in labour my father was stealing her jewellery to pay his gambling debts.

2. THE GAME OF THE NAME

My father having been born in Poland was a foreigner, and so was I. He did not become a British subject until he was naturalised in 1934. This had the effect of naturalising me too. The family name was Rumyaneck. It was not until I was six that the final form of our surname, Rumney, was settled on. Traditionally all Jewish children were given a Hebrew name which in many cases were anglicised at birth. My father's name was Mordecai, my mother's, Shifra; these later became Max and Sophie. My Hebrew name was Baruch but Boris was the name I was given. Some Anglicisation! For much of my early life I hated this name and could not understand how my parents could have failed to foresee what discomforts it would cause me. My mother was an intelligent and sensitive woman but she did have her blind spots, a residual foreignness. In my first year at grammar school I was the only boy who wore woollen underwear knitted by her. As soon as this was spotted in the changing rooms I was an object of derision and hilarity. From my very first year at primary (then called 'elementary') school, four years old, my classmates catcalled Boris Karloff, the most famous Hollywood horror movie actor of the 1930s or more humiliating still, Doris or Horace. Even now, some, misremembering my name, greet me with Basil. When I was eleven, for reasons quite obscure to me, our maths teacher Bill Bowker dubbed me Rudolf. Perhaps there was to his ear some Ruritanian association between that name and mine or he just liked the alliterative effect of Rudolf Rumney. Whatever the origins, I was for much of the rest of my school life known to all as Rudolf the Red Nosed Reindeer. I poured out the pain and shame of the teasing I had endured in a poem which I wrote in my mid-fifties called *I'll Tell You What's in a Name!* which ends with the following lines:

> *To give a name like Boris was crime enough*
> *Against a boy brought up the English way,*
> *Who wanted nothing more*
> *Than merge in the crowd,*
> *Unnoticed, not stand out,*
> *Wear grey shirt, school blazer, dark blue mac,*
> *And best of all to bear a name like Jack.*

Jack, the name I so envied, was that of my best friend Jack Fox. What I did not know at the time was that he was born Yaakov Fuchs. Jacob Fuchs to Jack Fox – a happier name change than mine.

Baruch in Hebrew means 'Blessed'. If you are blessed it means you are special and that is a terrible burden to impose on your child. You don't want to start by being special, you want to start ordinary – like Jack Fox – and build on that. By Jewish tradition I was special simply by reason of my sex and position in the family. I was a male child. I was the first son of the first son. I was the first grandchild of both sets of grandparents. And I remained an only child. I was adored and spoilt by my aunts and uncles. I retained my primacy in the family hierarchy for four years until my cousin Michael was born but regained it when his parents emigrated to America a year later. The weight of expectation on me was too heavy to bear, particularly as it became more and more clear as I got older that I was turning out to be an unexceptional little boy.

They did not leave me with Baruch but why not a more English alternative like Bernard, say, rather than Boris? Too ordinary maybe? My name still arouses curiosity. "Are you Russian?" "Yes," I reply quite truthfully, "Both sets of my grandparents emigrated from the Imperial Russian Empire before the First World War".

When I was seventeen I romanticised my origins by claiming to friends that when I was born my mother was a Russian ballerina living in Paris. This story certainly impressed my first girlfriend, Naomi Epps – originally Nechemah Epstein.

I've only met one other Boris – a neighbour Boris Sackville (formerly Sakharov) but until the advent of Boris Johnson, it was not a name you came across very often in England. We frequently spotted each other coming off the train at Blackheath Station and from a distance one would call out "Hi, Boris", the other reply "Hi, Boris". Dozens of heads would swivel in our direction. They must have thought we were crazy.

Very little about my family history is straightforward; even the origin of Rumyaneck is shrouded in ambiguity. The word 'rumianek' is Polish for camomile. When in my late teens I asked my father for an explanation, he said, "You've got to understand, my boy, that your grandfather Aaron came from a long rabbinic line. One of them had healing powers and women of his congregation would go to him with their ailments. And for whatever the complaint, he had a universal panacea – camomile. So he became known as Reb Rumianek – Rabbi Camomile."

Although my father was a great romancer and fantasist, I both believed and loved that story. My cousin David was sceptical. His more prosaic explanation was that one of our forebears somewhere in Poland had been a smallholder who cultivated camomile commercially for use both as beverage and medicine.

In my twenties, I reproached my father, "Why did you change our name? Rumyaneck has both character and poetry."

"I didn't want to", he replied, "But I kept getting letters addressed to Mr. Maxie Maniac and felt enough was enough."

For about a year my parents experimented with Romaine until the name Rumney was finally settled on. My grandparents remained Aaron and Esther Rumyaneck; one half of the family followed my father's choice, the other half opted for the more aristocratic Romney.

Because Rumney is the anglicised version of a town to the east of Cardiff I am sometimes asked if my family come from South Wales. Such muddles make me feel like reverting to my truly rooted name, Baruch Rumyaneck.

3. A DIVIDED HOUSE

From the age of two until I was seven, I lived with my parents and my maternal grandparents, Simon and Rose Dushman (born Simeon Dushina and Shoshana Hatchik) in Albion Road, Stoke Newington. We spent most of our time in a large basement room, which served as kitchen, laundry, dining room and playroom. This was Grandma's domain and the heart of family life. Shelves contained jars of fermenting black cherries soon to be cherry brandy, pickling cucumbers and curdling milk, the latter a great delicacy, but not to me. I ate, played and drew at the large oilcloth covered table. It was there that I discovered the pleasures of being read to and then of reading on my own, comics of the time, *Tiny Tots* and *Chicks' Own* and when I was six, sign of increasing seniority and sophistication, *Rainbow* and *Tiger Tim*. Here I was bathed in a tin bath and my hair washed, roughly and impatiently by my mother and gently and lovingly by Grandma.

During these years Grandma was in her fifties but I thought of her as a very old lady, always encased in a shapeless pinafore dress which divested her of all womanliness and made her look stouter than she was. Slow moving and soft voiced she spoke English well but with a heavy Jewish, Eastern European accent. Although an untutored lady, she was bright; unlike my grandfather, she had taught herself to read English and was an avid reader of the *Daily Mirror*. But mainly she poured her energies into producing the finest Jewish cuisine. Friday was Sabbath eve and at nightfall we all gathered at the kitchen table.

The religious formalities out of the way, cold fried fish (halibut, haddock, plaice), or cold gefilte fish, most commonly carp, minced, patted and rolled into balls and poached – "Mind the bones darling!" – was served accompanied by *chrain*, a pungent sauce made from a mixture of ground horseradish and cooked beetroot.

Saturday lunch was the meal of the week. For me it started on Friday morning when my grandmother brought home the freshly slaughtered broiler chicken and I watched her with rapt attention as she opened up and eviscerated the still warm fowl. She then separated out the giblets: heart, liver, kidneys, feet and shell-less, half-formed, all-yellow eggs. These were all thrown into the pot with the cut-into-pieces chicken carcass, neck and feet, carrots, turnips, onions and *petrouchka* [parsley root] added and all boiled into a soup. At lunch vermicelli was added to make the incomparable *lokshen* soup; as the old joke has it, Jewish penicillin. After soup, the boiled chicken was parcelled out and served up with vegetables. The smallest portion was reserved for me. I noticed things like that even then. They were my early experiences of hierarchies and inequality on which my later socialism was founded. Baked apples with raisins for finishers; finishing the adults off, they staggered to bed for their *shobbes schlaf,* Sabbath sleep, leaving me, bored, to amuse myself at the kitchen table.

Up a flight to the ground floor of this end of a terrace of three houses, built by Thomas Cubitt in the 1820s. Here was the business owned by Grandpa and my uncle Percy, making up women's outer clothing. This was a busy place, noisy with the buzz of a bank of six sewing machines and the clump and hissing steam of the 7lb iron wielded by the presser.

Uncle Percy's skill was in arranging pieces of stiff, brown paper, the template of a dress or coat, in the most economic pattern over several layers of cloth, before using his large tailor's shears to cut out the sections used to make up of the garments. By dint of this geometric talent, he was able to make, say, eighteen garments out of a given roll of cloth where the manufacturer had estimated for a maximum of sixteen only. By the custom of the trade the extra two garments were known as *cabbage* and were the outdoor tailors' to keep as their own.

My thimbled grandpa, a tape measure round his neck and his mouth full of pins, sat on a table, nimbly sewing the seams, hems and lapels of coats and costumes. One of seven children, at the age of seven his education was brought to an end and he was recruited full-time into his father's tailoring business. Grandpa was short in height but sturdy. Always dapper and smartly turned out in grey tweed suits, collar and tie, right up until his death at the age of ninety-six. He had a soft, nut-brown face, toothbrush moustache and round glasses to correct short sight caused by such close work from so early an age. His voice was thick and with an incorrigible foreign accent; though a man of few words, the words he uttered were law both in workplace and home. Much later in life after watching *Othello* on television his sole comment was "*Voss voz dot mit der henkerchiff?*" [What was that with the handkerchief?]

The workshop for me was a place of endless fascination and a cornucopia of playthings: scissors, thimbles, cotton reels, buttons and several mannequins, full bosomed and full hipped, on rotatable stands instead of legs, which I twirled and spun round and round and swathed in discarded offcuts of lining material and woollen cloth. Best of all was the secure feeling of being surrounded by benevolent adults, tolerant of my curiosity and childish pursuits.

My parents' flat was on the second floor and consisted of kitchen, living room and their bedroom, in which I slept until the age of seven. I always had tea in the kitchen and enjoyed that cosy and intimate time with my mother, intensified by a table containing my favourite things: buttered *Hovis* toast and a soft boiled egg, two chocolate fingers and jelly and custard. After tea I'd go off on my own to the living room to listen to Henry Hall's band on the wireless. His signature tune, *Here's to theNext Time* and the 1934 hits *Who's Afraid of the Big Bad Wolf* and *I Love You, Yes I Do* were particular favourites, still embedded in my memory.

I adored my mother. She was beautiful. Petite, with long raven-black hair, vivid, expressive features, energetic and with great vitality - when thirteen she had won the London Schoolgirls 100 yards' sprint. She was loving to me but fiery tempered and unpredictable. All was going well, we were on the best of terms, I was being a good boy and then I would do something to displease or anger her and out of the blue, she would slap my face hard. It hurt and continued to sting for several minutes. But far worse it damaged my sense of myself. Without having any notion of what I had done wrong I had become a bad boy.

On my fourth birthday one of the tiny lifeboats attached to a model liner, a present from an aunt, was lost somewhere between being handed to me at the front door of the house and our flat. I searched and searched, running up and down the dimly-lit, uncarpeted stairs many times without any luck. I still mourn the loss of that lifeboat. It stands as a paradigm for all the many objects I have lost over time.

It was bedtime. My parents wanted to go to the pictures. I lay in my cot and I cried and I cried. "I don't want you to go." My mother got very angry and tore up my *Chicks Own* because I'd been a bad boy. I was very upset because she had only read me two of the stories. I wept myself to sleep.

About the same time, I had a dream that an ogre came to eat me up. My father told me that dreams that frightened you were called nightmares. The dream woke me up and I shouted for Mummy and Daddy. My father came in, picked me up, held me very tight and carried me into the living room. The light was on, the fire was burning and I felt a huge sense of warmth and security, sitting on my father's lap. This was my father at his best: warm and loving. I did not yet know him at his worst. Nor do I have any sense of him as a constant presence in the house. Perhaps he was at business (as my parents called work) and I was in bed before he got home or, knowing what I know now, he was engaged in monkey business. Shortly after his death in 1981, I wrote a poem:

> *Dads don't die, they're rocks, big rocks*
> *Designed to save their sons from knocks.*

Potent portents of the man you hope to be,
The twig that fell not far from the tree.
For me it was more complicated,
Though basic genes were replicated
He stayed to me a lifelong riddle,
Elusive, split right down the middle,
One half, clever, bright, a real charmer,
The other, gambler, liar, serial harmer.

I was six. There was palpable tension in the house. I picked up titbits. Adolf Hitler was to make a major speech that night. My parents were going to listen to it on the radio. I would be in bed by then. I understood something very grown-up was going on but did not know what. I was in bed but still awake. Coming from the living room I could hear Hitler's harsh voice and the huge roars of applause and *'sieg heiling'*. I did not understand one word but somehow I knew it was bad.

4. A DIFFERENT KIND

Every Saturday after lunch my parents and I would walk the mile or so to 63, Downs Road, Clapton, the home of my father's parents, Aaron and Esther Rumyaneck. The whole family and assorted friends congregated there. Picture a typical occasion in, say, early 1934. Hubbub, tumult, clamour. I bang away discordantly on the piano. My father is playing chess with a younger brother, the only silent ones present, though there'll be plenty of passionate argument when the game is over. Uncles Judah and Sam and uncle-by-marriage-to-be, Alf are discussing – which really means shouting each other down - the utter failure of the National Government to implement even the most milk-and-water socialist policies. Aaron, whom I knew as Zaida, to distinguish him from Grandpa Simon, is declaiming to anyone who'll listen, verses from his poem, *Hitler's Glocken Klangen* [Hitler's Bells Are Ringing], taking occasional time out to roll his special Turkish cigarettes.

Esther, Buba, to me, and her daughters (my aunts, Rosa and Ray), my mother and various fiancées, girlfriends and female relatives chatter animatedly in Yiddish (Buba having no English despite having lived in England for thirty years) while they prepare tea: crusty black rye bread, chopped liver, chopped hardboiled egg and onions, bagels, smoked salmon, cream cheese, various types of herring and large black olives bought straight from the barrel. A banquet of my favourite foods. As the family begins to tuck in the noise abates but only a little.

5. PATRIARCH, PEDAGOGUE & POET

Too late to fully chronicle the life of Aaron Rumyaneck. There are so many gaps. He died in 1945 when I was 15, then too young and uninterested to ferret out the facts of his remarkable life. He was born in 1878 in Bialystok, a town in north-eastern Poland, with a population of 66,000 of which three quarters were Jewish. During the 1880s and 1890s the Jewish community thrived culturally and intellectually, and socialist and Zionist organisations multiplied. In particular, during this period the study and use of Hebrew as a living (rather than biblical) language became popular amongst those who supported Zionism or were intending to emigrate to Palestine.

Nothing is known about Aaron's family, his early years, his education or the development of his ideas. But as a child and young man he must have been a remarkably talented scholar who probably obtained his mastery of Hebrew, biblical and Talmudic studies at a *yeshiva* [religious college].

Early in his adult life he became a peripatetic teacher. Records show that he stayed in a number of Polish towns with Jewish populations, among them Blonie, where his eldest son, my father, was born, and Sochaczew where a prominent Jewish family put him up in their courtyard and where he taught students biblical subjects and Hebrew and also established a Zionist study group. A report states that 'because of him the first scandal broke out between the observant Jews and Zionists who interpreted his words, which injured the honour of the observant Jews.' The meaning of this is obscure and I can only speculate that the observant Jews disapproved of Zionist aspirations in the way in which ultra-orthodox Jews in Mea Sherim, Jerusalem, today refuse to recognise the authority or existence of Israel as a state.

At some point he fetched up in Turek where his third-born, my Uncle Sam, was born. A history of the Jews in Turek recounts that Aaron, 'a leading pedagogue, was recruited to satisfy a continuing thirst for knowledge and assisted by able instructors, Mr. Rumyaneck's classes revolutionised the entire teaching system. His courses included Hebrew and Jewish literature, mathematics and the Talmud. Notable scholars emerged from that school.' A receipt dated 1908 sent to him in Turek for a donation to the *Odessa Committee for the Support of the Children of Israel Working the Land in Syria and Mastering Crafts in Syria and the Holy Land* shows his continuing Zionist belief that the Jewish problem could be solved only by the return of the Jewish people to the land of Israel – apparently expanded to include Syria!

The family eventually came to England some time between 1908 and 1910. Whether this was because Aaron had secured a teaching job in Leeds or because of the pogroms which swept through Poland in 1905-6, I cannot say. Bialystok was worst hit with 66 people killed and 60 injured.

Aaron was appointed headmaster of a *Talmud Torah* [religious school] in Leeds and by then the father of six children, he tried to supplement his low salary through at least two unsuccessful business ventures: *A. Rumyaneck, Woollen and General Manufacturers' Agent (telegrams: Pracmattia, Leeds)* and *The Oriental Cigarette Comp, Expert Tobacco Blenders, Cigarette Manufacturers & Cigar Merchants* whose logo consisted of a star within a crescent moon, both within a Star of David. He also ran a herring delivery business.

My father spoke little of his early days as a small foreign boy but two memories particularly stood out for him: reading comics beneath the bedclothes by torchlight as a way of learning English and being hauled out of bed at 6am for Hebrew studies under Aaron's tutelage and then delivering deli herrings to Aaron's customers before getting off to school.

Did Aaron lose or leave his teaching post because of his Zionist views or some other arcane religious or political difference? He was an officer of the Leeds branch of the *League for Jewish Emancipation*, an organisation first created in 1914 to further Zionist aspirations through political action and this may have been considered incompatible with the religious principles of the Talmud Torah of which he was principal. But I can think of no other reason why he left Leeds for Hackney in about 1925 other than economic hardship.

And it was in Hackney that at the age of four I first got to know him, a short, portly, shambly man with a crumpled face. Always unshaven, grey stubble covering his face, he greeted me by nuzzling his bristly cheeks against mine. His voice was throaty and phlegmy, brought on by smoking too many cigars and cigarettes of his own manufacture. He spoke to me of matters of which I had not the faintest comprehension. I believe that his scholarly interests had stripped him of all understanding of how to engage with children. I both feared and was fascinated by him.

Aaron had the unhealthy look of a man who rarely left the house. I never saw him out of doors. During the Saturday afternoon gatherings, some of the family with me in tow, would take a walk on Hackney Downs but Aaron never accompanied us. As far as I know from the time he left Leeds until his death he had no earned income of any kind and I can only assume that he and Esther were supported by those of his children who could afford it.

His main achievement during this period was the publication in 1933 of his privately printed epic poem *Hitler's Bells Are Ringing*. With remarkable prescience this work prophesied the destruction of the Jews by the Nazis and that Germany would go to war against Britain and France. As he saw it, the political solution for the Jews, was the establishment of a Jewish state in Palestine and for the world at large, the total boycott of German goods. He must have been influenced by a pamphlet published by *Captain Webber's Boycott Organisation in London* in 1933 which proclaimed: 'Peace or War – which shall it be? Hitler's policy in Germany a grave danger to world peace. Do your duty – boycott German goods – buy British and give more work to British unemployed'.

Such a boycott was during this period supported by various Zionist, trade union and socialist organisations in USA, Britain and Poland. Ironically its successful implementation was scuppered by the appeasing actions of more conservative Jewish organisations and the whole enterprise fizzled out. Some commentators and historians have expressed the view that if such a boycott had been successfully enforced, the Nazi government would have collapsed because of the economic crisis which would have followed.

I tell you, England, I warn you Frenchmen
My path to victory is strewn with roses.
My army is mighty, the legions are strong.
Hocus-Pocus – One Two! That is my goal
To destroy everything that lives
Peacefully with the Jew – rulers of nations…

In towns, death marches, evil spirits cry out
Elsewhere, in camps, cruelly the dead fall
Like ears of corn in a field – endless
Here, there, death and murder
Hocus-Pocus, One Two! Provoke, martyrs, every party
Jews, Christians, all alike, but first the Jews.

(Excerpt from *Hitler's Bells Are Ringing*
translated anonymously from the Yiddish)

6. ALBION ROAD STOKE NEWINGTON

The large front room of the first floor was the equivalent of the parlour. It was never used either for living in or entertaining. Dust sheets covered all the furniture except for a large wind-up cabinet gramophone in which my mother kept her shellac records. She sometimes played these to me; mainly Strauss waltzes and Caruso singing arias from the Italian operas. I feel as if I have known *The Blue Danube*, *La Donna e Mobile* and *Your Tiny Hand Is Frozen* for ever. This was the room to which I often escaped to spend time on my own.

It held a powerful fascination for me. I was not barred from entering it but it did feel like forbidden, alien territory, so silent and bleak compared to the vitality and busyness of the rest of the house. Winter or summer it felt cold and with its long draped curtains always drawn, perpetually shrouded in gloom.

On one occasion when I was about five or six, I entered the room and found myself attracted by my reflection in the uncovered full length mirror. I stared at myself as if at a stranger. What I saw was a handsome, serious-faced little boy with dark brown, wavy hair, brown eyes, wearing a long-sleeved brown pullover. I was in a brown study, almost a trancelike state as I became lost in the image of my own gaze and felt as if I was on the point of experiencing some revelation, a presence, an intimation of some kind. Still in this state, I was summoned downstairs, the moment shattered but I've often wondered about its meaning. Perhaps it was the dawning of self-awareness, of the consciousness of my own separate existence; more prosaic than being vouchsafed the secret of life but still an important developmental step. I was on the necessary road of separating from my parents, ceasing to be their little boy, their creature and embarking on the hard task of becoming an individual in my own right.

This was indeed a lost moment, and I often wonder whether the apprehension of something to be revealed was intuitively true or merely a childish illusion. To try to understand it better, possibly even recapture the moment, I stand in front of a full-length mirror for several minutes staring into my eyes. The experiment is an utter failure. I cannot reconnect with my child self. All I see is a face familiar from thousands of shaves, hundreds of haircuts; the face of an old man with lined, Semitic features and with the disagreeable look one sees in so many aged faces. A face I recognise as mine but which seems to bear very little relation to the eager flames of hope and curiosity which still burn brightly within me. And the sadness is that although that boy still lives on, too many years and too much living makes it impossible for me to speak his words, his memories. Try as I might I am unable to get inside him, imagine what he thought about the life he was living or what his opinions were or indeed, whether he had any.

My impressions were of the most primitive kind: I loved and needed the parental figures around me, adored going out, particularly on buses, trams or trains, enjoyed my food, being read and sung to, listening to music on the radio, rushing out to the Walls' 'STOP ME AND BUY ONE' tricyclist. Also playing in a desultory kind of way, I rode my red front wheel pedal tricycle. I had a fort and lead soldiers, a platoon of two dozen scarlet-coated, busbied Grenadier Guards, some standing, others kneeling, or lying flat on their stomachs; all with their rifles at the ready. It was clear that I was not officer material by the lack of flair with which I deployed my little army. I marched them up the castle ramp and I marched them down again, *bang bang bang* and it was all over. Because of my careless handling of them, my poor Guardsmen suffered friendly fire injuries and losses of their heads and rifles and in the case of the standers and kneelers the bases on which they balanced.

I had a small windup gramophone and one record which I played again and again.

> *Little man, you're crying, I know why you're blue,*
> *Someone stole your kiddie car away.*
> *You'd better go to sleep now,*
> *Little man you've had a busy day*
>
> *Put away your soldiers, the battle has been won*
> *The enemy is put to flight*
> *It's time to go to bed now, your busy day is done.*
> *The war is over for tonight.*

In my case it was: *Put away your soldiers, the battle has been lost.*

I had a profusion of pencils and crayons and drew and coloured unimaginatively, trains, boats, aeroplanes, houses, always the same, never improving. Art was the only subject I failed in my O-level examination. My favourite toy was a clockwork train set which went round and round the single circular track. I longed for a more complex system, particularly a junction or two for greater variety and so that I could control the train's direction but this was a yearning which like so many of my childhood desires was never realised.

In part I put my lack of creativity in play down to being an only child. There were advantages of course. I had no rivals to usurp my little princedom. I had a monopoly of my parents' love but the weight of their focus on and their expectations of me – to be good, to be clever, to be successful – were too much to bear. My mother told me that if she were to have a little girl she would call her Miriam so for several years I waited for the arrival of my little sister but she never came and for the whole of my life I have carried an image of Miriam, the sister I never had, somewhere in my memory backpack: what being an only child meant for me in those early years was being a solitary child. I never had a playmate and the lack of stimulus did not fuel my creativity but stultified it. I think I was a child who craved action, going to the park, the fun of the children's playground. As the firstborn I had no cousins to visit and play with. I cannot remember any time whilst I lived in Albion Road visiting or being visited by other children for a play date.

My earliest memory is of sitting, possibly in my pushchair, in the garden which had a lawn kept trim by my grandfather who also tended the hollyhocks and roses which were the first flowers I ever knew the names of. It was a perfect summer's day and it was the azure blue sky which had my rapt attention. There were kites in the sky over Clissold Park and biplanes hauling advertising slogans and skywriting leaving trails of words I could not yet read. It was in this garden that my father conducted for my eyes an experiment to demonstrate 'nature red in tooth and claw'. Showing remarkable hand-to-eye coordination, he caught a fly in midair and then holding it delicately by one wing, placed it on a spider's web. With a twig he captured the spider as it rushed out to anaesthetise and bundle up its prey and placed it in a stoppered bottle. He repeated this process and we then watched the two captive spiders fight each other to the death. I was horrified but fascinated. I never knew whether my father had put on this show as a lesson in natural science, to show off his physical dexterity or as an expression of an innate sadism. It certainly constellated something quite voyeuristic in me. Although he was no angel, I can recall no other example of deliberate acts of cruelty on his part. In his relationship with me, I experienced him as benign; perhaps he found his attacking style of chess as a legitimate outlet for his aggressive impulses.

7. THE OUTSIDE WORLD

My mother took me shopping in Stoke Newington High Street, to boring Marks & Spencer for items of clothing and to exciting Woolworths where I would drag her reluctantly to the toy counter. Those I would beg for were the superbly engineered model cars, planes and other technological wonders of German manufacture.

"You can't have one. Look, here's a nice colouring book."

"Why can't I have one?"

"Because I say so. They're made in Germany and we're Jewish and the Germans hate the Jews."

"Why do the Germans hate the Jews?"

"Enough Boris. If you don't keep quiet, you won't get a thing."

So off I went, disgruntled, none the wiser, clutching 'a nice colouring book'.

It was in Stoke Newington High Street that I had my first lesson in law. Seeing a policeman pass, I asked my mother what the folded cloth object slung across his shoulder was. 'It's a sack to put naughty boys in and take them to the Police Station.' It was in fact a cape. Was I terrified? I don't think so. I wasn't a naughty boy; they were the rough, ragged non-Jewish boys I was forbidden contact with. Anyway I wasn't rough. I was always clean and neatly dressed. But the threat did help instil in me a respect for the law – except for minor tax dodges – which has lasted all my life. I would have made a good policeman.

I loved it when my mother took me to nearby Clissold Park, originally the landscaped grounds of a grand Georgian mansion. There were deer and a menagerie of rabbits, goats and peacocks and a boating lake. After a cursory look at the rabbits – 'Look, aren't they sweet, darling!' – I tugged my mother away towards the playground where she helped me climb into one of the cradled infants' swings and did what all mothers do, to my exuberant joy in the rising and falling motions. Higher! Higher! I always felt shortchanged. Impatient to move on, she never wanted to keep going for long enough to satisfy my desire for more. A couple of slides and, too soon, we were off, back across the park to tea and Henry Hall's dance band.

On one occasion, my mother uncharacteristically left me in the sandpit in the charge of another mother. Freed from her restrictive presence, I played with other children in the pit and was having the time of my life when she returned and found my hair, ears clothes and the rest of me drenched in sand. After venting her fury on the poor woman who had been looking after me, she yanked me homewards, telling me off for getting in such a state. Bewildered and downcast, as usual I did not know what I was supposed to have done wrong. What did she expect, I now ask, but back then I was her creature, her little Boris. I had been a 'bad boy', guilty as charged.

At weekends it was my grandfather who took me to the park. His was a more sedate pace than my mother's who always seemed in a hurry, with me trotting at her side. He made for the bandstand enclosure where we could sit on dark-green slatted seats to hear whatever brass or military band was playing that day. I loved those occasions and got to know much popular music: medleys from Gilbert and Sullivan, marches, polkas and tunes from the 1914-18 war, *Tipperary*, *Pack up your Troubles* and touchingly sentimental, *Keep the Home Fires Burning*. Though most of our time together was spent in silence, I felt safe and secure in his presence. He wasn't exciting like my mother but he wasn't excitable either.

The house next door to ours was the factory/family residence of Mr Pollard who manufactured fur clothing: coats, jackets and fox fur stoles. I had the impression that they were far wealthier and more successful than our family. They certainly kept their distance from us and that may have been because, unlike my grandparents, they were second or third generation Jews or Jews from Germany who looked down on *Litvaks*, that is Jews from Eastern Europe. Whatever the reason, there was no social contact between the two families which in my lonely state was a shame because there were two children: Sarah, several years older, but Alan was my junior by only five days. He would have been an ideal playmate. I used to see him playing with his sister in the next garden and pined to join them.

I also learnt the heartburn of envy from Alan. On his sixth birthday I spotted him riding his new tricycle, one with a saddle, pedals with a chain and brakes. I ached for such a trike; at that moment my own red trike with front wheel pedals became a despised object and I never rode it again. Alan was bigger and cleverer than me. We went to the same primary school and he had a natural ease and confidence, a coterie of friends and hangers-on, all of which consumed me with envious longing.

On the day after my seventh birthday I approached him in the school playground and said,

"I've had a good idea! Everybody gets a second birthday five days after their first."

Alan looked at me wide eyed. After a few seconds he replied in a voice suffused with contempt,

"That's the stupidest idea I've ever heard."

One morning, having turned four, I was catapulted into school life: Hawksley Road Elementary School, just round the corner from our house. There had been no warning or preparation but I settled in comfortably without any symptoms of separation or abandonment. Too comfortably from what my mother told me much later in life. Apparently I talked so much on that first day, the teacher asked my mother to take me away. She protested vehemently and I was allowed to stay. But my mother seemed to be in complete agreement with the teacher because imprinted in my psyche is her frequent complaint 'Boris, did anyone ever tell you that you talk too much?' And this from an indefatigable talker herself; perhaps she could not stand the competition. What I do realise now is that until I went to school I had had no experience of sharing and competing for space with other children and this was a lesson that I had slowly and painfully to learn.

I did well enough at school but my belief in my omniscience suffered a shock (the humiliation of the event still remains with me) when I volunteered to spell '*express*' and omitted the final 's' even though I had spent time practising the previous evening. My artistic incompetence and lack of creativity was confirmed by the constant comparisons I made between my stilted work and the imaginative, colourful paintings of my classmates. We sculpted in plasticine in which I showed the same stodgy stolidity, producing primitive boats or railway engines again and again. In adult life I wrote a poem about these experiences which ended with the lines:

> *When all I made looked like a turd*
> *No wonder that I chose the word.*

Things were no happier for me in the playground. At playtime, groups of kids played and sang songs and jingles but I remained firmly on the outside, knowing neither the rules of the games nor the words of the songs. The girls particularly seemed to have acquired a complex social sense and sophisticated knowledge of the world of which I was ignorant. They all seemed so confident in their handling of friendships and rivalries and in their mini-adult assurance. All I could do was watch and shuffle, chuff-chuff and choo-choo around the playground as a railway engine, moving my arms like pistons and emitting a hiss of steam noises, whilst yearning for acceptance into the community of my peers.

My sense of an unappreciated self was increased when my teacher adjudged that I had committed some misdemeanour deserving of punishment. Again, I have no memory of what I was supposed to have done wrong; after all my belief in myself was as *good boy*. Perhaps she experienced me as cheeky or impertinent, though my intention would only have been to please or impress. Whatever the offence had been, the punishment was the same as that which she administered to all naughty children. I was called to the front of the class, the right leg of my short pants raised up and I was slapped, hard, several times, on the back of my thigh. It was not so much the pain that hurt as the public humiliation. It was going home time and I ran off howling to my mother who was waiting for me at the school gates. She comforted me but once again the message had been conveyed to me that I was a 'bad boy'.

My ambition in my class was to be first, the chosen one. Not in an academic sense but first in alphabetical order, the first to say 'Present' when the register was called. As we sat in alphabetical order, it was Monty Abrahams, front left desk, who occupied the pole position. Changes of the family name being in the air, I devised a name for this purpose, Boris Abcdana. It never occurred to me that I would have been trumped by, say, a Ronnie Aaronovitch.

I wonder now where my father was during this period. Surely it was his job to introduce his son to the external world, to prepare him for the tasks that lay ahead. It's not that I have no sense of him, he obviously was a day-to-day presence in my family life but I have only a few recollections of spending time with him, being taken out or read to by him. Throughout my life so many of the outings he planned ended in disappointment, failure or worse still, disaster. At some point during the Albion Road period – I was about six – he decided to take me to the Monument in the City of London, built in 1677 and designed by Sir Christopher Wren to commemorate the Great Fire of London. When we arrived, my father made for the ticket office, discovered the clerk engaged in attempting to solve a chess problem and within minutes a board was out and set up and a game was in progress while I, fed up and bored, hung about for what seemed an eternity when the contest became the best of three. By the time the last game had ended dusk had fallen, it was closing time and without having climbed the 311 steps to the viewing platform for an all-round view of pre-blitz London, we set off in search of a bus home.

8. MY FATHER – A CLEVER FOOL
Part 1

I cannot grasp my father. Or pin him down. He eludes me, slides away, slippery customer that he was. All I can do is speculate in trying to make sense of his contradictions. He was born in Poland in 1901. At the age of 16, after matriculating at Leeds Grammar School, he came to London to study mathematics at Queen Mary College, in the East End of London, living at an uncle's nearby. Free from Aaron's rigours and rigidities, he neglected his studies and spent his days (and probably his nights too) playing chess and cards. He soon dropped out of college and earned a crust as a Hebrew teacher. Sometime in the early 1920s the Rumyaneck family moved en bloc to Old Hill Street, Stoke Newington where Max lived until he married my mother, Sophie, in 1927.

He met her at a Jewish young people's dating and mating place masquerading as a Zionist society. It wasn't surprising that she fell in love with him. Physically Max was no Adonis but he was good-looking, a little above medium height, bespectacled, neat-featured with a cupid's bow of a mouth and a dimple in his chin in which his mother claimed she used to lodge a pea when he was a child. Even more seductively, he was softly, melodiously spoken with the gift of the gab. He was a real *schmoozer* – that's 'talker' in Yiddish but its incorporation of 'ooze' is apt; he oozed charm from every pore. There was also a touch of flashiness and aggrandisement about him, particularly in social situations. When a bookkeeper he claimed to be an accountant, and after retirement pretended that he had been a teacher even though he had been one for only a short period as a young man.

Of course he could have been an accountant or a teacher. Or many other things. The world was his oyster but he failed to crack it open. There is a sense in which he was a truly tragic figure. He had fatal flaws. Immoderation. Impulsiveness. Risk-taking. This was manifested in his chess-playing preferences. The Queen's side opening was not for him; he had neither the stomach nor the capacity for the slow, obsessive and analytic skills required for such a game. He would always play a King's side gambit instead, with its greater opportunities for brilliant attacking strategies, the showier the better. The apotheosis of his game was a Queen sacrifice followed by a checkmate, two or three moves later. He was county champion of Hertfordshire in 1948 and 1949 and I followed him around during both the eliminating rounds and the finals, watching his games and bursting with pride when he was presented with the victor's trophy.

Max taught me chess and chess notation. I learnt a few gambits and the general principles of play but though keen I was an indifferent player. As with so many things, I could never give him a decent game, let alone beat him. The only time I won, and then only just, was with him playing blindfold. He always had to give me a handicap in any contest, except in our political debates where his dialectical talents so far exceeded mine that in later life, I could only silence (rather than vanquish) him by shouting him down. He didn't hide his contempt for my political views. In my teens I was a fervent Labour supporter but still believed in our constitutional democracy and the independence of our courts as guardians of our individual freedoms. With his belief in Marxism and his Communist sympathies he dubbed me 'a little liberal'. This juxtaposition of 'little' and 'liberal' infuriated me. I was liberal in many of my views but was not a Liberal and resented the sneering implication that I was just a naive, wishy-washy kid.

His other passion was mathematics. Pre-war, when they were in their heyday, he was an enthusiastic player of the football pools. He claimed that he was one of the first to adopt a system of permutations and combinations which vastly increased his chances of winning – but win he never did. The Theory of Numbers (prime numbers especially) was his particular love and one in which he did a considerable amount of original work, publishing papers with titles such as *Equations in Polynomials* and *Digital Invariants*, in the *Mathematical Gazette* and other specialist journals. He corresponded with academics throughout the world and whilst in the army – a clerk in the Royal Army Pay Corps – was taken under the wing of Professor Goodman, head of the Mathematics Department of Reading University, who offered him a place there once he returned to Civvie Street. He applied for a grant so that he could take up the place, but was turned down on the ground that his education had not been interrupted by his military service. I wonder (very tentatively) whether embarking on a mathematical career might have been the saving of him.

He also wrote a series of articles for *Personalities*, the house magazine of the Government censorship agency in Liverpool and later the *Royal Army Pay Corps Journal*, bearing such titles as 'Shakespeare and Chess', 'Shakespeare and Bridge' and 'Shakespeare as Army Pay Clerk'. Here are a few quotations in support of his thesis that 'Shakespeare was an enthusiastic devotee of this most social of games', from the second of these:

'I'll call for clubs.' (Henry VI.1.3)
'Why then I'll double thy folly.' (Two Gentlemen of Verona II.4)
'Look how our partners are rapt.' (Macbeth I.3)
'We will yet have more tricks.' (Merry Wives of Windsor III.2)

You have to admire his dogged persistence in his scouring the Bard's plays for appropriate quotations to support his *esprit de jeu* and his innovative way of demonstrating that you can call on Shakespeare in aid of virtually any crazy notion.

I know I'm boasting but there is much to boast about. My friends adored him. He showed great personal interest in every one of them, entertaining them with his stories and erudition and initiating them into the complexities of chess and the magical qualities of numbers. But he was a riven man with a deep and dark secret and shadow side – the liar, the cheat and the gambler who ended up in old age a defeated man. He protested his love for my mother but let her down again and again. There were three separations to my knowledge, the first when I was eight years old. They all followed the same pattern: borrowing from work colleagues on lying pretexts, gambling the money away (he never seemed to bet successfully) and, being unable to repay, either lost his job or took flight.

The first time was when he was employed by Marks & Spencer as a trainee manager. One day, all was normal. The next, Mum told me we were leaving the flat I loved in Blackheath, cases were packed and we lunched on egg and chips at a nearby cafe. Of that day which ended up with my mother and me moving into a garret room in 38 Alkham Road, Stoke Newington – without my father who had been abandoned for reasons of which I knew nothing. My only memory is of the deliciousness of that egg and chips.

Within a year my father had redeemed himself by getting a job at Brodericks, a chain of furniture retailers, and my parents were back together again. They were negotiating the tenancy of a flat when the war began. I was evacuated with my school to Peterborough and Brodericks relocated to Reading. Within three months the three of us joined up in Liverpool where my father had secured, heaven knows through what inflation of his fluency in French and German or other chicanery, a job at the Censorship. Life proceeded smoothly, and for me with great interest and excitement until the air raids brought interest and excitement of a more lethal nature and we evacuated to West Kirby on the Wirral peninsular. My parents separated again in the summer of 1942 and my mother and I moved to Letchworth. Once we had settled there, I set about nagging her to tell me why Dad had left us, where he'd gone to and what he was doing. And in particular why he wasn't coming to Letchworth to see us. Mum proffered a severely simplified version of events.

"Well, Dad spent all his wages betting on horses. He never won, so he lost all his money week after week and we had no money to buy food or any clothes or to pay the rent so we had to leave Dad for the time being and come and live with Grandma and Grandpa".

I was a problem solver even then.

"Why didn't you meet Dad every week and get him to hand over his wages so he couldn't gamble them away?"

"It's not that simple, darling".

But it was that simple. Many years later, after their third separation, my mother insisted as a condition of taking him back that he would hand her his wage packet unopened every payday.

9. INTRODUCTION TO JUDAISM

There wasn't much talk of religion or God in Albion Road. What operated there was the show, not tell, of life. I was devoted to my father who, inheriting something of his father, Aaron's pedagogy, was a great teller, but because of his absences from home much of the time, what went on in the house, directed by Simon and Rose, had a far greater impact on me during the years we lived with them.

I have no evidence that Simon was a God-fearing man. It was much more a question of living life as a Jew, expressing in his daily life his Jewishness and the continuity of tradition through a day-to-day observance of rituals associated with high days and holy days, the Sabbath, circumcision, bar-mitzvahs, weddings, funerals and mourning.

There was also a perceived difference, a huge gulf between the Jew and the Gentile. The latter was to be feared as well as held in contempt. Of the many Yiddish folk songs I heard as a child, the most pernicious compared the sober Jew, attending synagogue and engaging in Torah studies, to the Gentile, frequenter of the tavern. The refrain contains the line *Oy, oy, oy! Shikker is der goy* [List, list, list! The Gentile is pissed]

Difference was inculcated in me through the medium of language, especially Yiddish; language I heard from my earliest days. I picked up the meaning of: *shaygets* and *shiksas*, respectively, young male and female non-Jews, *kosher*, foods you were by law permitted to eat, *trayfe*, an animal not slain according to ritual laws or any food not kosher such as pork or shellfish.

At a formal level *goy* is not a value laden word, though sometimes used pejoratively. *Yok*, a non-Jewish male, is insulting in the way that attributions such as *yid*, *froggie* or *kraut* are.

Anti-Semitism was so pervasive and ubiquitous that Jews tended to keep themselves to themselves. Nearly two millennia of anti-Semitism and, persecution, pogroms and expulsions had made Jews everywhere suspicious of the non-Jewish worlds. Consequently, none of my family had any non-Jewish friends and from an early age I became very aware of the Jewish/Gentile divide and of my own Jewish identity.

Language was a great divider. Both my maternal grandparents and Simon emigrated from Eastern Europe to England as adults and spoke broken and limited English. Between themselves and with my parents, Yiddish was spoken. My parents spoke only in English to me but although I never spoke Yiddish, I was in time able to get the gist of what they were saying and gradually picked up a large vocabulary of Yiddish words and phrases. Yiddish is such a rich and expressive language that I regret never having mastered it.

But the greatest divider of all was the Law. From the Law so many other differences flow. And the Law is the word of God in the form of the Torah, the Pentateuch, the first five books of the Old Testament. Literally the word of God, spoken to his chosen people, the Jews. It constitutes the foundation of Judaism and the source of countless rabbinical commentaries and interpretations which make up the corpus of religious, dietary, family and moral law. The truth is that my grandparents did not keep to the letter of Judaic law. They were not strictly orthodox. They did keep the Sabbath in principle but not the more arcane minutiae. They turned the lights on and off and my grandma, Rose, felt no spiritual conflict in lighting the gas cooker or cooking. The strictly orthodox would employ a *shabbes goy* [Sabbath Gentile] to carry out such tasks which were classed as labour and forbidden on the Sabbath.

Dietary laws too are governed by the Torah. These were broadly observed by Rose, so no meal contained a combination of meat and dairy ingredients, nor did we eat porcine products or shellfish, though there was a blissful occasion when on a day trip with Simon to Southend-On-Sea, I was introduced to the salty taste and rubbery texture of boiled shrimps, pink and sold in their shells by the gill at a stall at the end of the pier.

Like most Jews we had a *mezuzah* screwed into the front door post. This was a small metal disc in which was placed a piece of parchment inscribed on one side with a text from Deuteronomy and on the other with the divine name, *Shaddai*.

We shared a house with Simon and Rose for two periods of my life, from three to seven and from twenty to twenty-nine. A fixed point of our family life, a three-line whip, was the Sabbath eve grace followed by the Sabbath evening meal. The table was laid with *challah*, the plaited Sabbath bread, glazed with egg white and covered with an embroidered linen cloth, also a bottle of wine and a silver goblet. At the crack of dusk, Sabbath had arrived. Fresh candles in the two silver Corinthian candlesticks were solemnly lit by Rose. Simon then filled the goblet with wine and having thanked God for creating the fruit of the vine took a sip and passed the goblet for each member of the family to drink. The wine was of a sweet muscatel variety and as a small child was my first experience of alcohol. I loved its syrupy taste and the warm feeling as it descended my gullet en route to my tummy. Wine on an empty stomach! I may not have become tipsy but I was certainly suffused by a glow of contentment for the rest of the evening. Next, Simon uncovered the *challah*, recited a short blessing, praising God for creating the bread of the Earth, broke pieces off the loaf, added a little salt and distributed them to the family. The rituals done, Rose brought the meal to the table. These were joyous occasions; the one night the family could be relied on to be together, the pleasure of eating delicious food together, the familiarity of the rituals, the relaxation induced by the end of the working week. And as a child I got to stay up late.

Throughout their lives my grandparents kept the main holy days and religious festivals. The first, *Pesach* [Passover], was around Easter time and commemorated Israel's deliverance from enslavement in Egypt over 3200 years ago as recounted in Exodus. This festival and the preparations for it were of immense excitement to me whose life consisted of long stretches of routine, interspersed with little patches of heightened life, a tempo over which I had little control.

The first intimation of *Pesach* was the sudden withdrawal of all our everyday crockery, cutlery, glassware and cooking utensils and the appearance of their substitutes (so as to avoid contamination) for the whole of the eight day *Pesach* period. On the night before the first celebratory *Seder* [order of procedure], I would join my grandparents in the ritual search for *chometz*; that is any foodstuff containing yeast which you weren't allowed to eat during *Pesach*. The object of the exercise was to hunt down and root out any *chometz* in the house, any residual foodstuffs containing yeast such as bread or biscuits, but if you are a stickler which in those days my grandparents were, you threw away anything which did not bear the imprimatur of the *Beth Din*, the rabbinical court. Armed with torches we scoured the house from top to bottom, looking under furniture, peering into cupboards and wardrobes in case a rogue crust of bread or illicit biscuit was lurking there. Needless to say we never did find any 'chometz' but I had great fun and felt that I was engaged in something really important and grown-up.

The first night *Seder*, a combined banquet and religious service held in our basement kitchen was attended by my grandparents, their son, Percy, my parents and me, the service element being led by Simon and the banquet prepared and served by Rose. As the youngest present I had a short but starring role early in the proceedings, the posing of the *Fier Kashers* [The Four Questions] to Simon in Hebrew, the child wanting to know why this night was different from all other nights. I knew no Hebrew then, nor had I yet learnt to read it, so my father guided me through the questions; he asked, I repeated. The, to me, boring service then continued by my grandfather reading lengthy explanations from the *Hagaddah* [Tale] in response to the child's curiosity, relieved towards the end of the first half by tasty snacks of matzo, bitter herbs (symbolic of the

Jews long captivity) leavened by a confection of crushed apples, raisins, nuts and cinnamon, and several swigs of wine, all preceded by short blessings. Then, hors d'oeuvres to the main feast, sliced hard-boiled eggs in mildly salted water, the latter representing the tears shed by mothers in Egypt whose babies were snatched from them. By the time supper was over it was long past my bedtime and I was excused the second half of the service.

For the next eight days our usual diet was transformed by the omnipresence of matzo instead of bread. For me it was a period of the utmost bliss; there was nothing more consistently delicious than this simple concoction made of flour and water and baked to a satisfying, teeth crunching crispness, spread with butter and sprinkled with salt. During this period Rose made my all-time favourite lunch, boiled pinkish Vienna sausages thin and curved with chewy skins and firm meat within, served with matzobrow, made from broken pieces of water-moistened matzo, mixed in with beaten egg, and fried.

Simon was not a regular attender at *schul* [synagogue] but he was a member of the Egerton Road Synagogue in Stamford Hill and often took me to Saturday morning services. At the entrance was a throng of people dressed in their Saturday best, the men besuited, shaking hands, wishing each other good *yom tov* [holy day] and exchanging news and gossip. The women who also wore suits (then known as costumes) and hats and many sporting expensive fur coats or fur stoles, were more restrained as they made their way to the women's gallery, men and women being separated in Orthodox synagogues by rabbinic diktat. Once in the main body of the *schul*, I was absorbed by the bustle and the clamour of a hundred conversations as the male congregants wrapped themselves in their *tallises* [prayer shawls] and flicked through their prayer books. The rabbi raised his hand and the *shammes* [sideman, verger] called the congregation to order so the service could begin. Throughout my childhood I was terrified of the *shammes*, always an elderly man with a disapproving expression. He paced the aisles on the lookout for misdemeanours and hushing the chatterers with a stern '*Shah!*' [Silence]: the jealous Judaic God incarnate. The service felt interminable, seemingly a never-ending recitation of long tracts of Hebrew liturgy, incomprehensible to me and probably incomprehensible to the majority of the congregants who as young boys would have attended a school to learn to read Hebrew, without the need to understand the meaning of the words. My grandfather was a fluent Hebrew reader but barely understood a word of the texts he gabbled with the others at breakneck speed as they bobbed and bowed in rhythm to the words.

Halfway through the service my interest, excitement even, was revived by the revealing of the *Torah* to the congregation. These were amongst the synagogue's most revered and valuable treasures. Egerton Road owned several, locked in a curtained cupboard known as the Ark. They were in scroll form, hand written on parchment and dressed in purple, dark green or deep blue velvet.

The wooden handles were topped by ornate silver knobs and the effect of richly appareled authority, completed by a medallion affixed to a silver chain necklace across the velvet cover. To me this always felt like a moment of true theatre. A hush fell on the congregation. The rabbi approached the Ark, drew the curtains, opened the cupboard doors and lifted out one of the Torah scrolls. Having taken it to the altar, with great care and ceremony, he removed the ornamental accoutrements and coverings as if he were undressing a beloved, until only the bare scroll remained which he bore aloft among the congregants, most of whom were by then in a state of spiritual exaltation. They vied to touch, to stroke, to kiss the scroll, muttering players as they did so. These were moments of high drama; God's own words uttered directly to and only to the Jewish people, made flesh in an object beyond price.

Once some kind of normality had been restored, the rabbi returned to the altar where he selected the portion of the law to be read that day and called to read it a man chosen because he was a Cohen, a member of the priestly caste. Bursting with pride, a congregant, ordinary except for the name he bore, Mr. Cohen would approach the altar to murmurs of encouragement and approbation from all quarters of the synagogue. The rabbi would ensure the scroll was held open at the proper place and with a silver pointer would guide the reader along the text of his portion.

His duty done Mr. Cohen returned to his place where his neighbours would greet him, shake his hand and congratulate him on the honour bestowed on him. Meanwhile the rabbi dressed the scroll and returned it to the Ark. This was always a sad moment for me, the Torah was out of sight, with the fall of the velvet curtain the play was over. Unfortunately, it wasn't. It should have been but there were still masses of liturgy to be recited before we were released and could go home for our Sabbath lunch.

My grandmother had a short repertoire but everything she produced was of several star Michelin quality. There'd be chopped chicken liver or chopped hard-boiled egg and onion for starters, then the pièce de résistance, chicken soup with carrots and vermicelli, rich and healing and the only dish I know with a bouquet analogous to a fine wine. Roast chicken and accompaniments to finish. Priorities have changed; today children get the best. the most succulent and the biggest bits. They get served first. Then my grandfather got the choice portions of the bird, the other adults, breast or leg and were served in order of seniority. I was at the bottom of the food chain. I got a wing and if I was lucky the heart or a foot. 'It's not fair!', I thought. My undiminished habit of gnawing my chicken bones until not a shred or splinter of meat remains harks back to those unjustly apportioned helpings.

The other major holy days observed by Simon were *Rosh Hashanah* and *Yom Kippur.* The former falls in September and commemorates the Jewish New Year. I accompanied Simon to synagogue but the liturgy and the chanting were as never-ending and boring as ever. There was, however, one moment of theatrical intensity, the blowing of the *Shofar* [the ram's horn] with its doleful and minatory sound, blown by a *Tokia* [blaster] in long, short and staccato blasts which followed a set sequence prescribed by Talmudic law. Every time I heard it, I was both enthralled and terrified by its archaic and primitive sight and sound.

Ten days later followed *Yom Kippur,* the Day of Atonement, the most solemn day in the Jewish calendar. The obligation to fast from sunrise to sunset is only one of several prohibitions regulating the conduct of pious Jews on this day. Even Simon, relatively relaxed in his religious approach, would fast and spend from dawn to dusk praying in the synagogue. As a child I was exempt the full rigours of fasting and spent only the morning with Simon before being taken home for a light lunch. The more concrete purpose of the day was to reflect on the wrongs done and offences committed during the previous year and seek pardon and forgiveness both from the persons wronged and through prayer, from God Himself. The congregants accompanied the cataloguing of their offences with much histrionic breast-beating and this was the only part of the service which roused me from my torpor. I understand now that a more spiritual soul-searching function of this day is that, freed from the mundane demands of working, washing, preparing and eating food, you could, in a more meditative, contemplative state go through a process of reassessment, and reappraise your life in terms of its meaning and consider what changes you needed to make for greater realisation of the self.

Where was my father in all this synagogue to-ing and fro-ing? I have no idea. He wasn't religious but he was militantly Jewish. Did he have other fish to fry? Working? Gambling? Playing chess? But I wish he had spent more time with me.

Simon and Rose did not observe the other holy days but *Hanukkah*, the Feast of Lights, usually falling in December, was celebrated. It is not a religious festival but commemorates the victory of the Jewish Maccabees over Syrian tyrants in 167 BC. My grandparents lit candles for nine days, one on the first evening, adding one light each subsequent night on the nine branched *menorah* candlestick. I waited with growing impatience for the ninth night and for the menorah to be complete in all its glowing radiance.

Hanukkah was the nearest (in time as well as character) that Jews have to Christmas, with presents for children and tasty delicacies such as *latkes* [potato pancakes]. In fact, even during this period, a gesture, presumably for my sake, was made towards Christmas. We laboured over multi-coloured paperchains which we trailed across the kitchen/living room as well as hanging ready-made decorations. On Christmas morning by my bedside I'd find an assortment of comic annuals and a net stocking crammed full of little toys, games and sweetmeats. This was emblematic of the movement away from strict dietary and other observances and towards a degree of secularisation brought about by the difficulties of following a fully Judaic life during the war.

At the age of seven I announced to my family that I did not believe in God. I felt nervous in denying His existence but no thunderbolt struck me in retribution for my blasphemy. I haven't believed in Him since. So where does that leave this poor, conflicted Jewish atheist; as a Jew or non-Jew? I did not know then that my father was an atheist and my mother was probably one too.

10. CHARLTON ROAD BLACKHEATH

In April 1937 my father was accepted for a managerial traineeship at the Woolwich branch of Marks & Spencer so we moved from Albion Road to a large first-floor flat in Charlton Road, Blackheath. This felt like a fresh start for all of us. For me at the age of seven, because for the first time I had a bedroom of my own, a proper bed instead of the cot which I had more than outgrown by the time we left Stoke Newington. For my mother, because it was always her dream to be looked after financially and emotionally by her man, to have absolute trust in and security provided by him so that she could realise my phantom sister, Miriam and perhaps more. And for my father, the beginning of a career with prospects to match his many talents.

I do not have a full list of his jobs before this time. His marriage certificate shows his occupation as Hebrew Teacher. My grandfather Aaron maintained a rigorous teaching regime. Because my father had to rise at 6am for Hebrew and Talmudic studies for two hours, before going to school, he became a fluent Hebraist but I know nothing of the nature of his teaching; whether as a private tutor, at a *Cheder* [Hebrew school] or in some other capacity.

On my birth certificate he describes himself as a *Foyles' Departmental Manager*. He was employed by Foyles in Charing Cross Road to create and run a Hebrew, Judaica and Yiddish Department. Later he had some kind of association with a Mr. Bierman. He went to an office every day, to a mysterious, very grown-up world called business. Sometimes my mother would take me to meet him from work. It was always a snug and secure moment for me to be out with both my parents who were delighted to be with each other again. My mother would always brightly greet my father with the words *Etwas niaes?* [Any news]. She was greedy, ravenous for news; to be reassured that she was at the centre of my father's life, taken notice of, her existence acknowledged. My mother's feeling of being an outsider and of exclusion could easily be evoked. Her father and brother were in business together, the business was in the house where they lived and all family conversations were dominated by business. No contribution from my mother was sought or encouraged. In later life she would complain that in any new social situation she was ignored, not welcomed in. Others would not 'come forward', they were already well entrenched in impenetrable groupings.

Everything seemed calm and well-regulated in our new home. I felt very cosy and contained, playing on the newly carpeted floors. My set of coloured pencils served as trains and I constructed an elaborate railway system with stations and routes criss-crossing the whole of the living room floor. I was enrolled at Sherrington Road Elementary School, with its smaller scale buildings and light airy classrooms, smarter than my gloomy Victorian Stoke Newington school. I was impressed by the printed workbooks with their sums ready for you to answer: *(9x6) -(8x4) = ?*. I tore into them with great confidence and delight, took my results to Miss for marking and amongst all ticks there was one cross. Spelling, yes, but in arithmetic this had never happened to me before.

But I loved the area. I've lived in Blackheath for most of my life and I still love it. What I remember of this period are times out of the house rather than in it. My father taking me to our local library at Charlton House, a beautiful Jacobean mansion. Walks across Blackheath to one of its ponds to sail my little boat. Visits to Greenwich Park where my father explained the meaning of longitude, astronomy and telescope. On our walks he also told me about palindromes ("Able was I 'ere I saw Elba") and combined a lesson in mental arithmetic with what seemed to me to be something akin to magic. He would issue a series of commands:

"Think of a number. Multiply it by 3. Take away 2. Double it. Add the number you first thought of. What do you get?"

"31"

"5 was the number you first thought of".

That was my clever daddy. The great entertaining educator, a wizard with words and when he was with you, you couldn't ask for a more delightful, charming companion. But two excursions ended disastrously. The first wasn't his fault. We went to the Greenwich Maritime Museum where I was both fascinated and appalled by the carefully laid out clothes Nelson was wearing when he received his fatal wound at the Battle of Trafalgar. There was a large bullet hole in the shoulder of his coat and bloodstains on an undergarment. In the same room was the painting of him dying on the deck of HMS Victory, bloody and pale. This was my first encounter with human death. I was haunted by bad dreams and nightmares for many weeks afterwards.

One day in late July, we set out for a day trip to Herne Bay. I was fine messing about with my bucket and spade and making sandcastles. Fine eating the egg and cress sandwiches my mother had made for our lunch. But my father had a more ambitious plans for me; he wanted to teach me to swim. So we left the safety of the sand, paddled a little way into the undependable sea where he supported my chest and midriff for what seemed an interminable time while I splashed and swallowed large amounts of seawater and became very cold and miserable. Back on dry land my father rubbed me down impatiently, leaving me cold, damp and sandy. I arrived home cold, my clothes still damp, where my mother, anxious for me and angry with my father for his incompetence and clumsiness, gave me a hot bath and put me to bed. In practical matters Dad was often incompetent and clumsy.

The next morning, I woke up with a high temperature and other symptoms of a severe chill. I was in bed for a week but was judged well enough to go to the wedding of my aunt Rosa in North London. I felt fine but I wasn't. While changing buses in Poplar I was violently sick but we all pushed on to Egerton Road Synagogue, arriving too late for the ceremony itself. The pre-dinner reception was in full swing. There was *tummel* [tumult], *geshrai* [shouting] and multi-decibellous conversations, cries of *mazeltov* [good luck] to the newlyweds and 'Such a handsome *boychik*, your Boris, *kineahora*'. Kineahora is Yiddish mumbo-jumbo used to ward off the evil eye. Kisses were proffered by ancient relatives; whether it was these or the eating of a single olive which caused me to vomit again, I cannot say, but much to my disappointment at missing the wedding feast, my parents made their farewells and took me home.

Back in my sick bed for two weeks or so, my condition deteriorated into such a seriously chesty cough that my mother took me to the outpatients' department of Great Ormond Street Children's' Hospital. On the short walk from the bus, I had to make frequent stops because I was struggling for breath. Chest X-rays were taken and I was diagnosed as having bronchitis, severe enough for me to be admitted as an inpatient. As soon as I understood what was in store for me, I howled, cried, sobbed, clung to my mother and begged her not to leave me. In my terror of the threatened separation, I found the strength to keep up my heartbroken appeals for what seemed like hours and was mollified into submission only when she promised that she would stay and sleep in the hospital while I was there. Secure in the knowledge of my mother's presence, I spent a peaceful night in the ward, waking once only and seeing the night nurse sitting at her desk writing, her lamp glowing and illuminating the darkness. In the morning I waited for my mother to appear. From the window by my bed I could see across a courtyard into another ward and looked for her in the belief that was where she was staying

"When is my mummy coming?" I asked a nurse.
"Visiting hours are after lunch, dear."
"Can't she come now? She's staying here."
"Mothers don't stay in the hospital, dear."
"But she said."
"Well she said wrong."

And with that she went about her duties. Right on two o'clock my mother was there by my bedside with books and toys.

"You didn't stay here," I said accusingly.

"I couldn't. They wouldn't let me."

"But you promised!"

I felt betrayed, affronted. At some level I was aware that she had lied to pacify me into a state of compliance. And this from a mother who had impressed on me that lying was the worst of all sins. 'Boris, you must never, never lie.' I had so fully internalised this that all my life I have been a bad liar. I had learnt a harsh lesson. Grown-ups lied, even my mother lied. I had been given permission to lie too.

The ward was full of children, most of whom seemed sicker than I. I was goggle-eyed at the sight of a boy whose face was painted in Gentian Violet. A little girl clumped up and down the ward in iron leg braces. I knew I was getting better when I was allowed to dress and more importantly, use the toilet instead of the bedpan which I so hated that I very soon became constipated and was given some loathsome laxative.

Back home in Blackheath after my discharge from hospital, more bad news. Another separation was imminent. On medical advice my mother was sending me to a convalescent home in Southbourne, near Bournemouth.

"It's just a few weeks, darling.

I was sullen. I protested, "I don't want to go."

"It's a seaside, darling."

As if that consoled me.

11. CONVALESCENT HOME

A week later, at the beginning of September, my mother waved goodbye to me as the Bournemouth Belle stuttered and puffed its way out of Waterloo Station. I was easily distractible. I loved trains. I had a window seat. I had no thought or fear of the unknown life I was hurtling towards. I had never been on such a long journey. At Southampton, I caught sight of the ocean-going liners, including the Queen Mary, docked there. As I sped through the New Forest we passed a level crossing, where there was a group of girls in riding gear, on horses. Exciting but frustrating, brief glimpses, out of sight before I could take them in.

There were other children bound for the home. We alighted at Christchurch and were met by staff who carried our luggage from the station past the massive Priory Church and over the bridge across the River Avon, straight into Bellevue Road where my new home was.

There were about twenty of us convalescents recovering from I knew not what illnesses. I settled down quickly to our routine institutional activities. It felt like a holiday to begin with, still summer and every afternoon we crocodiled to Southbourne's sandy beaches where we played and watched the giant ships on the horizon pass en route to New York. On our walks I quickly attached myself to our attractive, dark haired nurse. She was a refugee from Austria and we talked about the annexation of Austria by Germany which I knew had just happened although I only had the sketchiest notion of what it was all about. But I think she was impressed by the very fact that I knew of the existence of such events and I basked in her favour until she left unexpectedly at the end of September. All such adult actions, entrances and exits were mysterious, sudden and unexpected. I was bereft; even more so when her replacement appeared: a large boned, blonde dominatrix, nice to begin with but she soon showed her true colours as the niceness dissolved into harsh bossiness, rough handling as she washed my face and combed my hair and impatience if I dawdled or had difficulty with my buttons. More importantly, I failed utterly to ingratiate myself with her.

With the advent of autumn our trips to the beach ended and we spent our afternoons in the garden. It was acorn season and we were all busy collecting them. Quite unasked, a pretty girl I hardly knew kept bringing along little handfuls which she gifted to my pile. After a while she came along empty-handed and announced that she was no longer going to collect for me but for him – pointing to another boy who already had several female acolytes busily searching for choice acorns on his behalf, for all the world like dwarfs building up the Nibelung hoard. How was I to understand this at the age of seven? Was he the king of the castle and I the dirty rascal?

There were more serious ways in which things took a turn for the worse as autumn wore on. The regime was, by the standards of the time, not cruel but the carers weren't kind either. Most of the time we were left to our own devices; there was no stimulus and no schooling. We were cooped up in the playroom with its stale old toys. There was no adult to supervise, amuse or instruct us. We couldn't go out except en masse for our strictly regulated afternoon walk and then only if it wasn't raining. We were stupefied by boredom. To show any kind of spirit was dangerous. On one occasion I was punished for complaining that our breakfast butter was rancid – even though it was.

One thing matron did take a keen interest in was our bowel movements. Once a week whether we had been motionless or not, we lined up for spoonfuls of castor oil. If we rejected or refused to swallow the vile stuff our noses were pinched until we did. My stay was supposedly for six weeks and the system was that when a child was about to return home, if male, he was put into an institutional uniform of grey shorts and red jersey so that his own clothes could be washed and packed ready for departure. One day I was given the red jersey and I knew I was on my way. A couple of weeks passed; I was still in my red jersey but not yet on a train to London. Time dragged and then one morning I was back in my own clothes again. Not a word was said but the other children knew in the strange way they have of snuffling out information which they can use to hurt you.

"You're not going home, you're not going home", they jeered and sang in unison. I was downcast and uncomprehending. Why the volte-face? In fact, I stayed at the home until the following April. I became quite depressed and cut-off. I put my spirit into cold storage during this time. Every day was the same, tame and uneventful. I didn't even go to church on Sundays because I was Jewish and spent that time by myself in the playroom.

During the whole of my time in Southbourne my parents never came to visit me. My grandfather Simon came once and that day stands out like a brief flash of light and lightheartedness in the bleak flatlands of my daily life in the home. It was just before Christmas and we took a bus to Bournemouth. The shops were lit up and the streets thronged with shoppers. We went to a tearoom near the pier, a large high-domed room, illuminated by chandeliers, crowded, abuzz with chatter and clattering tea-trays and 'nippies' bustling about. I faced a screen showing Walt Disney cartoon shorts: Mickey Mouse and Donald Duck. Simon ordered egg and salmon paste and cucumber sandwiches, chocolate eclairs and macaroons. Then a bus back to reality. Eggs were not part of our standard diet; they had to be paid for as an extra. Simon left money for a dozen so I had a daily boiled egg for breakfast until on the thirteenth day, no egg.

12. BACK TO CHARLTON ROAD

One morning in April 1938 I was again given the red jersey. I was on my way home. Or was I? I still loved my mother but had lost some of my trust in her. But soon I was on the train back to London, met by my uncle Percy who took me home where a clockwork train set was waiting for me; circular lay-out but no junction. "Where's mummy?" I asked. She was at work and returned later as did my father.

I bore my mother a grudge for many years for her seven-month abandonment of me. It was a sore place and I kept returning to it.

"Why did you keep me there for so long?"

"You'd been so ill we thought it best for you to spend the winter there"

"Well why didn't you come to see me?"

"We thought you'd feel worse when we left."

As an adult I wonder who'd have felt worse, her or me. If Dad had been up to his old tricks again, things might have been difficult between him and Mum who was working at Tate & Lyle's and it might have suited them to have me out of their care. Or worse still, out of their hair, as an interference in their social and cultural life and in their new or rediscovered freedom from the constraints of my presence. I could never get to the bottom of it; whenever I raised it, and I raised it often, she would respond along the lines of 'why do you keep going on about it. You know it upsets me. Don't be a *nudnik*' [a nag or bore]. So my mother's upset trumped mine. I think that what I wanted was not so much an explanation, though that would have been nice, but an apology and acknowledgement that this had been a miserable and distressing period of my life.

I was happy to be home but my euphoria was short lived. Because my mother was working she employed a 15-year-old girl called Mary to look after me during the day. I took to her instantly; she was tall, pretty, warm and friendly. Despite the age gap (I was eight at the time) we became good mates. She took me for walks in the park or on the Heath and sometimes to the council flat in Charlton where she lived with her family. She was a natural gymnast and once in demonstrating a cartwheel I caught the briefest glimpse of her bottom. She was knickerless so I saw the pubic bush and the split (yet another one). It was the first time I had seen a woman's genitals although when I was four I had once witnessed my mother nude and had noted *le difference*. With all due respect to Sigmund Freud and Simone De Beauvoir's *The Second Sex*, I did not conclude that a female was merely a castrated male, but I did find the sight of Mary one of intense interest and importance although I did not then have any inkling of what or why. Nobody told me anything. I wanted to know how babies came into existence and being a logical child had worked out that there was no effect without cause. When age 9, at one of the family's Saturday afternoon teas, in front of my parents and ten other adults, I asked my carefully thought out question 'does a mummy take some special medicine when she wants to have a baby?'

The entire gathering dissolved into laughter. Still nobody told me anything. I had to wait another year before I learned from other boys how impregnation occurred.

One afternoon Mary, a few other children who had joined us from nowhere and I were having a joyful time playing at a horse trough opposite our house. We splashed each other, creating effective scoops with our hands. I was in the thick of the fray and spray, soaked through, hair and face dripping, not having enjoyed myself so much since the beach at Southbourne. When the battle was at its height my mother appeared, off early from work. Predictably she was furious. She sacked Mary on the spot and hauled me home. I was not punished but in my heart I knew I had been to blame and felt guilty about Mary's dismissal.

13. BACK TO STOKE NEWINGTON

Within days, so it seemed, we moved out of our flat. This wasn't due to Mary's departure. My father was dismissed from his job at Marks & Spencer and my mother was leaving him. I don't know the details but I imagine his dismissal followed his lifelong pattern. He would borrow money from work colleagues by telling them lying hard luck stories.

'My wife is ill and needs an operation'. Or, 'My son is recovering from TB at a convalescent home and we're a bit short on this month's fees'. He was very plausible and successful in gulling people into parting with their money which he used to gamble or to pay off his gambling debts. Of course the loans were never repaid and the word leaked out to management who sacked him on the spot for misconduct. This behaviour must have been going on while I was in Southbourne and my father's gambled away salary was the reason for my mother needing to take a job.

Naturally I knew nothing of this at the time and no explanation for our return to North London was given. Once again adult decisions were being made beyond my comprehension; they were like immutable laws of nature. I just went along with them. My mother and I ended up that day in a garret flat at 32, Alkham Road. It was sparsely furnished with a double bed which I shared with my mother, a table, a couple of chairs and a coal fire. A sink and gas oven on the landing served as our kitchen. Three flights down was the coal cellar where our coal was stored. It was my job as the only male to keep our scuttle filled. The lavatory was also there, airless, smelly and stocked with shiny, slippery *San Izal* toilet paper. Inefficient in function, it was a good read with its rhyming couplets and wise saws printed on every sheet.

I became increasingly self-sufficient from the time of this move. Mummy, who had now become 'Mum', went off to work (I have no idea where or to what) before I got up and I made my own breakfast: eggs on toast and a cup of tea. I went to school on my own. Benthal Road Elementary School was not far away but it provided the base from which I was able to venture further afield. My grandparents had by then moved, clothing factory and all, to 49 Amherst Road between Mare Street and Hackney Downs Station. Because my mother was working and in 1938-9 state schools did not provide meals, grandma Rose made me lunch. As her house was about a mile from the school and time was short, I took the suburban steam train from Rectory Road Station to Hackney Downs, the next stop. Lunch break began at midday and my train left at six minutes past. As soon as we were dismissed, I was out of the classroom like a shot, sprinted to the station, bought my penny return and was soon eating whatever delicious dish grandma had prepared for me. This daily journey, ideal training for thirty years of commuting to come, worked without a hitch until one day we were held back for an address by the headmistress, probably something to do with gas mask practice or evacuation arrangements in the event of war. The classroom clock ticked round to 12:02. I put up my hand.

"Please Miss, I've got a train to catch".

"So have we all" she replied with great sarcasm. I knew this to be patently untrue. I was the only one. Didn't she believe me? A put down which I felt was unjustly aimed at and wounded my well-meaning self.

Because of my illness and convalescence, I had missed a lot of schooling and had some catching up to do. All the work seemed harder and more complicated and with the additional burden of grappling with joined up handwriting, I struggled to keep up.

It was a period of general anxiety which communicated itself to us children through images of Hitler and German military might on the Pathe and Movietone news, grave grown-up conversations, gas mask practice, and Munich.

I was taken by my mother and father – he seemed to be back on the scene dating my mother but not yet living with us – and my uncles Alf and Jack and Aunts Rosa and Ray to a huge May Day 1939 rally in Hyde Park. I was bored by the speeches but the park itself was heavily fortified with anti-aircraft gun emplacements and barrage balloons and it was these that were the focus of my interest. Later we walked across the park, down Constitutional Hill and The Mall to the Strand Lyons Corner House for tea. The adults were on their third cups, deep in conversation when I slipped away to Charing Cross Station where I revelled in the steam and murk and smoke, the clatter of porters' barrows, the guards' whistles and sounds of trains on the move. Suddenly my rageful mother, having guessed where I had wandered off to, appeared.

'How dare you go off like that? We've been worried sick. Never, never do that again, do you hear me?'

Unchastened, I couldn't understand why she didn't trust me to look after myself. I was a big boy and had only been away a few minutes. Or so it seemed.

She was at it again at the beginning of the school summer holiday. I had taken to spending time at Hackney Station where a porter had befriended me and beguiled me with railway lore, including the fact that if you stood on an electrified line with both feet you wouldn't get electrocuted. Hackney Station was on the Broad Street to Poplar line, opened in 1865 and by the look of the rolling stock nothing had changed since. Mum gave me permission and the return fare to travel to Broad Street but I discovered on arrival at the station that there was no train due for two hours. I made a quick decision to go to Hackney Downs station where trains went to Liverpool Street and were more frequent. To get there I had to pass my grandparents' house and I was spotted. As I was climbing the stairs to the platform, I was summoned by my mother's imperious, pellucid voice. "Boris, come down at once!"

I gave her a summary of the facts: I had already bought my ticket, Liverpool Street was next to Broad Street, what difference? All in vain.

"You naughty boy! You said Broad Street and that meant Broad Street. You're coming back with me this minute, d'you hear me?"

Another outing spoilt by her inflexibility and imperviousness to reason.

In a parallel world to the looming war, we children continued to live our own lives, consumed by our own fads, fancies and fashions. Conkers, marbles, cigarette cards, comics, tops, yo-yos. It was the playground which provided our real training for life because all life was there: arena, stadium, marketplace, club and debating chamber. Pecking orders and hierarchies were determined by strength, popularity and combat or innate leadership qualities. Gender differences were becoming more apparent; the boys were rougher, louder, and more competitive, the girls skipped, played hopscotch or hung around, chatting in little groups. This was the turbulent and volatile society to which I yearned for membership and to make my mark. The way in which craze succeeded craze was bewildering and mysterious. On Tuesday we were all happily playing marbles and then out of the blue on Wednesday yo-yos materialised and everyone had one. How did this happen? It was like birds knowing when and where to migrate. In my desire to conform I scrupulously observed and followed every fad as it occurred, but my real passion was for collecting cigarette cards and so for me the arrival of that season was one of great excitement. This was when the vast majority of the adult population smoked and to ensure brand loyalty, tobacco companies included in each packet of cigarettes, a picture card of, say, a famous footballer or a ship of the Royal Navy, the idea being to suck the smoker into collecting the whole set of fifty cards. Both my parents smoked and I augmented my collection by the common practice of begging strangers in the street for any 'spare' cards.

During the card season, one corner of the playground became a market for the sale and swapping of cards, another for the game of 'flickers' in which one boy placed against the wall one large card or five small ones and another would flick cards from his own resources at those cards. If he succeeded in knocking one down, the cards were his, if he failed the other boy retained the flicked card. I had a stock of about ten large cards and set up my stall against all challengers. Unfortunately, the first to play against me was Sam Levine, renowned in the school as the demon flicker. Within minutes he had toppled all my cards with no loss to himself. I was devastated. I had lost all my capital with no return. I have been an ultra-cautious investor ever since.

Without warning the aeroplane season arrived. I'm not talking about sophisticated, remote-controlled scale models. A ragbag miscellany of ingeniously home-constructed paper and balsa wood gliders, Dinky toy models, cheap clockwork planes with rotating propellers. I had nothing, nor did I have either the competence or the means to make or acquire one. I felt an immense sense of shame in being excluded from the collective activity. One day before returning to afternoon school I popped into Hackney's Woolworths, and browsing at the toy counter saw something that immediately became a painfully intense object of desire, a balsa glider, easy to assemble, with a catapult contraption to launch it, price 3d (just over 1p). I didn't have a farthing to my name. I had to have that glider. There was no assistant at the counter or within sight. Completely on impulse, I picked one up, stuffed it under my pullover and left the store. I was a thief. It was all so easy but the actual magnitude of what I had done hit me the moment I was out in the street. My primitive but powerful conscience kicked in, following which an internal trial took place in which I was charged, tried and found guilty of stealing. I returned to Woolworths and replaced the glider. I had arrested myself from embarking on a life of crime.

During that summer of 1939, things were looking up for Dad and Mum, and by extension for me. Dad now had the job at Brodericks, I assume that he convinced my mother that he had turned over a new leaf, had kicked his addiction. We took an unfurnished flat in Stoke Newington but war came before we could move in.

I had one peak experience before war precipitated our dispersion from London. Simon took me on a boat trip. Not once round the lighthouse, not twice round the lake at Finsbury Park, but on the Royal Eagle, the flagship of the Eagle paddle steamer fleet which plied from Tower Pier to Ramsgate calling at Greenwich, Southend-On-Sea, Herne Bay and Margate. The entire voyage there and back took twelve hours. The engine room with its huge, rhythmically rumbling and hissing brass pistons was open to view and amidships the saloon bar emitted a yeasty, beery smell as though ale had slopped over all the deck and perhaps it had. The first excitement occurred within minutes of the boat departing; Tower Bridge opened to let us through. Cheering crowds on the upper level of the bridge waved at us as we passed below as if we were at the beginning of a long sea journey. We were the blessed ones. I felt very privileged and special.

14. EVACUATION

At 6am on Saturday, 2nd September 1939 I stood in the school playground, gas mask over my shoulder, clutching a suitcase just like all the other children in my class. I had no idea where I was going. A bus drew up. I clung to my mother for one last desperate hug and a smothering of kisses, boarded the bus and in a moment I was off on the most convoluted journey of my life. The bus took us to Manor House tube station, then by tube to Oakwood where we waited for an age for another bus to New Barnet. By being strategically placed when our train drew up and a bit of pushing and squeezing, I secured my cherished window seat and with the help of my unobscured view and the cheese and pickle on rye bread sandwiches my mother had made me, I was once again able to cut myself off from what lay ahead. Where were we going? Who would I be staying with? Would they be kind to me? These questions must have been lurking in some corner of my mind.

After lengthy stops and delays we pulled into Peterborough station and a bus was waiting to take us to Walton, a suburb on the north side. Late that afternoon I was taken to meet my randomly selected foster parents, Mr and Mrs Brooksbank who lived in a small terraced house at 60 Churchfield Road. There was a roast pork dinner waiting for me in the oven. As I ate this unfamiliar but delicious meal, by way of introduction, I chattered about myself, revealed that I was Jewish, that I wasn't supposed to eat pork but I didn't mind in the slightest. This was just as well because pork and its derivatives constituted a large part of our diet. I met their two boys, Hayden, a 3-year-old toddler and a little baby, Mervyn, and experienced the novel smells which pervaded the house: baby poo, wet nappies, Ostermilk and Gentile cooking, a mixture of dripping, bacon and boiled cabbage. Mrs Brooksbank was tall, a big-boned, fleshy, fresh faced woman, of few words. Perhaps that's how she seemed to me, as my mother was small and of many words. She, Mrs B, was not particularly maternal, or even friendly towards me. That was not surprising as she was busy and preoccupied with her own young family. I'll never know whether they took on the burden of an extra child as a patriotic duty or, taking advantage of a spare bedroom, they saw a way of making a few bob.

Mr. Brooksbank was initially very matey. On the first morning, soon after breakfast, he showed me the recreation ground, just a quick climb over the fence of his back garden. It was already crowded with local children and evacuees clustered around the swings, singing *Found a Peanut* to the tune of *Bonnie Clementine*. Easy to learn, it consisted of seven verses:

Found a peanut, found a peanut, found a peanut, just now.
Where d'you find it, where d'you find it, where d'you find it, just now?
In the dustbin, in the dustbin, in the dustbin, just now.
What's it taste like, what's it taste like, what's it taste like, just now?
Bloomin' awful, bloomin' awful, bloomin' awful, just now.
Serves you right, serves you right, serves you right, just now.
Same to you, same to you, same to you, just now.

Being immediately absorbed into this community, joining in the communal sing-song and learning to swing on the big boys' swings banished my sadness at leaving my parents. I felt accepted and part of things in a way I never had at school in London.

Later that morning a few of us wandered off to see our new school just opposite the rec and met a couple of women who told us that Neville Chamberlain had just declared war on Germany. I was excited rather than worried or shocked by the news. I had been living with my people's arch enemy for several years. War had been in the air for a long time. Now we'd show 'em!

Lunch consisted of my first-ever Sunday roast: beef, Yorkshire pudding and all the trimmings topped by an abundance of thick darkbrown gravy; a revelation, so different from my Jewish gastronomic experience. That afternoon, Mr Brooksbank took me for a trip in his rickety Austin 7; first to Stamford to see the George Inn sign straddling what was then the A1 and then on to nearby Wittering airfield where we saw Hurricanes taking off on training exercises.

He was a skilled worker in a local factory engaged in war production, probably no more than thirty, dark complexioned with black, slicked down, Brylcreemed hair and with the wiry leanness so common to working men in the first half of the last century. He had a practical competence and knew about things of which my father was totally ignorant. This first day felt like the beginning of a holiday. I liked being an evacuee. But my unconscious had other ideas. I began to wet the bed. Not nightly, but I often woke up in the morning having soaked my pyjamas and sheets. Mrs Brooksbank did not respond harshly or punish me but she must have been fed up with the frequent sheet changes and extra laundry I caused and there was a distinct cooling towards this voluble, cocky, Jewish Londoner with his enuretic tendencies.

My parents came to visit me once only. I was delighted to see them but all I can remember of that day is of sitting with them on a bench by Walton Station level crossing, nursing a small fart bubble back and forth along the fissure of my buttocks, memorable because it was a new skill learnt in secret on that very occasion. Shortly after their visit Dad was posted to Broderick's Reading branch and day trips to see me were then out of the question. They sent me frequent postcards, one of which described how on a glorious autumn day they strolled through Reading town centre sharing a large bag of succulent tomatoes. I was baffled by their eccentricity. Why would anyone want to eat tomatoes on their own, for pleasure, like toffees? The ways of adults were beyond me.

We evacuees of course had no school of our own and we shared the primary school opposite the rec with the local children; they attended in the morning and we in the afternoon. There was one weekly highlight. A teacher came round with a trolley of books for you to choose from and it was yours to read for the next hour and following weeks. Completely at random, I selected Richmal Crompton's *Just William*. From the first page I was totally absorbed, shushed for laughing aloud. In the William books I discovered the sheer joy of and total immersion in reading.

It was also in Peterborough that I finally came out of my social isolation. I took Marion Chadwick, fair-haired and pretty, the cleverest in my class, to the rec via our back garden. In gentlemanly fashion I helped her over the fence in full view of Mr and Mrs B. and for several days had to endure their teasing of my politeness – presumably unheard of in our part of Peterborough – and my obvious infatuation. It was true; I was besotted with Marion. But it was a pure and innocent love and the sexualisation by adults of this pre-sexual friendship made it into something shameful and embarrassing.

Friendships with boys were much less problematic and excited no adult comment. In the rec, the playground and the street, a cheeky chappie side of me was constellated. I found that I could make other kids laugh and was accepted into a gang consisting of both local and London boys and for the first time I tasted freedom away from adult surveillance. We roamed the surrounding countryside, swishing sticks along muddy paths, stopping at hedgerows to pick blackberries. We traversed the woods and were chased by farmers when caught in the act of scrumping. I was also introduced to bawdy humour. I spotted a metal sign embossed PCWW [Peterborough Council Water Works].

"What does that stand for?" I asked.

"Peter's Cock Wants Washing", someone snapped back. This was the wittiest, the funniest thing I had ever heard.

I was taken to see *Snow White*. I loved the antics of the dwarves, individually, so well characterised but was terrified by the evil Queen at the moment when she disguised herself as an old crone.

Also with the whole family crammed into the Austin 7, we went on a trip to visit Mr B's mother. The route took us through the mediaeval centres and across the ancient bridges of Wisbech, Downham Market and Kings Lynn, and we stopped at Hunstanton to gawp and marvel at its stratified, multi-coloured cliffs. Mrs Brooksbank senior lived in an isolated, tumbledown cottage, surrounded by a great expanse of flatland, bounded by the Great Ouse. The old lady I'm sure was harmless enough but dressed in all black, bent and toothless, she resembled the witch in Snow White and I was very relieved when after tea, Mr B. took me for a walk to see the Great Ouse, a straight wide sheet of water between high banks 'to protect the land from flooding', Mr B explained.

These excursions were brief shafts of light in an otherwise increasingly bleak landscape. Back at home I was treated with coolness and Mr B began to cuff or slap me for disobedience or other minor faults, such as coming home late or with muddy shoes. On one occasion he hit me when I told him that I had been out with the gang even though I had never been expressly prohibited from doing so. As the nights closed in, so did I, and I began to fill an exercise book with sums and other things I had learnt or thought of or imagined. I wrote out and memorised Walter de la Mare's 'The Scarecrow', the first poem which had any emotional impact on me. I was too young to make the symbolic connection with my miserable situation expressed in the first quatrain.

> *All winter through I bow my head*
> *Beneath the driving rain;*
> *The North Wind powders me with snow*
> *And blows me black again*

But as hinted at in the final quatrain, I needed only patience and to tough it out to realise a happy outcome and a return to my own family.

> *Soon I shall gaze across a sea*
> *Of sun–begotten grain,*
> *Which my unflinching watch hath sealed*
> *For harvest once again.*

By the end of November 1939 I probably looked like a scarecrow myself. Dirty, unkempt and un-cared for, I was suffering from a croupy cough, and had come out in spots and boils all over my face and body. It was in this condition that grandfather Simon found me when he came unexpectedly to visit me in early December. He took one look at me, packed my belongings and brought me back to London that very day.

15. LIVERPOOL

My parents were no longer in Reading; a month before I left Peterborough, they had moved to Liverpool, the home of the huge clearing sheds of the giant football pools, Littlewoods and Vernons. Because it was a major port, at the outbreak of war these buildings were taken over by the Ministry of Information for the censorship of mail to and from abroad, and my father, eager to avoid the draft and claiming a greater knowledge of French and German than he in fact had, bluffed his way into a job there.

After staying with my grandparents for a few days, they put me on a train in the care of a portly middle-aged man. They entrusted the safety of a nine-year-old to a stranger. I didn't mind at all. Wondrous things to see and experience: the complexities of the junctions and marshalling yards at Rugby and Crewe and crossing the bridge over the River Mersey at Runcorn. My parents were waiting for me at Lime Street station. It was dusk and the sky was fiery red. As our tram climbed Brownlow Hill, the sandstone mass of the Anglican Cathedral loomed on our right. My father told me about the Mersey ferries, the overhead railway, the Mersey Tunnel with its JUNCTION in the middle. I decided to explore the city and its tram system as soon as I could.

We occupied the top flat of no. 32 Bentley Road, a flatlet house. Mrs Fraser, an elderly woman whose sole companion was an equally elderly Pekinese dog, was our landlady. There was a matey, louche atmosphere to the place. A ground floor room was occupied by a very attractive couple, handsome Alex Parker and blonde beauty, Pat Potter. Rare in our circles to know an unmarried, cohabiting pair. My bourgeois parents were entranced. They quickly struck up a friendship with Pat and Alex and soon were introduced to and absorbed by a bohemian, pub crawling group of artists, poets, dancers, socialists and assorted intelligentsia.

I too found my place in the house. I was of use. I ran errands. For money. I fetched milk, bread, carrots. I'm sure that this early work experience of self-employment laid the foundations of my future freelance careers. Money in exchange for services.

I also gained a reputation for enterprise. The winter of 1940 was exceptionally cold. Coal was in short supply. Our usual coalman failed to appear. We were all freezing. One morning at the bottom of our road I spotted a horse-drawn cart laden with bulging coal sacks. I directed the coalman to no. 32 where he was relieved of his entire load. I was generously tipped by grateful lodgers.

But the greatest benefit of my parents' preoccupation with their new-found social life was the freedom it offered me. I wasn't at school so I could come and go as I pleased. I mastered the tram system, travelled on the overhead railway which traversed the length of the docks, pottered around Pier Head, took the ferry to New Brighton with its beaches and fairgrounds and, as a budding young cineaste, frequented the repertory cinemas in Lime Street showing double features of American crime films and thrillers – admission 6d and no enforcement of having to be accompanied by an adult.

I keenly followed the progress of the war. Fiercely patriotic but naïve, in early 1940 during the Phoney War I had no doubts that the combined military might of Great Britain, France and their imperial allies, hugely outnumbering the German forces as it did, would soon defeat the comically Chaplinesque Adolf Hitler. The war map of Europe on my bedroom wall showed these statistics: Strength of Armies: France 3 million, Great Britain 1.5 million, Germany 2 million. I did my arithmetic. No contest.

Being first up in the morning I dashed downstairs to the hall to read the newspapers which had been delivered; the *News Chronicle* (ours) and three copies of the *Daily Express*, and on Sunday, *Reynolds News* (ours) and the *Sunday Express*. Things began to get bad with the German invasion of Norway which was when I started to listen to the 9 o'clock news with my parents, read by Alvar Liddell in the beautifully modulated tones of what now sounds the extraordinary BBC accent of the time. As spring wore on, the news worsened by the day and my parents became increasingly concerned. Winston Churchill became Prime Minister and we listened to all his broadcasts following Dunkirk and the fall of France and during the Battle of Britain. I was only a child. I believed all our propaganda. I did not in any way comprehend the danger we were in, both as a nation and as Jews.

The adults were busy and even more preoccupied than before. Dad joined the Local Defence Volunteers, soon renamed the Home Guard, and was off training with broomsticks at the weekends. Mum started to look for war work.

But my life as a small boy just went on being a small boy's life. I had never had a pet. Not a dog, cat, guinea pig or even a mouse. Well, we had mice but they were lured into small wooden cages and drowned. My uncle Jack owned a cat, I'm sure only for the punning possibilities of the name he gave it: Catastrophe. Mr. and Mrs. Lewis lived in the flat below ours. He worked in the toy department of John Lewis. Could there have ever been a better job than that? He gave me a very good deal on Dinky toy warplanes of which I was a devoted collector. Thereby hangs a tail, attached to an eager wire-haired terrier called Spot belonging to the Lewises. I became very attached to him and was allowed to take him for walks in Sefton Park on condition that I never let him off his lead. For many weeks I conscientiously stuck to this rule but on one occasion Spot strained so doggedly against the leash that I, being deluded enough to believe that he knew who was master, was tempted to set him free. Off he shot into the distance and out of my sight. I ran after him, shouting his name but he had disappeared. With increasing panic, I searched the park until dark when finally, with a heavy heart and huge anxiety I returned home and confessed the loss to his owners. They immediately set off and soon returned with a cheerfully bounding, tail-wagging Spot. No reproaches were made, no punishment administered but I was never allowed to walk Spot again.

I had no schooling for several months and often having nothing better to do mooched around the city centre. I happened upon the Natural History Museum which was closed 'for the duration', but with the help of some smooth talking, I induced a guide to take me on a private tour. He diligently showed me round what he considered the most interesting exhibits for a small boy: large stuffed mammals and birds and case after case of butterflies, moths and beetles and I politely followed him. Eventually I summoned up the courage to enquire about what was really on my mind.

'Do you have any stuffed ladies without clothes on?'

My guide was shocked and disappointed, looked at me with disapproval and without a further word ushered me out of the building.

After the Easter holidays I was put into St Margaret of Antioch C of E Primary School – afternoons only because of wartime shortages of staff. Best of all I was admitted into a small gang from whom (at last!) I learned the basic facts of human reproduction. I wasn't horrified, it made perfect sense and I felt a great sense of relief at having broken into the taboo subject. My first comment to my friends founded on the daily indoctrination at our church school was 'That means God must have done it to Mary.' Even at that age I wasn't buying in to any notion of an Immaculate Conception. I consider myself lucky that my Christian friends didn't beat me up. Generously they continued my sex education with dirty jokes and ditties, involving such characters as a young swain, an old man and his daughter, Fuckerada and Dick and Mary at the dairy.

But there were rough, tough kids in the class. I didn't speak Scouse and was mocked for my posh London accent. During my months in Liverpool, fed by my mother whenever I was hungry on a diet of raw onion sandwiches, I'd become quite fat and was nicknamed Porky. I was shoved about, tripped up, pinched and elbowed, in classroom and playground. Just high-spirited horseplay, but I wasn't used to it.

There was great excitement at home; my father had drawn the favourite, *Mac Moffat*, in the office Grand National sweepstake. The winner would scoop £40 – worth about £2000 in today's money. Dad promised me that if he won he would buy me an electric train set with junctions. After school on the day of the race I dashed out of the gates and asked the goldfish vendor stationed there,

"Who won the National?"

"*Bogstar!*"

I was devastated. No train set for me. I trundled home. I needed comfort. My parents were out and had left me a note 'Gone to Aintree with Pat and Alex' I made myself an onion sandwich and waited for them to return but did not see them until the next morning; they'd been pub-crawling with thousands of other racegoers

But my disappointment disappeared when the next weekend my uncle David, newly qualified and enlisted in the *Royal Army Medical Corps*, came to visit us on embarkation leave, resplendent in his Captain's uniform. We all had tea at the *Adelphi Hotel* and the grown-ups talked grown-up talk while I wolfed *Kunzle* cakes and listened to the pianist playing *I've Never Had a Lesson in my Life but I know All About Love", We're Going to Hang out the Washing on the Siegfried Line* and *Two Sleepy People*. As we parted David handed me a package. A present! I willed it to contain *Dinky* toys. A flight of *Fokkers*! A squadron of *Spitfires*! Once home I tore off the wrappings. A two volumes set of *French for Beginners*. What an inept birthday present for a ten-year-old. What a failure of imagination. All these years on I understand why. He then had no children of his own. But more importantly, he had never wanted to be a doctor; he had a flair for languages and they were his true love. I memorised 'Un, deux, trois' to 'dix' on page 1 but then never opened *French for Beginners* again.

It was the long summer holiday; time of boredom for ten-year-old boys everywhere. My best friend, Leonard, and I made our way down to Pier Head in the hope of adventure. Trams congregated, ferries disgorged passengers from Birkenhead and Wallasey, people bustled about; it was a place of arrival and departure to and from faraway places. Anything could happen there. We soon became fed up. We had no money and no plan. We sat on the same bench as a seedy, shabby man. He offered us bars of chocolate. 'Yes please!' He went off to the Nestles slot machine and bought us each a penny bar. While I ate mine, he put his arm around my shoulder and fondled my ear. I didn't like the physical contact but was enjoying the chocolate. Leonard whose thigh the man had been squeezing stood up saying,

"We'd better go. We'll be late for tea."

"There's plenty of time." the man responded. "Come on! I'll take you for a ride on the Overhead Railway."

This was the treat; the excitement we had been craving. Three stops and we alighted. He held our hands.

"Come and see my house." he said.

We made our way through a maze of mean, dockside streets until we came to a dilapidated house where he announced,

"Here we are"

Beyond the front door stretched a long, ill lit and dingy corridor receding into total darkness.

"Come on in and we'll have a cup of tea".

Not on your Nellie!

"Quick, scarper!" I shouted sensing danger, and off we ran all the way back to Pier Head. To our relief the man made no attempt to follow us. Discussing what had happened, Leonard and I concluded that the man had been up to no good and should be reported to the police. We made our way to Dale Street Police Station where we presented ourselves at the enquiry desk and assuming the role of spokesboy I said,

"A man tried to kidnap us."

Soon we were in an interview room making a statement to a young detective constable.

"Why did you go with him?" he asked

"We were on the spree." I replied, delighted to have the opportunity of using vocabulary picked up from one of my comics.

Leonard's parents and mine were contacted and came to pick us up. Arrangements were made for us to come back the next day and take the police to the house where the attempted abduction had taken place. This was the real adventure – to be at the centre of a police investigation. Helping them with their enquiries.

My parents were not cross with me and were even accepting of our spree-seeking motivation. But then my father's notion of appropriate punishment was extremely bizarre. The previous week we were walking in Sefton Park and a passing gang of youths shouted insulting comments about my parents. 'Fuck off', I called after them. And for this, for rushing to defend the honour of my father and mother, I was punished. Dad made me write out the word 'Fuck' 1000 times.

Boring, but also strangely enjoyable. I was also punished for the Pier Head incident although that was not my parents' intention. They decided not to cooperate with the police and cancelled our appointment at Dale Street. To this day I have never understood their reason for this. Was it fear of getting involved or of publicity? Whatever the reason I was deeply disappointed.

But I suffered a further punishment even more severe. My fantasy is that it arose as an indirect result of Leonard's parents being far less forgiving than mine and that he, fearful of painful retribution, claimed that I was the sole initiator of our encounter with the paedophile, for this is what our parents, but not we, knew him to be. And that he further asserted that he was an unwilling participant in what had occurred but I had persuaded him to accompany the man or even in some diabolical way compelled him to do so.

'It was his fault Dad. He made me.'

So Leonard (in my imagination) escaped punishment but not me. For in consequence of their belief in my bad influence on their son, my malign propensity to lead him astray or into danger, he was forbidden any further contact or association with me. Innocent of all crime or wrongdoing, I lost my best, and only, friend. I never saw Leonard again.

With his loss I was very much on my own and had to create my own amusements. I marched up and down Bentley Road alternating the British army's quick march with the German goose-step. A Captain Mainwaring type, straight out of 'Dads Army', witnessing the latter, accused me of being unpatriotic and ordered me to stop.

Two girls about my age in their navy blue school uniforms and velour hats used to walk along Bentley Road every afternoon on their way home. They were very pretty and I wanted to make contact with them. I didn't have the faintest idea how. So purely to attract their attention, and not out of malicious intent, I threw stones, not at them, but along the pavement towards them. Result, but not the one I had hoped for. The next day they appeared at the front door of no. 32 and complained to my mother. She was of course angry with me.

'That was a most ungentlemanly thing to do, Boris Rumney. Go to their house right away and tell them you're sorry.'

Conscience stricken, I did more than that. I dug into my money box and bought the girls each a monster bar of Cadburys Milk Chocolate. I rang the bell of their pastiche Jacobean house round the corner from us in Lodge Lane and when the girls' mother came to the door, I was at my most polite and courtly, made my apologies and handed over my gifts. I must have made such a favourable impression that I was instantly forgiven and invited to tea the following Sunday.

My hosts were the Sonnabends, a wealthy Jewish family, refugees from Germany and their lodge was my Brideshead and I, Charles Ryder in miniature, to their Flytes. During the summer of that year I was a frequent guest at their table at which they served sandwiches, salads, delicacies and patisserie of a variety and refinement of a completely different order to the eastern European and plain English fare I was used to. We played in their sumptuous garden and large lawn, ideal for our games. These afternoons gave me an experience of a world of other possibilities and a first glimpse into a more gracious style of living which came to an end with the approach of autumn and the first German air raids.

After the fall of France, the residents of no. 32 cooperated in taking precautions against German bombing. Mrs Fraser designated the cellar as our air raid shelter and we spent a weekend furnishing it with easy chairs, table and a bed for me as the only child in the house. The first raids started in August and then occurred with increasing frequency and intensity. As soon as the siren sounded we all dashed downstairs. I very soon got used to the routine and lay on my bed listening to the characteristic, intermittent throb and drone of the German bombers, the sound of anti-aircraft fire and exploding bombs until I fell fast asleep. I was unperturbed by the commotion as I did not have the capacity to envision a bomb falling on our house.

On 29th November I slept through the siren. Dad shook me awake. 'Hurry Boris, there's an air raid.' Mum, Dad and I quickly made our way downstairs. On reaching the ground floor I popped into the toilet, saying that I would follow on down to the cellar. Pee done, I was just reaching for the chain to flush, when there was a large explosion and the skylight fell in with large shards of glass crashing into the hall immediately outside the loo. Thus by a second I escaped death or serious injury.

The next morning Mum and I walked the neighbourhood. We discovered that Granby Street where we shopped daily had been badly hit and that the land mine which had blown out all our windows, had destroyed a jute factory in Lodge Lane. The Sonnabends' lodge was unscathed. Later that day we left Liverpool never to return.

16. WEST KIRBY

The night of the destruction of the nearby jute factory and the consequential blast damage to our house was one air raid too many for my *geshrockener* [easily scared] mother. The next afternoon, she and I (I imagine my father was at work) took the little electric train from Liverpool Central Station to West Kirby, a small seaside town on the River Dee side of the Wirral peninsular. We were refugees and had no idea where we were going to live. The first night was spent lodging with an old lady in a house just down the road from Calday Grammar School. No electricity, no gas. The house was lit by a few oil lamps which cast eerie shadows everywhere. A few other evacuees had found their way there and we all sat down in silence to a frugal meal of soft boiled eggs, which I could not bear, meanly buttered, thick cut white bread and cups of tepid, milky tea. My prevailing feeling was of overwhelming boredom, immobilised and silenced in a dark flickering room amongst this group of depressed and traumatised people. There were no books or comics; I had left all mine in Liverpool and anyway there wasn't enough light to read by. With no radio to listen to the 9 o'clock news, there was nothing for it but to go to bed immediately after tea and lie awake to the sinister sound of wave after wave of German bombers on their way to Liverpool. A few minutes later came the distant bangs and booms of anti-aircraft fire, bombs and land mines.

After the gloom of this ill-lit house, it was a joy to wake up to a crisp, sunny morning and the invigorating smell of the sea and be back in the world and on the move again, this time to an unoccupied house in the old village of West Kirby where we met Pat Parker and her sister Effie. A blazing row erupted between Pat and Effie; Pat had secured a tenancy of the house and wanted us, the three Rumneys to share it with her and Alex. Effie believed that she had a prior claim as sister and played the sibling card for all it was worth but Pat was adamant and we became the favoured co-tenants. Effie stormed off and we never saw her again.

I was of course just a passive observer in all these events, trailing after my mother. I never wondered then, as I wonder now, how all these arrangements to meet were made: how my mother knew to get to that place or that house, how my father knew when and where to join us. Did my mother telephone him at work? Write him letters? He must have been staying in Liverpool in the bombing whilst my mother was fixing up our accommodation. Did he stay at Bentley Road or elsewhere? How were our belongings transported from Liverpool to West Kirby?

Our house was in the heart of the Village, a simple cottage, with whitewashed walls, sparsely furnished and next door to an abandoned abattoir. I had a room of my own and in the evenings when I was in bed I had my first taste of classical music listening to Alex's shellac records of Tchaikovsky's *1st Piano Concerto*, Borodin's *Polovtsian Dances* and piano works of Chopin. For years I would whistle melodies from these works in buses, shops or other public places in the hope that others would recognise them - and me as a sensitive, music-loving boy. They never did of course; I could have saved my breath.

Shortly after moving in, I contracted a severe bronchitis which kept me in bed for two weeks. It was during this time that I first experienced the pleasures of adult books. There was a general store nearby which also contained a small circulating library. The first book my mother borrowed for me was a *Saint* book by Leslie Charteris, an Agatha Christie of his day. I was hooked. I read the whole of his oeuvre during my illness, forcing my mother to visit the library more and more frequently as my reading speeded up during this period of enforced immobility.

Less than two hundred yards from our house was a popular West Kirby pub, the *Ring O' Bells*, at which, virtually every evening, my parents and Pat and Alex would join what I imagine to be a louche and bohemian crowd. Pat and Alex introduced my parents to a completely different social milieu and despite the increasing hardships of war or perhaps because of them, this was a particularly exciting and carefree time for them. It was for me too. Freed from the constraints of adult oversight, I became part of a small gang of village boys for whom one of the rooms of the disused slaughterhouse became our meeting place and where we sat eating Smith's crisps and anything else we could lay our hands on, drinking bottles of *Tizer the Appetizer* and consciously modelling ourselves on Richmal Crompton's William and his friends. Perhaps at some level too, we were in our boyish way, aping the ribald adult behaviour up at the *Ring O' Bells*.

Once I was over my bout of bronchitis, I was enrolled at the local elementary school, scarcely two minutes' walk from my house. It was a Church of England school, next to the village church itself. Our classrooms were large and airy but instead of the conventional arrangement of desks in rows, work tables were laid out in a single row along three sides of the room with boys occupying one half and girls the other. Sitting opposite me was Hilary, sturdy in body and limb, fair-haired and rosy cheeked. I was immediately infatuated. I wouldn't have put it that way at the time even if I'd known the word. I confided to Robert Ellis who I thought was my friend that I thought Hilary the nicest girl in the class. The traitorous Robert spread this delicious piece of gossip. It was taken for granted that I was in love and the class collectively dubbed me 'Hilary'. This wasn't the only nickname I was shamed by bearing. My mother's daily diet of onion sandwiches continued unabated and I was still as fat as I had been in Liverpool. Here I was imaginatively named 'Barrage Balloon', soon to be shortened to 'Barrage'. This was just the start of a number of humiliations I suffered in West Kirby.

After virtually a year without schooling, I had fallen behind and did not shine academically. There was one-hour-long period once a week which I adored above all other lessons. Called *Free Composition*, we were allowed to write on any subject of our choice. It was the first time I experienced the sheer joy and pleasure of writing. As my imagination began to flow so did my pen and I write now in the hope of re-experiencing that first exquisite flush of creativity. But *'rarely, rarely, comest thou, spirit of delight'*.

In Liverpool I had written only one major work, a limerick which I still think wasn't bad for a boy of ten.

> *There was once a female Finn*
> *Who really committed a sin.*
> *She made friends with Goring*
> *Who thought her adoring*
> *And asked her to visit Berlin.*

Was it in the hope of self-publishing that at the same time I became interested in printing? The small ads section of the *Liverpool Echo* advertised small hand printing presses at the price of 7/6d, a little under 40p in today's money, but then way beyond my means. My savings from errands run for the residents of 32 Bentley Road did however allow me to buy a much cheaper alternative; a special jelly and ink. Much to my mother's annoyance I got her to liquefy the jelly in a large pan and then pour the liquid into a flat dish. Once solidified I was ready to print by creating a master copy with the special ink and placing it face down on the jelly. The advertising blurb claimed that you could print off thirty copies per operation but I found they came out blurred, smudged and illegible. This was the end of my career as a printer, but my obsession with the process continued undiminished. Almost too good to be true, there was a boy in my class called Leonard Gould whose father owned the only printing works in West Kirby. I assiduously cultivated his friendship and soon was rewarded with an invitation to tea and a visit to the family printing presses. I was shown how type was set, saw the printing presses in action churning out catalogues and *The Hoylake and West Kirby Recorder* and to my acquisitive delight was given a parting present of a set of lead typeface letters. Back in Leonard's house we played with his complex and many junctioned electric train set. I could not imagine a life richer than lucky old Leonard's. One of the compositions I wrote, I entitled *A Day in the Life of a Printer* in which I enumerated the books and publications printed by my fantasised printer self: '...and then I set up the type for *The Boys' Bumper Book of Tricks and Puzzles* and ran off 5000 copies'.

The boys' pack leader in our class was a tough, strong boy known as Pobbo, who already had a reputation as an exceptional swimmer. I felt that Pobbo belonged to a completely different species of human being to me; he was born with leadership genes and he evoked automatic deference in you. His best friend and lieutenant was a freckled open-faced boy called George Clague who eventually became my best friend. Another distinguished member of our class was the son of the local butcher, Tom Tutty, who organised a masturbation circle (I spotted them once – literally a circle) which used to convene on the Grange, a wooded, thickly thicketed area overlooking the River Dee. I was invited to join but even then, out of a kind of modesty and preference for privacy, I declined.

West Kirby is on the estuary of the River Dee, at that point about five miles wide. Across the Dee you could see the Welsh hills and on a very clear day Snowdonia itself. The tide goes out for miles, broken up by runnels and small gullies. During those times we often walked out with sandwiches and a flask of tea for a picnic onto the Hilbre Islands about a mile offshore. The main island was a meteorological station and access to it forbidden but this did not apply to the rocks, small coves and the caves of its foreshore.

There were elements in these trips which I, cautious of physical danger, did not heighten my enjoyment. There were quicksands to be avoided and the incoming tide was rapid and powerful. I had fantasies of blundering into a quicksand, being sucked into it up to my waist, my friends watching from a safe distance, fearful of being drawn in themselves. Me, flailing helplessly, sinking inexorably until I was submerged to my mouth and nostrils, the taste of coarse wet sand clogging my airways, spluttering, gasping, choking, darkness.

That never happened of course but I did have a near death experience. Because of the huge fluctuations in the tide, West Kirby had constructed a semicircular sea wall to contain the sea for about a mile along its main promenade and a lido was built there. In the summer term my class was taken there for a weekly dip. There were no formal swimming lessons but all the children seemed able to swim, except me. Fed up with pottering about in my depth and despite my usual timidity, I struck out in a kind of doggy paddle. It seemed to work. I made progress. I exulted. It was so easy, I could swim. Then I went under. I irrupted into a different world, one of darkness and silence. I surfaced once, then twice. My eyes stung, I swallowed water, my chest tightened, then someone pulled me to the surface and brought me to the poolside, fighting for breath. No teacher had dived in to save me in the nick of time. My rescuer was a classmate. For a brief period, I was the centre of attention and I bragged about the incident afterwards. But I said nothing to my mother; she would have forbidden me to enter the sea again or even learn to swim – as her mother had forbidden her.

My parents seemed to figure very little during this period. I was free to come and go as I pleased. I joined the Scouts mainly because after each meeting you could buy sweets, chocolates and cakes, a primary consideration in those days of shortages and rationing. Inspired by the *William* books I was borrowing weekly from the West Kirby public library and made feasible by access to unlimited amounts of confectionery, I organised a party for a few friends, funded by an equal contribution from each of us. I was responsible for the provisions and the venue was the Lido.

After the next scout meeting I bought quantities of chocolate and Lyons chocolate rolls and from a local shop, bottles of *Tizer*. I struggled to convey these goodies in an open cardboard box the half mile or so from my home on a blazing June afternoon and by the time I reached the Lido, the chocolate had melted and the chocolate rolls had congealed and were adhering to the silver foil wrapping. The lukewarm *Tizer,* shaken during its transportation, foamed like champagne when opened. If lickable and smearable were edible the party was a great success but not for me. It was the first time I had hosted a social occasion and I felt responsible for failing my friends. I left the Scouts shortly afterwards. I could not get to grips with the complexity of knots. All my life I have never got beyond the Granny and the Reef.

At this time failure was around in a far more serious way. I was shortly to take *the Scholarship*, later called the 11+. I was desperate to pass and go to Calday Grammar School. I have no idea where these academic aspirations came from. Perhaps because I was judged to be a clever boy when younger. Or parental expectations picked up by me over the years, the emphasis on learning and brilliance in the wider Rumney family. Whatever it was, because of the lengthy interruptions to my schooling between the ages of seven and ten, I needed someone to help me prepare for the scholarship tests in maths, English and general knowledge. Dad was busy commuting to work in Liverpool every day and tied to Home Guard exercises, some overnight fire watching and fun and games at the *Ring O'Bells*. Nonetheless I believe he could have done better than he did.

He gave me no personal coaching at all and without researching the standards required, set me test papers devised by him, of such complexity, not to say opacity, that they were far beyond my understanding and in any event bore no relation whatsoever to the nature of the papers which were actually set.

I felt confident going into the exam. I knew a lot. I was a bright kid. But once I read the first test paper, the questions made no sense. I stared at them uncomprehendingly. I had never done the work on which they were based. I felt empty and panicky. Shaky and miserable, I went into the playground, ostensibly to have a pee, but really to try and calm myself and collect my thoughts. To no purpose; the questions and problems set were just as baffling when I returned to my place.

Two months later the results were read out in class. Three girls and Alan Fairbanks, our cleverest pupils, had passed. I had failed. Later William Watson confronted me.

"You bin cryin'. Just 'cos your name weren't called!"

"Haven't been crying", but it was true, I had stifled my sobs but my eyes were full of tears and my voice was quavery. The news spread and the classroom resounded to jeers of 'Crybaby'. My failure and breakdown invoked far greater interest (and retribution) than the success of the four class members.

Returning home from school one day, early in July, I was unable to open the front door. I knocked and a woman leaned out of my bedroom window and shouted belligerently 'Go away, we don't want you here!' It was our landlord's family come to reclaim their property. We had been evicted. Both my parents were out and I had no idea what time they'd be back so I explained the situation to my friend Bob McDonald's mother who lived in the cottage opposite ours. She was a plump, motherly woman who tut-tutted at my predicament and the landlords' (as I now know) unlawful re-entry and gave me shelter. When my mother returned it was arranged that I would stay overnight with Mrs MacDonald and – the apparently inconsequential details one remembers – I breakfasted there as well, on eggs, bacon, fried bread, toast and marmalade; ordinary fare, but to me, never having experienced such dishes before, a Proustian moment.

The problem for me about our eviction was that I was infused with a deep sense of guilt because I thought it was all my fault. A few weeks before, a young male member of the landlord family came to the door asking for his fishing rod which he had left behind in a cupboard adjacent to my bedroom. He found the rod but was upset because there was a section missing. I held my tongue but was full of anxiety because some time before this I had discovered the rod and the various uses to which I could put it: swishing, fencing, a rifle, a cane, a spear, a walking stick. And as a punishment for the theft of their property, the landlords had turfed us out. I was to blame and to avoid reprisals myself, dared not confess my transgression.

Where my parents and Pat and Alex stayed the night I have no idea. Nor if they took any action against the landlords. Did they manage to retrieve all our clothing and possessions? None of these important issues were shared with me. I was just taken off by my mother to Liverpool Lime Street station. We boarded a train to Leeds, packed with civilians and servicemen. I was disgruntled because I didn't have a window seat and was even more fed up later in the journey because there were so many cuttings and tunnels between Manchester and our destination. I was on my way to stay with my grandparents, Aaron and Esther, whilst my parents found new accommodation for us. My grandparents had evacuated to Leeds at the beginning of the war, never imagining that the industrial towns of the North would be within Hitler's bombers' reach within a year.

We took the tram from Leeds Central Station to Moortown and my grandparents' house in Sholebroke Road, a house sparsely furnished and dimly lit. My mother left to return to the Wirral the same day leaving me bereft and bored in the care of my grandparents. As Esther spoke only Yiddish, we were unable to have much in the way of conversation but at least that had the advantage of silence. Aaron was desperate to communicate his poetry to me as he had no one else to share it with. He was in the process of writing a poetic saga in Yiddish and day after day he read me sections of it, first in Yiddish, then in English, interspersed with lengthy commentaries on the poem's genesis, its mythology and allegorical and symbolic significance and meaning. It was all totally over my head. I didn't understand a word. In addition, I had to bear his squeezes and cuddles, the nuzzling of his grizzled unshaven cheeks against mine. There were no books or toys to keep me occupied so I devised a complex public transport system in their living room using a set of Lotto cards as the buses and the Lotto counters as passengers.

Both food and money were in short supply and to make matters worse Esther was a poor cook, producing thin soups, greasy stews and watery vegetables. Not only that, but there was never enough to eat and I felt perpetually hungry. Aaron was diabetic and there was in the kitchen his ever full tin of Ryvita from which I stole to supplement my meagre diet.

Apart from my daily helpings of Aaron's magnum opus, life at Sholebroke Road was dreary, deadly dull and lacking spark and animation. I began to explore the city using the tram system with its maximum fare of 1d for children. I ventured as far afield as Roundhay Park, Leeds' largest open space, the ruins of Kirkstall Abbey and the great stately home of Temple Newsam. I went to the local cinema; the films I mainly wanted to see were thrillers which were barred to children unaccompanied by a grown-up. The common practice was to approach an adult entering the cinema and ask 'Please will you take me in?' And more often than not they would oblige. It was outside the cinema that I became friendly with some other boys and we formed ourselves into a little gang.

It was in this gang that I first discovered that I had incipient legal skills. We decided to formalise our corporate identity by drafting some rules of membership admission, purposes and conduct. At our rule drafting meeting I naturally and without opposition took over the role of drafting the wording (it wasn't just because I had the pencil and paper) and in my childish way produced something quite lucid and creditable. So the summer days passed; we roamed Roundhay Park, fished for tadpoles in the lake, went to the pictures, hung about in Leeds shopping centre and found a florin and blued it all on ice cream sundaes.

One day my aunts Rosa and Ray came down from London with their husbands, Alf and Jack, chauffeured by Alf in his Ford 8, ELA 655. The object was to combine seeing Aaron and Esther with a day out. I was taken along too, squashed into the back seat of the Ford with my two aunts as we journeyed to Knaresborough where we stayed for an hour or so. I went off by myself, first exploring the mediaeval centre of the town and then setting off along the River Nidd to see *Mother Shipton's Cave*, the legendary birthplace of Ursula Shipton, soothsayer and prophetess and dropping a penny into the *Petrifying Wishing Well*, yearning to be reunited with my parents. On the way back to Leeds we passed through Harrogate and I regretted that there was no time to stop and explore what even to my inexperienced eye seemed a very distinguished town. Rosa was keen to see Carmen Miranda in *Down Argentine Way,* a film then currently showing in central Leeds. It wasn't a film I would have chosen myself but it was in Technicolor and I enjoyed the flamboyance of Miranda's dresses and the Latin American rhythms and dances.

My parents had found accommodation in a modern semi-detached house at 84, Gleggside on the outskirts of West Kirby which we were to share with the owners Mr and Mrs Weir and I returned to our new home in early September just before the beginning of the autumn term. I was not sorry to leave Sholebroke Road.

17. CALDAY GRAMMAR SCHOOL

Ashton, Bennett, Blazer, Bellini, Broadhurst, Cannon, Cook, Cross, Davey, Davis, Delamere, Ellis, Ellison... Mould, Osborne, Playfair, Soar...

Their names are implanted indelibly in my memory, half my form mates at Calday Grammar School, where, having failed the scholarship, I became a paying pupil.

So in September 1941 I was catapulted into a new home, new school, new subjects and activities. With the adaptability and acceptance of youth I took it all in my stride: Latin, French, Algebra, Geometry and Woodwork. Homework. Rugby football. Initially I felt something of a yokel. The boys in my class seemed so knowledgeable, so sophisticated, and so witty. A small coterie, an elite, was dedicated to the music of *Harry Gold and his Pieces of Eight* who broadcast weekly and whose jazz rhythms were replicated on desktops by that curious mimicry of syncopated jazz drumming produced by hiss and teeth – *tsss-ta, ta-tsss-ta, ta-tsss-ta*.

This group, academically as well as in most other ways, more advanced than me, had gone through prep school together and had been close friends for several years. I yearned to be part of it.

My collection of bus and tram tickets was of no interest. My slender knowledge of the music of Tchaikovsky and Chopin cut no ice. My in-depth knowledge of the works of Richmal Crompton and Leslie Charteris did not impress. So I attempted a riskier tactic. Our maths master was teaching us about geometric shapes.

"Does anyone know what a polygon is?"

I put up my hand.

"A dead parrot, Sir."

I'd been waiting to be asked this question since I had seen the joke some months before in an ancient comic book. My reward was class hilarity and an order to report myself to the headmaster, Mr Glasspool, for impertinence. I left the classroom steeling myself for a beating. The head, an elderly man, preoccupied with the responsibility of running a school, inflated, due to the war, to 600 pupils, told me to curb my cheek in future and so I *'scaped a whipping*. My attempt to curry class favour was not successful; in fact, a week later I suffered a further setback. We were changing for rugby and neighbouring classmates spotted that I was wearing cream-coloured woollen underpants, with buttoned flies and a matching vest, with tape ties instead of buttons. These had been knitted by my mother. Deviating from the norm of white cotton elasticated pants and sleeveless vests, I was for several weeks the object of derision, the butt of remarks including words such as pansy and sissy and poof. Ever since that shaming episode, any possibility of desiring dandydom was squashed; all I craved was sartorial anonymity.

After school one day, I was on my way home when I suddenly found myself surrounded by about eight of my classmates shouting, "Jew, Jew, smelly old Jew." I was utterly shocked; this atavistic expression of hatred had come completely out of the blue. I had believed all these boys to be my friends. Near to tears I cried out,

"Why are you doing this? I've done nothing to hurt you."

"Oh yes you have" one wag replied. "You've hurt my nose." This riposte was greeted with hoots of laughter.

"I'll fight any one of you." I challenged.

"Super, anyone here would beat you. Choose."

I looked round. Alan Mould was one of their number. He was supposed to be my friend, a special friend. I felt a particular sense of betrayal. He was bigger and heavier than me but I didn't care. I pointed to him.

"Mould!" I said.

It was agreed that the fight would take place on the playing fields next day during morning break. Did I sleep that night? I can't remember but I certainly sat through the first lessons of the morning in a state of nervous excitement. The bell went and the whole class made for the rugby field. Word of the fight must have spread because half the school gathered round Mould and me as we're squared up to each other. We sparred for a few seconds and then I unleashed a right-hander which caught him full on the nose. He fell to the ground, blood gushing from his face. His seconds agreed that he was not fit to continue.

Back in the classroom I felt like a hero, exonerated, exultant as if I had been set and passed with flying colours a test of my courage. Our teacher took one look at my bloodied opponent and said, not unkindly "Get off to the washrooms Mould and clean yourself up." My feeling of triumph changed to apprehension; fighting was forbidden and I feared that I was to be called to account. My fears were unfounded; no accusation was made. It was as if news of the incident had reached the staff common room and a tacit agreement had been reached that no disciplinary action be taken.

The next day Mrs Mould engineered a meeting with my mother to complain about my behaviour. My mother would have none of it; accusing Alan of anti-Semitism, she stood up for my right to defend my honour by fighting him. Her quick temper and fieriness could be a great asset when not directed at me.

The fight with Mould marked a turning point. The anti-Jewish jokes and taunts ceased. I was accepted as a fully-fledged member of my class for the rest of my time at Calday.

This incident coincided with my growing enthusiasm for rugby – I had a flair for tackling and was given the position of full-back in the class team. On my twelfth birthday, Soar, who at 5'6" lived up to his name, was streaming down the field towards our twenty-two. Only I stood between him and a try. I tackled him low and as he and I went down, his boot caught me a crack on the nose. Back at home I presided over my birthday tea with ten guests, jubilant at my own powers and sporting a sore and swollen nose. From that date it grew into the Semitic schnozzle which I bear today and in vain I have contended that its size and shape are due not to genetics but to my rugby injury.

As a postscript to this eventful day, after the party was over my mother reproached me for grabbing food before my guests. I was mystified. "But it's my birthday, my party" I said. My mother explained the duties of a host. And so the canons of hospitality were first inculcated in me.

In the summer term I fell in love with cricket which unlike most of the boys in my class, I had never played before. I was always hopeless with the bat but had some potential as a bowler. Osborne, the star batsmen in our class came over to my house a few times and on a piece of waste ground showed me how to bowl. From then on I played in every form game and in the evenings with a group of boys coached by an enthusiastic father on a greensward overlooking the River Dee estuary with the foothills of Snowdonia in the distance. We played until dusk set the sky over North Wales aflame with the most improbable sunsets, painted by Turner when he stayed at nearby Hoylake. But for us it was bad light stopped play.

The school did not provide lunch and several of us used to dash down the scrubland of Grange Hill to the British Restaurant in West Kirby for a nourishing, plentiful meal, price 9d. Stews, pies, roasts and extra potatoes and gravy for us growing lads and suet puddings and custard. British Restaurants were communal eating places designed to augment the meagre rations of wartime, numbering at their apogee, 2000 throughout the land.

All these school and out-of-school activities were taking place against the backdrop of the war in which I continued to take a keen interest. During 1941 and until October 1942 things were not going well, the air raids ground on, by the end of 1941, the Germans were at the gates of Moscow and in North Africa, Rommel's Afrika Corps had thrown the British Army back to within fifty miles of Alexandria. Stalingrad and El Alamein were yet to come. German bombers returning from Liverpool passed overhead. One night such a bomber randomly dropped a leftover bomb which hit and destroyed a house right in the middle of a huge field, a quarter of a mile from our own house killing all the occupants. Shortly after this incident the authorities delivered a Morrison shelter, a cage-like structure made of steel which nearly filled our living room. The top doubled as a table on which we ate our meals and I did my homework.

Nor were we at school immune from wartime activities. Whilst commercial activities, the sale and swapping of stamps, comics and other commodities continued unabated (I sold my entire ticket collection and used the proceeds to buy a Penny Black and Cape Triangular) we were now called on to give up our Saturdays to work our way through West Kirby, collecting any utensils or objects made of metal to be recycled into the war effort. Off we went, supervised by a master, trundling handcarts and wheelbarrows and humping sacks and other containers. There was real joy in this collective endeavour, in the feelings of virtue in making a contribution and getting out and about in the sharp winter sunshine. The adults, carrying out their aluminum pots and pans, tin baths and old iron kettles also brought glasses of orange squash and currant buns for us boys.

I had never handled, let alone used, a tool before I started woodwork lessons. To this day no craftsman, I did become reasonably proficient in the use of the plane and the chisel and progressed as far as making objects with dovetail joints. George Clague from my primary school days lived a few yards from my own house. Our proximity cemented our friendship and we were in and out of each other's houses all the time. George's father had a shed/workshop with a full set of tools and we set about creating our own assembly line, turning out model destroyers which we painted battleship grey and hawked door-to-door, first in Gleggside, and then further afield at the price of 2/6d each in aid of Hoylake's Warship Week. We sold twenty-eight models in all, raising a total sum of £3.10.0 towards Hoylake's adoption of the destroyer HMS Verdun.

As I became more immersed in school life and activities and formed new friendships, I saw less of George. Was this primitive snobbishness on my part? George was at a state secondary school; I was a grammar school gog consorting with other grammar school gogs. Or was it natural for me to have transferred my loyalty to my classmates? One evening I was at home, passing the time with a couple of boys from my class when George called round.

"I've got some news" he announced.

"Oh yes?" coolly, from me.

"I'm starting at Birkenhead School next term."

"Good" I said.

After he and the other boys had gone, my mother who had been present, told me off for not showing more interest in George's news. She was right. I was not a good friend. To this day I feel a pang for not responding more warmly to what was a life-changing event for George.

So far she had caught me out in the sins of greed and pride. I was not nice. I was yet to do worse. I became friendly with one of the boys, Cannon, Cook, Cross or Davey, I'm not sure, and he confided to me something discreditable he had done, something shameful like pooping in his pants or cheating in an exam and I spent a whole afternoon threatening him with exposure, even blackmailing him for a much desired Tuppenny Blue. He begged me not to, called on the debt due to our friendship and finally produced the Tuppenny Blue. I pulled back from the brink, claimed that I'd been teasing, just a little joke, couldn't he see the funny side? Of course he couldn't. I don't know what possessed me. Playing a role? The pleasure of unaccustomed power? Innate sadism? Just as with the near theft of the balsa glider three years previously, I stopped myself from embarking on a life of disrepute and following in my father's footsteps.

I suppose that somewhere along the line, I had internalised something of my mother's strong moral code and that might have acted as a brake on my nascent baser self. My parents and particularly my father figured very little in my life during this period. My energies were directed to school friends and school activities and to taking full advantage of the freedom from adult oversight owing to their wartime preoccupations and anxieties. I have no recollection of my father being around. Apart from commuting to and from his job in Liverpool, fire watching duties, Home Guard training and heaven knows what mischief kept him away for many evenings and weekends. At some level, I missed him, could have done with more of him, an older male who was interested in me and showed it. But reflecting on this issue, I would be foolish to ignore my mother's overarching influence on the formation of my conscience and moral code.

I cannot recall reading anything worthwhile during this period. We were members of West Kirby library, a charming 19th-century mansion set in a formal tree-lined garden and week after week I limited my borrowing to bound volumes of *Punch*. Good for developing my sense of humour, not so good for broadening my literary tastes. I avidly devoured comics: *Hotspur*, *Wizard* and the Billy Bunter stories in *Magnet* were my weeklies of choice. I also discovered interesting information about women's bodies, ailments and amatory concerns in the various women's' magazines subscribed to by Mrs Weir. My mother deemed them unsuitable for a young boy and while she did not actually forbid me to read them, they just disappeared from view.

That's another thing I could have done with my dad for. He was a voracious reader and could have introduced me to age appropriate literature. But West Kirby was my time of being a little animal, active, dirty minded, tree climbing, extrovert, cheeky and at times, not at all nice to know. In other words, I lived in a small boy's paradise. Too good to last, I was soon to be ejected. Mum broke the news to me one Saturday in late June. We were to leave West Kirby on Monday.

On Sunday at low tide, I walked with friends to Hilbre Island where we shared a picnic of egg sandwiches and my mother's famous ginger cake washed down with *Tizer*. We trudged back to the mainland as the tide turned, paddling through the incoming gullies and rivulets. The sun beat down as we pottered along the beach towards Hoylake past the Royal Liverpool Golf Club. I don't remember who I was with. I don't remember what I felt. I was living in the moment and the morrow could take care of itself. Impulse, physicality and friendships with other boys were the main drivers of behaviour. This was a time of great freedom for children. Adults, preoccupied with the rigours and uncertainties of wartime Britain were only too happy to let their children roam. In the case of my parents, my father's gambling was an additional distraction. But the bottom line was that I had no power to say no. When my mother told me that I had to leave my school, move from West Kirby and join my grandparents in Letchworth Garden City, I couldn't argue or express any feelings on the loss of a place in which I'd become very happy. One Monday in early July, clutching a suitcase, I found myself walking with my mother down Grange Hill towards the station. Boys from my class passed us on their way to school, puzzled that I was going in the opposite direction. 'Goodbye' I said to each of them. I knew that we were leaving. Without my father again. Mine not to reason why.

18. LETCHWORTH AND HITCHIN GRAMMAR SCHOOL 1942-43

In flight from West Kirby and my aberrant father, my mother had no-one else to turn to but her parents who had themselves fled to Letchworth Garden City, 40 miles north of bomb-ravaged London. They lived at 44 Norton Road, a large detached house owned by Mrs Richardson and occupied by her and her two adult children, Norma and Tom. Somehow space was found for my mother and me.

We arrived in Letchworth just before the long school holiday. I knew no one. I was bored, wandering round the town in search of friends, as in West Kirby, up to my old trick of whistling the opening of Tchaikovsky's 1st Piano Concerto in the hope that someone, child or adult, would show interest, perhaps even know it and recognise me as a soulmate. Tom had left school and worked at Kryn & Lahy, the local steel foundry. Norma was a moody young woman for whom I did not exist. Ungainly and spotty faced, she mooned in her room, playing and replaying her record of *Blues in the Night.* Sung by *Peggy Lee*, with *Benny Goodman and his Orchestra,* I heard it so often that I have retained some words all my life. *My mama done told me when I was in knee pants, my mama done told me this.*

While I whistled my way through my new neighbourhood, decisions were being made about me in which I played no part. Two hundred yards along Norton Road from where we lived was a modern state secondary school with spacious playing fields which my grandparents thought I should attend. If that had come about, I would have left school at fourteen, the age at which compulsory education then ended. And done what? Faut de mieux probably have become a trainee tailor in my grandfather's clothing factory. Tinker, tailor; the cherry stones had never foretold that occupation for me. I now imagine the family conference to determine my future.

MOTHER: Listen, Albert Einstein he isn't. But in West Kirby he was doing well at school.
GRANDPA: Why pay when there's a perfectly good school just down the road? And he can come home for lunch.

MOTHER: Because he would get a better education at grammar school.
GRANDPA: Education–shmeducation! Who needs it? I started work in my father's workshop at the age of seven and I've earned good money for sixty years.
GRANDMA: Fifty-eight years.
GRANDPA: Who's talking to you? You go find the money for the fees.

My mother was a determined, tenacious woman. Within a week of our arrival in Letchworth, she had found a clerical job at British Tabulating Machine Company which manufactured punch card machines and, during the war, code breaking equipment for Bletchley Park. Once she was earning her own money and freed from absolute dependence on my grandparents, she began to make enquiries and discovered that fees at Hitchin Grammar School were five guineas a term which she could manage on her own. I passed the entrance exam and was set to start there in the autumn term.

Meanwhile I had the summer months to get through. Twin girls of my age, evacuees from London, lived next door and I, hungry for companionship and in the absence of anything promising more fun, i.e. boys, introduced myself and inveigled an invitation into their garden. Stalemate! The twins were quiet, neat and ladylike but I was energetic boisterous and raring to go.

"I'll show you how to play Rugby" I said.

I fetched the ball I had borrowed from Tom and explained the rules. They joined in a half-hearted way. I demonstrated tackling on each of them in turn. Unhurt but muddied, they fled indoors and were forbidden to play with that rough boy, whose Rugby tuition was in parental eyes, just a ruse to disguise his impure intentions.

On Saturday afternoons grandpa and I would take a bus down to Letchworth cricket ground, a haven of peace, surrounded on all sides by a screen of trees. We sat in deckchairs in the baking sun, grandpa in his Sabbath best suit with waistcoat, fast asleep by the end of the first over. I woke him at the interval for money for tea and sandwiches. A foreigner, never having played or even seen cricket before, he must have been completely baffled. He admired strength; he was a small but strong and compact man himself. He told me that when young he would have liked to have been a weightlifter or wrestler and after retirement at the age of 79 he yearned to play bowls but was unable to gain admission to the local club, probably because he was foreign and Jewish.

The long, tedious summer at last came to an end and I plunged into the life of my new school. I also plunged into trouble within weeks. Jewish trouble. David Billson, in one class lower than mine, but bigger and tougher, lived a few hundred yards from me. As we were getting off the bus from Hitchin he said something insulting to me and I went for him. We scuffled and hurled punches at each other but before any real damage was inflicted, a couple of adults intervened and separated us.

A few days later I was standing in the queue waiting to go into the school dining hall when a boy asked,

"Are you a new boy?"

Before I could reply, Ian Chrisp piped up.

"No, he's a Jew boy."

Great mirth in the queue which was not a place in which to hurl myself on Ian. A few months later I launched a paper aeroplane (of my own secret design) into the same queue and was caught by the headmaster creeping along just behind me.

"Throwing things in school, boy! Wait for me outside my study."

Three strokes of the cane; this was my last brush with him for four years.

By a strange irony both Billson and Chrisp became good friends. Billson and I particularly, were best buddies for several years. I was a frequent guest at his house where we played board games, consequences and charades. His mother, a teacher, was very hospitable and a formidable tennis player. Occasionally she would take us down to Letchworth Tennis Club for a knock up. This was my only experience of the game, a lifelong regret. With Ian, also a close neighbour, I played cricket, evening after evening on the Norton Road School playing fields.

There was more pressing Jewish business on the agenda. The war had interrupted my Jewish education but now that I was within my grandparents' jurisdiction, they insisted that I be *bar mitzvahed*. My opinions or wishes in the matter were not a consideration. I was Jewish, ergo at the age of thirteen, I was to be *bar mitzvahed*. No ifs or buts. My grandparents were probably not even aware of the meaning of the ritual, which was the admission of the boy into the community, as a person old and mature enough to take full responsibility for his actions. Because of the war, a large number of Jewish families had evacuated to Letchworth and in the absence of a purpose-built synagogue they hired Howard Hall, a community centre, for Saturday services and other holy days. So as a first step, I had to regularly attend Sabbath services. Also because I was so far behind – and in any case there was no *Cheder*, a traditional school or class teaching the basics of Judaism and the Hebrew language, in Letchworth – an individual tutor had to be found. A colony of orthodox German Jews, refugees from Nazi Germany, had established themselves in Mullway on the north-west fringes of Letchworth. Not as extreme as the *Hasidim* of

Stamford Hill or Gateshead, they must have appeared alien to the local population who had probably never seen a Jew before the war, let alone these heavily bearded, Homburg-hatted, black-suited men, always bespectacled because their sight had been ruined by daily *Torah* studies since childhood. My tutor was a Dr Heineman, small, precise, distant, with a heavy German accent. I started weekly lessons with him in late October 1942; my *bar mitzvah* was scheduled for the Saturday after my birthday, the following February so time was short. I had to start from scratch, mastering the Hebrew alphabet, getting used to reading from right to left. Once I was proficient enough at reading, I had to learn my portion of the *Torah,* sung to a prescribed chant before the synagogue congregation. I remember and can chant most of my portion to this day. Looking back, what I find extraordinary is how mechanical I experienced the whole process.

By the time of my *bar mitzvah,* I could read Hebrew falteringly, my portion fluently, but had no idea of its meaning, significance or even where it came from in the Scriptures. Like so much of what was happening at this time of my life, I cannot get in touch with what, if anything, I thought about it all. It was one of those inexorable laws of nature you just obeyed. Another chore to add to an ever-increasing list as you got older. I was neither happy nor unhappy about it. Jewish boys got *bar mitzvahed* and that was that. Tradition, as *The Fiddler on the Roof* would have it. And though I have been an atheist all my life, I am pleased to have had a *barmitzvah*, become a fully paid up though non-observant Jew. Why am I pleased? I could offer sophistic reasons, plausible, psychological or anthropological explanations, but at its core it still remains a mystery to me.

The great day arrived. My grandparents and mother were present but not my father who as far as I was concerned had completely disappeared from my life. I chanted my portion word perfectly. Back home for a celebration meal of Vienna sausages and chips. Not a fountain pen in sight. A silver inkpot was my only present. No big deal. Today a *bar mitzvah* is a very big deal indeed. After the reading, at the end of the service, drinks and canapés for the whole congregation. Presents from everyone. Dinner and dance at the Dorchester Hotel for two hundred guests. More presents.

Alongside my Hebrew studies I was adjusting to my new school. It was smaller, less chaotic and more orderly then Calday. I settled down quickly in my allocated class, 2a, held my own academically and made new friends. Jack Fox, the only other Jewish boy in my year, became a lifelong friend. John Skinner lived in Hitchin in the flat above Burtons the Tailors with its mandatory snooker hall on the first floor. We played toy soldiers on the rooftop terrace with its views of the cattle market and graceful early

19th-century public library. Skinner's father was a Lt. Colonel in the Army who must have passed on his military genes to his son who by superior tactics invariably overwhelmed my ill-positioned forces.

About halfway through the first term I floated to my class the idea a publishing a weekly paper to be called the *2a Rag* and edited by me. It was to contain form news – a football match between 2a and 2b was imminent – and stories and articles of general interest. Contributions would be welcome, the editor's decision final. I wrote the first instalment of a serial entitled *The Thief of Weston School* and because I was let down by a promised contribution was forced to labour over an article distinguishing anhedral and dihedral aircraft wings. That was a real struggle for me, involving research into a subject about which I knew little and which interested me less. Over a whole weekend I worked like a mediaeval scribe, hand-writing two copies in neat copperplate. Mum stitched the copies into very small tabloid form and the first issue of the *2a Rag* was launched on the Monday. A great success, it was read eagerly, too eagerly. One copy was confiscated by a teacher from a boy reading it in class, the other by a prefect on the Hitchin to Letchworth bus on the afternoon of publication. I was not hauled off before the headmaster for distributing seditious literature. Not a word was said but the copies were never returned. There was never a second issue.

There was something very deadening about Hitchin Grammar School at that time. Initiatives were not encouraged. We might have got away with the *Rag* if I had first sought and obtained permission and then submitted the copy for approval prior to publication. When I was in the Sixth form I submitted a piece to the termly *Hitchin Grammar School Chronicle,* describing the desperation of an examinee confronted by questions he could not even understand, let alone begin to answer. The editor, Tommy Hall, a prissy contemporary, accepted it for publication. The next term I wrote a feature about Caves Milk Bar and Ice Cream Parlour where every day after school, boys from the Grammar School and girls from our sister High School, spilling out on to the pavement, congregated, gossiped, bantered, flirted and paired off. No worse written than the exam piece, it met the barrier of the editor's prudish disapproval and was rejected. Boys and girls mixing and mingling. Sexual undertones. Too transgressive. Not fit for publication. Nor was my manuscript returned to me.

19. LETCHWORTH 1943-45

Shortly after my *bar mitzvah* my grandparents returned to London. The German blitz on London had come to an end by June 1941 when the Luftwaffe was deployed in the invasion of Russia. With their departure our tenancy at 44 Norton Road ended but rooms were available next door at number 42. Detached like its neighbour, it was set in large and well-tended front and rear gardens. Built in the first decade of the 20th century, it still retained the original gas lighting.

Our landlady was a Mrs Strickland, an aged, tiny crone. Bent and supporting herself on a stick, she not only resembled a wicked witch but behaved like one. An embittered widow, she lived with her two middle-aged spinster daughters, tall and stick thin and as disgruntled and disagreeable as their mother.

A few days after moving in, my mother and I were in our little sitting-room, reading, when Mrs Strickland, without knocking, hobbled in and demanded that we turn off the lights as lights-out at 9:30 pm was 'a house rule'. My quick tempered mother refused, claiming that such a rule was absurd, whereupon Mrs Strickland made for the chain to douse the lights. My mother immediately grappled her away and bundled her out of the door. Mrs Strickland never tried to impose her lights-out rule again, but relations remained frosty for the remainder of our tenancy.

As there was no electricity in the house, we had to power our radio by an accumulator, a bulky battery which had to be recharged every week or so. We hired ours from a local store and it was one of my Saturday tasks to exchange the flat accumulator for a newly charged one. Food was strictly rationed and in short supply and I had to join long queues at the butcher and grocer to obtain our minute quantities of meat, bacon, butter, cheese and other basic foodstuffs. Mum worked Saturday mornings and once the shopping was done my next job was to clean the living room which, in addition to the use of a *Ewbank* to sweep the carpet and dusting all surfaces, included a meticulous polishing of the furniture. I didn't resent it; I enjoyed the structure created by my prescribed duties and executing them efficiently. There was also an even more powerful motivation: that of pleasing my mother, the glow of 'goodboyness' I felt when she came home from work, the pleasure of basking in her approval.

I also experienced a sense of containment provided by the structure of school and my close relationship with my mother although I continued to miss and yearn for my father. Until his return I was my mother's consort as I accompanied her to the pictures at the Broadway, a luxurious art deco cinema which I loved for its grandeur and the quality of the movies I saw there: *Casablanca*, *Brief Encounter*, *Double Indemnity*, Bing Crosby and Bob Hope in the *Road to...* series. The best of all to me, at that stage of my developing sense of humour, was my collapse into uncontrollable laughter caused by Danny Kaye's *Up in Arms*; in particular, the scene in which as a GI he is caught by his sergeant in the act of playing an illicit windup gramophone. To put the sergeant off the scent, he mimes the female ballad singer until the gramophone begins to wind down and he is forced to mimic a gradual descent into a tuneless *basso profundo*.

On sunny Sundays we would walk to the ancient little town of Baldock and have tea at the 14th Century Tea House where I discovered the Epicurean joy of Heinz Spaghetti on toast.

My best friend during these years was David Billson. Where had his anti-Semitism gone? Was I one of the 'but you're different' syndrome? I never explored it. I was pleased to have an Anglo-Saxon friend, well set up, nice looking, bright and with a good sense of humour – that is, he laughed at my jokes – to hang around with. I often spent time at his house where his mother, a former teacher devised quizzes and other amusements for us.

I had the sense that she rather disapproved of me. Her innate belief confirmed; here was one incarnate, a pushy Jew. It was something in her tone of voice, a slight snappiness when I won one of her general knowledge tests or word games. She crushed my jubilation with a prim,

"Now then Boris, no bragging!"

But that apart, she was a generous hostess. Despite rationing and food shortages, she always managed to rustle up a delicious sandwich and cake tea. David and I were able to use her membership of the Letchworth Tennis Club to use the courts and play a primitive game of patting the ball to and fro. One of my many regrets is that my friendship with David came to an end when I was fifteen and we drifted apart into different interests and activities.

In the heart of the shopping centre was Nott's bakery. Local opinion of the quality of its products was encapsulated in the following:

> *Eat Nott's bread,*
> *Shit like lead.*
> *Fart like thunder,*
> *No bloody wonder*

Double up humour for us kids, but the scabrous ditty didn't stop David and me popping into their first floor cafe on Saturday mornings and sharing a pot of coffee. Always crowded and lively with bustling waitresses, the clatter of crockery and what I imagined to be sophisticated adult conversation and laughter, it possessed one extraordinary element which made an indelible impact on me. The walls of the cafe were covered with brightly coloured murals, bucolic scenes of Mediterranean type countryside, iridescent, bursting with the ripe fruitfulness of harvest time and of bronzed, heavy limbed and big busted peasant women picking bunches of purple grapes.

I was ignorant of art then but now know that a local artist, Agnes Core Haggo, who painted the murals, probably in the 1930s, had been heavily influenced by the post-impressionists, Gauguin and Picasso. Because of the ideas elaborated in the book *Garden Cities of Tomorrow* by Ebenezer Howard, the city's founding father, Letchworth attracted numerous artists, architects and craftsmen to make their home there, drawn by socialist idealism, the promise of an urban utopia and the principles of the Arts and Crafts movement. Harold Gilman and William Ratcliffe, prominent members of the Camden Group of artists, lived there and Spencer Gore frequently stayed with Gilman and painted a number of landscapes of Letchworth, then in its early stages of development and still largely rural. Letchworth Museum and Art Gallery which in 2015 was absorbed into a much larger museum in Hitchin, had a collection of 150 works by a number of artists, mostly not well-known, painted during this early period. Clearly influenced by the Impressionists, they are of a high professional standard without being over-academic. I go into all this because of a retrospective pride in having lived in such an interesting and beautiful environment which I absorbed through my pores and about which I became curious only long after I had left it.

20. MY FATHER – A CLEVER FOOL
Part 2

From the age of twelve to fourteen, in relation to my schoolmates at Hitchin Grammar School I was suffused with shame and embarrassment. What to say when asked 'Where's your father? What does he do?' I had heard a vague rumour circulating among my aunts that he had applied to join the Navy. If that was true, what sort of fantasy world was he living in? An urban Jewish intellectual like my father in the Navy? The nearest he'd ever got to seafaring was on the Woolwich Free Ferry. But as a boy I understood none of that and would reply,

"He's in the Navy".

"Is he? Jolly good. Officer or rating?"

Feeling wretched, I would claim a commission for him. So I too became enmeshed in his world of deceit and subterfuge.

In 1944, a couple of years after they parted, my father made contact with us and plied my mother with gifts: perfume, chocolate and something then in extremely short supply – silk stockings. He enlisted or was conscripted into the Royal Army Pay Corps and started courting my mother (and me) by visiting during weekend leaves, taking us for lunch to the *George & Dragon* in Baldock and then onto the *Astoria* for the Sunday matinee.

My pleasure at his returning and taking my mother off my hands was reduced by a fear of being spotted by friends in the company of a private in a Pay Corps uniform rather than a gold braided naval officer. But perhaps they would think he wasn't my father. That's what our landlady believed and she forbade him from staying overnight. All very shaming but my mother managed to wheedle a council house share and once we had moved in, my father spent all his leaves with us and my parents' reconciliation was complete.

By then I was fifteen and the process of our getting to know each other again began. On Sunday mornings he and I would walk to the *Wilbury*, a pub on the town's edge where he introduced me to beer in the form of shandy and told me the most marvellous stories and dirty jokes which I retold with acclaim to my friends the next day. Books began to appear in the house: a three-volume illustrated set of Shakespeare (my first encounter with soft porn in *Venus and Adonis* and *The Rape of Lucretia*), Graham Greene's *Brighton Rock*, Nigel Balchin's *Mine Own Executioner* and John Cowper Powys's *A Glastonbury Romance*.

By Easter 1945, the war was almost over, the Russians were at the gates of Berlin and Germany was on the point of defeat. I had from the start been a passionate follower of the war's progress, but for a brief period during the school holidays I had more pressing preoccupations. The Jewish Passover festival coincided with Easter and my parents and I were celebrating it with my grandparents who lived in the upper part of a house in Clapton, East London.

An identical ritual had been taking place on the ground floor flat occupied by Mrs. Cohen with her family. Once the service was over she popped upstairs to invite me down to meet and play cards with her granddaughter, Beryl. Beryl Green of Neasden, north-west London, telephone number Gladstone 6800, had just turned thirteen. I was too shy to gaze; my glances were covert and brief. But I saw enough to be smitten in an instant: blue black tresses, long dark lashes, green, slightly slanting eyes, delicately defined lips. And sweeter than honey, crescent breasts and a guileless expression.

We played rummy. She shuffled cards with inexpert charm and dealt them out with such exquisite awkwardness. I was infatuated, a lost boy. Unfortunately not lost for words but fatuously talkative. I adopted a pose of world-weary cynicism, attacking my school ('lousy teaching'), my school dinners ('lousy cooking') and my local cinema ('lousy films'). Despite the gaucherie of my attempts to make an impression, she liked me enough to agree to meet me later that school holiday and I promised to write to make arrangements.

In my letter, I proposed I would cycle from Letchworth to her home and we would then go for a walk. I waited eagerly for a reply, desperate to be in her company and to share our deepest thoughts and feelings. But the adults in Beryl's life believed that she needed protection from this brash, forward boy who used ungentlemanly words like *lousy* and who therefore probably had ungentlemanly designs on her. She was forbidden to meet me and wrote a curt letter telling me that she couldn't make it. I confided my upset to my father, complaining that the grown-ups had no right to interfere and that we were old enough to make up our own minds about whether we became friends or not. "Never mind, my boy!" he replied. "Just call it *Easter Episode*." I couldn't and I didn't. I resented the reduction of my finest feelings of courtly love as an Episode. Thus did my father demonstrate his habitual ineptitude by favouring a flashy phrase rather than a show of empathy to his sorrowing son.

In 1946, a year after the end of the war, my father was demobbed and took up permanent residence with us. He found a job in a shop in Westbourne Grove, Bayswater which specialised in anodising old metal utensils. This was a thriving business in those days when kettles, pots and pans were in short supply.

He seemed reformed and rehabilitated. He was in steady work, with a weekly wage coming in. I was delighted but also to a lesser extent, disgruntled to have him back. He was, or so it seemed to me, so knowledgeable and sophisticated. He introduced me to James Joyce, Rabelais, Aldous Huxley and Bernard Shaw. *The Observer* and *The New Statesman* were delivered weekly. Fluent of speech, he was softly spoken with just a touch of Yorkshire brogue. Not a trace of a foreign Jewish accent even though he had not arrived in England until he was thirteen. I was proud to introduce my friends to him, relieved that I had a flesh and blood father to introduce them to. My friends loved him; he was charming and accessible, taught them crafty chess moves and entertained them with paradoxical mathematical puzzles. I basked in his popularity.

But there were formidable downsides to his return. He reasserted his authority over me and reappropriated his wife, my mother. She colluded in both these acts. She was back in love with him and he with her and there was very little room for a third. They were not only going through one of their many honeymoon phases but he also reclaimed his primacy as the top male in our little family. However, I had been surrogate husband to my mother for several years, her escort, her fetcher and carrier and confidante and adviser, probably in more ways than were healthy. On the one hand I welcomed my father taking the burden of my mother off my shoulders and allowing me to get on with the business of being a testosterone-fuelled, adolescent boy, and on the other hand I felt my nose put out of joint by the new alliance which I felt had been made for the sole purpose of showing me who was boss and excluding me from their coupledom. The changed emotional dynamics needed a lot of adjustment and I'm not sure that I managed this very successfully. Certainly my mother didn't think she had done so, as she admitted to me forty years later.

As an example of these teasing, mocking episodes by which my father asserted the re-appropriation of his wife, I came home one afternoon to find my parents out. I cycled over to some friends and returned early evening. My parents were in the sitting room enjoying a companionable cup of tea.

"Where have you been?" I demanded accusingly.

My father replied, "We've been to Bedford".

I was affronted. A trip, without them seeing whether I wanted to accompany them.

"Why didn't you ask me?"

"We didn't think you'd want to come; you see we've been to Bedfordshire" [Bed-for-sure]. A poor stale pun but it was being made clear to the pubescent son who had spent the afternoon in the marital bed and who belonged there

About a year after leaving the Army, Dad landed a plum job. My uncle

Percy, by then in partnership with my grandfather, was on the committee of the Master Ladies Tailors Organisation (MLTO). The secretaryship became vacant, Percy proposed my father as a replacement and he was offered the post.

MLTO was an employers' organisation and Dad's job involved negotiations with trade unions and relevant government departments, dealing with individual members' issues, arranging and attending conferences, members and board meetings and other administrative tasks. One such conference was held in Paris jointly with French confreres. Dad returned with a multi-coloured silk *Sulka* tie for me and a tale which for me at the age of eighteen represented the height of sophistication. He was being solicited very persistently by a prostitute at a nightclub at which he and a number of members had ended up. He bowed very politely, saying, "Pardonnez-moi madamoiselle, mais je suis homosexuel!"

One problem for me was that I was unable to compete with my father. He had to be sightless for me to beat him at chess. His dialectical skills exceeded mine to such an extent that I could never win an argument in any of our frequent discussions. I clearly had to find a way to differentiate myself from him, be my own man. When I was in the Army, in a letter, I accused him of attributing too high a value to logic, reason and rationality, leading to a coldness of approach to issues of a feeling or emotional nature. I instanced his lack of interest in music, art and nature. His response was one of anger. What effrontery to make these sweeping assertions about his character of which I knew nothing. By what right did I think I could malign him so? For my father to be so stung represented a victory of sorts and not just a pyrrhic victory because the point I was making about the preeminence of feeling represented the first stirrings of an attitude to mental life and mental functioning which led to my interest in psychoanalytic theory and in my mid-fifties to becoming a psychoanalytic psychotherapist.

21. PASSIONS 1943-46

MUSIC

Until I was fourteen I'd had no inclination to enlarge my repertoire of classical music. Then, my mother bought a second-hand portable, windup gramophone for £3 which she presented to me together with Tchaikovsky's Nutcracker Suite and a single 12-inch record of the first movement of Rachmaninov's 2nd piano Concerto which had become well known as the incidental music to the movie, *Brief Encounter*. In retrospect I wonder why she did not buy the whole work. Was it a question of money? It's too late to ask now but it is a minor resentment I can harbour along with the huge portfolio of more serious grievances.

Out of my own pocket money, I bought a tin of steel gramophone needles and played my minuscule collection until I knew them so well that I could sing along with all the melodies. I became hungry for more and Uncle Jack stepped in. He gave me a number of records he was prepared to discard from his own collection which included a pre-first World War recording by Arthur Nikisch and the Berlin Philharmonic Orchestra of Beethoven's 5th Symphony. The first movement was missing, cracked or perhaps retained by Uncle Jack. But what remained, changed me forever. Despite the primitive technology of both my gramophone and the acoustic recording, I had never before heard sounds like those unleashed by Beethoven. You can deconstruct and anatomise music into its constituent parts but although you can describe your own feelings as a response to what you hear, it is more difficult to explain precisely why it has that particular effect. What infused me with emotions I had never experienced were the transition between the scherzo and last movement and the opening bars of the last movement itself. The scherzo drops to piano and ends with the strings playing pizzicato. After a brief pause the strings and timpani play pianissimo, ending in a repeated group of three notes, dark and mysterious and gradually increasing in volume. Suddenly the whole orchestra blazes into sound, the brass, including trombones appearing in a symphony for the first time, joining in triumphantly. Sounds such as these had never been heard before 1808, and certainly not by me until 1944/5 and they made me weep; not tears of sadness, but of joy and relief because after the *sturm und drang* of the earlier movements, they spoke of hope and redemption. Although I did not make the connection until much later, this was a time in the later stages of the war, the Allies were closing in on Germany, victory was in sight and indeed the world was indeed moving forward into the *broad sunlit uplands* as foretold by Winston Churchill. Beethoven's music caught our collective mood precisely: at the end of the periods of struggle and darkness, humanity and human values would prevail.

After some weeks I yearned for the missing first movement, famous for its four note opening, three short, one long, representing the Morse code letter 'V' for Victory, embodied in Churchill's two-fingered salute. I made the trip to a second-hand record emporium in Berwick Street, Soho. There were no Nikisch to be found, so I bought one performed by Landon Ronald and the Royal Albert Hall Orchestra, recorded electrically in 1925. A much better sound and different interpretation, chalk to cheese compared to my earlier version but I didn't care, I had the complete work. Anyway, after four years of war we were used to shortages and things you wanted not being available. Shopkeepers would greet one's request with an incredulous "Don't you know there's a war on?" The government exhorted us to *make do and mend* and certainly in my early explorations into the world of music that is what I gladly did.

Once embarked on my musical journey, I couldn't get enough of it. The radio provided an introduction to and enlargement of the canon. Sunday was homework day, made bearable by the Sunday afternoon concert. Most Wednesdays I rushed home from school in time to listen to the weekly five o'clock concert. Tommy Hall was the only other boy in my class with whom I could share my passion and discuss the music we had both heard on the radio. We had very different musical tastes and argued incessantly. His favourite composer was Mozart; at that time, I found him too cool and preferred the music of the Romantic School starting with Beethoven and culminating in the heart–on–sleeve emotionality of Tchaikovsky and Rachmaninov. Apart from Tommy, my developing cultural interests began to differentiate and isolate me from my contemporaries.

There was very little live music available in Hitchin or Letchworth. I spent most of the Christmas 1945 holiday at my grandparents in London and went to my first concert at the Royal Albert Hall on Sunday afternoon, the 30th December. I bought a four-shilling ticket for the arena and was overwhelmed from the moment I was seated, by a combination of the vastness of the hall's space, the opulence of its interior and being present in a place packed with adults who seemed so confident in those surroundings. I felt that I was about to participate in some religious ritual in a great cathedral.

I watched fascinated as the members of the London Symphony

Orchestra took their places on the platform and began tuning up. The conductor, Morris Miles appeared, raised his baton and launched the orchestra into the overture to Wagner's *The Flying Dutchman*. I sat transfixed at the opening bars, shimmering violins holding one note, soon joined by strident, whooping brass and thunderous timpani, Wagner's heart-stopping depiction of a violent storm at sea. The main work was Sibelius' 2nd Symphony which with its unfamiliar harmonies I found difficult, except for the big, lush tune in the last movement.

The experience was something akin to a drug-induced high. I was addicted. I had no money but would allow nothing to stand in my way to obtain my fix. My grandparents hosted a weekly poker school and the custom was for a percentage of all cash changing hands to be donated to the JNF (*Jewish National Fund*) and deposited in one of their metal collecting boxes. The box lived on a cabinet among the family photos, a pair of Corinthian columned silver Sabbath candlesticks and a bulldog nutcracker, awaiting the monthly JNF collector. I discovered that by holding the box upside down and shaking it vigorously, half crowns and florins would spill out of its slender aperture. I was not greedy and took just enough for my ticket and bus fares. I knew it was wrong but in some obscure way, felt that taking from a charity box was not taking from my grandparents. But of course I was stealing from them and from my people as well.

However, repeated criminal acts funded concerts for the remainder of that holiday and the Easter of 1946 when I again stayed with my grandparents, ostensibly to revise for School Certificate. The Albert Hall became a familiar venue, door-to-door from Stoke Newington on the 73 bus. Amongst other gorgeous works, I heard the Beethoven and Brahms violin concertos for the first time, played by Tzigeti and Bronislaw Huberman, two of the great virtuosi of the day.

The Beethoven and Brahms were the works I decided to buy recordings of with legitimate money given to me on my sixteenth birthday. On a midweek visit to London I went to the large HMV store in Oxford Street, spacious, as quiet as a church and virtually empty of customers. I discovered from the young woman assistant that she had two recordings of each concerto in stock, one by Jascha Heifetz, the other by Yehudi Menuhin.

"Which one is better?" I asked.

"Well, it's a matter of taste".

"But how can I choose when I haven't heard them?"

"Take them upstairs and listen to them yourself."

It transpired that on the first floor there was a whole suite of listening rooms, each furnished with two easy chairs and the most up-to-date gramophone equipment. The assistant had handed me the four bulky albums; each two sided 12-inch shellac record had about eight minutes playing time and I settled down with feelings of wonder and well-being for the rest of the afternoon listening to all four albums. At the end I made my choices, Yehudi Menuhin for the Beethoven and Heifetz for the Brahms. I thought the next time I would come with sandwiches and a bottle of lemonade, stay the whole day and then tell the assistant that nothing was to my taste

In 1946, during the summer holidays, I once again stayed with my grandparents so that I could go to my first promenade concerts before the autumn term began. I went to three within a week and whether the JNF or I paid for my tickets I cannot recall. I loved the mateyness of the prom queue, the shared enthusiasm of the prommers and the eclectic nature of the programmes. I was exposed to composers whose music I had never heard before: Prokofiev, Bartok, Richard Strauss, and Vaughan Williams. The composer, Constant Lambert conducted his own cantata, the exciting *Rio Grande* with its jazzy rhythms. The distinguished pianist Moseiwitch played Beethoven's Emperor Concerto and another first was Sibelius' 5th Symphony. After the concert, a young man I had met in the queue and I walked down Exhibition Road together to South Kensington station.

"So how did you like the Sibelius?" he asked.

"Not very much."

"Seriously? He's one of the greats. What else have you heard?"

I felt a little under pressure.

"Oh, the 2nd Symphony and *Finlandia* and *Valse Triste*."

"Just that? You poor chap! Do persevere! There's a violin concerto and the rest of the symphonies..."

He had recited most of the Finn's oeuvre by the time we reached the station and parted. I left him with familiar feelings: of not being up to snuff, being inexcusably ignorant and disappointing my knowledgeable friend. But I did persevere, became enamoured of the dour composer and got my parents to give me his 5th Symphony for my seventeenth birthday.

Footnote: The Third Programme (reincarnated as Radio 3 in 1970) began transmission on 29th September 1946. I was there. That night I listened to the inaugural concert, all music of celebration, including a Festival overture written especially for the occasion by Benjamin Britten. From that day music, ancient and modern, was available every day and the world of us music lovers would never be the same again.

CHESS

It was in the family DNA only in a metaphorical sense. My father was a brilliant player, I, though enthusiastic and identifying with him in my love of the game, was an indifferent one. I played a lot in my adolescent years, mainly in the school reading room after lunch where half a dozen or so keen players would convene. Jack loved the game as much as I did, but something in his DNA had been passed on to him by his great-uncle Miguel Najdorf, a world-class grandmaster who died in 1997. Jack played an attacking and aggressive game. He was certainly the strongest player in the school, generally beating me with ease, and would if he had persevered, and not switched his drives in the direction of girls, have made it at least to county standard. I, on the other hand, played a tentative, wait-and-see game which got me through the opening stages but I never really had any clear tactical sense once the opening positions had been established. I was reactive rather than proactive. Because of my father's passion for the game, it was one of the few things he had the patience to teach me and it was because of him that I learnt the Kings Gambit, if white and the French Defence, if black. I also learnt chess notation and played out games of masters such as Alekhine and Capablanca, for all the good it did me; the brilliance of their play was far beyond my understanding.

One evening Jack and I ventured into one of the weekly meetings of the Letchworth Chess Club. The members welcomed us two 15-year-olds and we were offered games. My opponent was an old man whom we later nicknamed Snorter because he snorted and snuffled as he shortsightedly dipped his head to and fro over the board. I quickly established a winning position but was unable to deliver the coup de grace and was eventually forced to resign.

Thinking about these events now, I wonder to what extent my game suffered because I could not beat my father in anything requiring intellectual or cerebral skills. Freud's biographer, the psycho-analyst Ernest Jones, wrote a paper in which he theorised that the great 19th century champion Morphy was unconsciously re-enacting the Oedipus complex, the King representing the Father who had to be overcome in order to win the Queen, representing Mother. I on the other hand could never beat my father and this disabled me from playing better than I did. The truth of course is that I had no real aptitude or talent for the game and gave it up by the time I was sixteen.

CYCLING

It began with a bang. I set off down the hill on a borrowed bike, got into a wobble, lost control and crashed into a wooden fence. It hurt. My left elbow began to swell. Thus began my cycling career. Suspecting a fracture, my mother sent me off to the Three Counties Hospital, Arlesey, two miles from Letchworth. For us schoolboys, Arlesey was the hospital, known to us as the nuthouse or loony bin. *They should cart you off to Arlesey* was a common insult. But Arlesey had during the war ceased to be a dedicated lunatic asylum, as such institutions were then known and shared its buildings and facilities with the London Royal Free Hospital, evacuated from its own premises. My elbow was x-rayed and I was examined by an orthopaedic consultant, in the presence of a number of medical students. A small fracture was diagnosed and a plaster and sling applied. I was fascinated by the whole process and for the first time, at the age of fourteen, knew with absolute certainty and assurance that that was what I wanted to be, Dr. Boris Rumney. My life's work.

As soon as my arm was healed, I was back on a bike, learned to ride properly and bought a second-hand bicycle, no gears, and semi-dropped handlebars for £5. Jack, of course had a three geared, fully dropped handlebars, racer. From then on I cycled everywhere, more and more adventurously as I became increasingly confident: making solitary trips to Cambridge, stopping for a row on the Cam, and to Bedford, passing RAF Cardington with its huge sheds, formerly housing immense airships but then two-a-penny barrage balloons.

To provide a focus for my forays into the countryside I invented a hobby for myself: collecting pub names. The only rule was non-repetition, once one Red Lion was seen, no further one could be entered in my little blue notebook. This obsessive hunt for new names motivated me to explore every street of every town or village I visited. This activity was a variant of that practised by many of my peers who stood for hours on Hitchin Station, collecting and marking off in their little books, locomotive names and numbers, as they flashed past, Edinburgh or London bound. They were a band of brothers, united by a common passion, whereas I pursued a solitary path; no one else I knew collected pub names and I had no friend with whom to share its intense fascination. But what we had in common was a passion for the construction of lists.

I cycled to Enfield to stay the weekend with Uncle Alf and Aunt Rosa. On Saturday evening I went off to the cinema to see some forgettable Hollywood movie and sitting through an interminable theatre organ interlude, belting out popular ballads, I got into conversation with the young man sitting next to me in which we bemoaned the state of the cinema and popular culture generally. We arranged to go for a walk the next morning on Enfield Chase. I cycled over to meet him and on the walk he steadied the slow pace of my bike by holding on to my saddle, at the same time, inadvertently, or so I thought, touching, not to say stroking, the upper part of my buttocks. He told me that he had friends with a flat in Islington and I would be welcome to stay with them (and him) and we would all go to the Sadlers Wells Ballet. I felt thrilled, honoured even, to be invited to spend time with such interesting adults but my parents forbad me to go. I protested, begged them to let me, that here was my entrée into the cultured crowd I had been longing for but they were adamant.

In 1945 my father, a private in the Royal Army Pay Corps, was stationed in Whitchurch, Hampshire and soon after Summer Term had ended I set off to spend a few days with him there. I had no anxiety about cycling on some of the busiest A roads in the country because traffic was so light. Petrol for private cars was strictly rationed and most freight was transported by rail. As I passed Elstree Film Studios, I stopped to watch an open-air scene of a large crowd paying homage to whom I thought were an enthroned king and queen elevated as if on a stage, being filmed in close proximity to the road. The movie was an adaptation of George Bernard Shaw's play *Caesar and Cleopatra*, one of the most expensive films ever made in the UK. It was a spectacular flop. It was a hot day and pausing only for a swim in the pool forming part of a roadhouse on the A30, I arrived at the lodgings arranged by Dad in time for supper.

Dad was on duty during the day so I explored the surrounding countryside, cycling to Winchester and Salisbury for the cathedrals, then on to Stonehenge, back through the New Forest to Hythe, ferry to Southampton and then back to Whitchurch. Everything felt empty and simple, the roads both free of traffic, street furniture and markings, no queues or charges for entry to cathedrals. Ancient villages were neither cosmeticised nor surrounded by unimaginatively designed and out of keeping housing developments. Stonehenge was unbounded and unfenced, there were no visitors' buildings and no shop. I just left my bike on the grass and wandered among the stones, alone, the only visitor that afternoon. Cycling through Southampton I was stunned by how German bombing had flattened the whole of the city; in shock and awe I passed acre after acre of rubbled wasteland as I cycled north from the harbour.

I spent the evenings with Dad at *The Pineapple,* the Whitchurch pub favoured by the Pay Corps lower ranks, middle-aged, solid men; bank clerks and bookkeepers in civilian life, too old or unfit for active service. They were a friendly, jovial lot, particularly after a pint or two. My father with his charm, gift of the gab and quiet sense of humour seemed to be central to the group and I was proud of his popularity and pleased to be a witness to the vitality and sense of fun of such a bunch of men of the world. Technically because of my age I was in contravention of the law by being on licensed premises but the pub staff turned a blind eye as my father was a regular and even allowed him to buy me half a pint of shandy every night.

I cycled back to Letchworth on 6th August 1945. My father returned home by train on the same day to start a week's leave. I arrived home with a celebratory supper on the table and just before the 6 o'clock news. The newsreader, dulcet voiced, unflappable Alvar Liddell, more animated than usual, announced that the Americans had dropped an atomic bomb on Hiroshima. We knew then that the war against Japan was over.

The next summer, 1946, after completing our School Certificate exams, Dennis Doughty and I set off on the A1, the Great North Road, on the August Bank Holiday weekend, then falling on the beginning of the month. This premier trunk road was almost deserted, private car traffic was still light even though the war against Japan had been over for a year and Dennis and I were able without danger to cycle side-by-side. I was infused with a sense of wonder and beauty at the things we saw and the places we visited, the cathedrals and mediaeval city centres in Peterborough, Lincoln and York, the first experience of youth hostelling and of meeting girls of our own age. In one hostel I met a bright faced, curly haired girl, my age, also waiting for School Cert results and a music lover. I imagined we could have been soul-mates but parted the next morning, she south, I north. The last lap from York to Whitby across the Yorkshire Moors was the most strenuous: the long climb up to the moors followed by the exhilaration of freewheeling at breathtaking speed down the other side to Whitby. We arrived at sunset in time to see the fishing fleet leaving the harbour for the North Sea fishing grounds. The youth hostel, next door to the Abbey was incomparably positioned high above the harbour and accessed from the quayside by 199 steps, which presented difficulty only when we had to haul our bikes to the top.

The return home by a different route was uneventful until about twenty miles from home my bike suffered some catastrophic mechanical failure. Stranded miles away from any town with a bicycle repair facility, my bike and I hitched a lift on a lorry en route for Letchworth while Dennis on his reliable Raleigh cycled home on his own.

The bike was reparable only at great cost so I discarded and never replaced it. In September I moved up to the Sixth Form. It was beneath the dignity for us sixth formers to cycle. Only boys did that. We walked or used public transport; Philip Dean whose father owned the greengrocers in Station Road even drove to school in a green Triumph sports car and parked it outside the headmaster's study.

Peace had returned and plenty was on its way and I arrived at school on the first day of term in September 1946 full of optimism and determination to keep up the good work.

22. CONTEMPORANEOUS EVIDENCE:
Diary Interlude Jan-May 1946

Diary For 1946, I wrote on the first page, adding 'Private' three times, 'Strictly Private And Confidential'in bold capitals and for good measure, in poorly executed gothic-horror letters:

'A CURSE ON THOSE WHO WOULD READ THIS BOOK'.

I have no idea what motivated the desire to keep a journal because that is what it was, although I would not have then known the difference. January 1st starts off very low-key. I was spending part of the school Christmas holidays at my grandparents in London. *Pretty boring*. The first words, the first sentence. Although I seem to keep myself extremely busy in a multitude of activities, boredom is something of a leitmotif during the early months:

3RD JAN	*Evening dull as usual*
5TH JAN	*Another dull evening*
13TH JAN	*A very uninteresting day. I am getting utterly sick and fed up of Letchworth.*
21ST JAN	*On the whole a dull day.*
10TH FEB	*My birthday, Sixteen at last! But a dull day.*

A similar entry on 18th Feb, but no complaints of boredom for the remainder of the journal. In fact there is a hint of life being lived at a more intense level on New Year's Day. *Mrs Cohen returned to 141B and the Greens were supposed to come back for dinner. I hoped Beryl might turn up but as it happened none of them did.* On the 6th Jan *I heard that B was coming on Monday but I was past caring.* The next day *I heard from grandma that Mrs Cohen didn't want me to see Beryl and had said that I was getting too big for my boots, whatever that meant.* Later that day, returning to 141B, *I rang the bell and who should open it but Beryl. Naturally I was very fidgety upstairs. Therefore, at 3pm I decided to go up*

West. *I saw her and said goodbye before I went. But while waiting for a 653, she, her sister Yvonne and a friend of Yvonne's came dashing out of 141B and caught the same 653 as I did. And then I travelled with her from 141B to Piccadilly. The conversation was general and when I left her at Piccadilly I came to these conclusions: 1. She was not as pretty as last time. 2. She was unintelligent. 3. She was much smaller than me than last time. 4. She had gone skinny. 5. She liked Frank Sinatra. Then I knew. I no longer had the slightest desire to be friends with Beryl.* Denial by rationalisation? I'm not sure. Perhaps I had matured since the previous Easter and was no longer the besotted boy I was then. But I think there is an unconscious hint that not all feeling for her had been expunged by the reasons so cogently expressed on 7th Jan. For on the 11th May, *I saw George Raft and Ava Gardner in 'Whistle Stop' which wasn't a good picture but I like Ava Gardner very much; she looks a lot like Beryl.*

I may have matured since first meeting Beryl but nonetheless immaturity and an affinity to young Adrian Mole, without the laughs, pervades the journal. My rejection by Beryl and the hostility to my overtures towards her by her family were not only wounding but sapped for a couple of years any earlier confidence I might have developed in my relationships with girls. Although on 11th Jan I announced that since that encounter with Beryl I was n*ot so interested in girls as before. You would have thought the opposite.* It is clear the interest remains and is expressed in my witnessing the amorous antics of school friends and my own transient meetings with girls. As for the first: the 4th Feb, *Whiteman and Dave Billson in the bus coming home got on very well with two girls they have had their eyes on lately. It was amusing to watch.* Then something more solid, Jack's first love, similar to my abortive ardour for Beryl. 23rd Feb: *Jack told Dennis Doughty and me that he had become friendly with Marion Hooper that St Francis School girl, pretty but oh so childish.* 4th Mar: *I went to Baldock with Jack to have a milkshake but of course Jack went to see Marion.* 13th Mar: *I heard that Fox had given up his little blonde friend.* 22nd Mar: *Jack told me a whole story on how he dropped Marian Hooper.*

As to the brief encounters with girls, I sense a yearning at odds with my proud proclamation of 'uninterest'. 5th Jan: *In the queue for the theatre I talked to a girl of about 18 who goes to Cambridge. We talked mainly of art and theatres. Back at the Savoy I met the girl's friend as well, very pretty I thought.* 28th April: At an Albert Hall concert *I met a boy of about 15 with two girls, one of whom I thought was one of the nicest girls I have ever met. She liked good music, spoke well, was intelligent and was* very *attractive. What luck I have!?* Just a fleeting meeting. So during this period I did not have a friendship with a single girl and this remained the position until I met Naomi in July 1947. All my friends were male and the journal makes it clear that my closest were Jack and Dennis Doughty with whom I did most of my hanging out.

My father, although still in the army during this whole period was frequently at home and his own passion for and deep knowledge of chess stimulated Jack and me to study the game and we too became enthusiastic players. In terms of subject matter, chess related entries are the most numerous. The first on 28th Jan starts quietly: *Played Folland chess after dinner. Won one, lost one.* The next day I play Jack, my most regular opponent. On 1st Feb my father entered the lists as our chess mentor. *Dad first played Jack and me simultaneously and of course won hands down, then he played us blindfold, also winning.* By the 5th Feb I had become so enthusiastic that I went down town and ordered Chess Monthly. On 8th Feb, Dad as tutor *went over the French Defence pretty thoroughly.* The next day *I went to Foyles but there were no decent chess books, not even there.* On my 16th birthday *Dad showed me the King's Gambit in* detail. On the 12th Feb I was myself the instructor and *taught Wilson how to play chess, sorry, the moves of chess.* The next day I report that *he seems to be progressing quite fast.* I went to Letchworth Chess Club on the 19th and *played three games with adults and lost in all, but very honourably.* On the 28th Jack fails to appear for a prearranged chess session with me and my father and I realise that his pursuit of Marion Hooper took precedence over our beloved game, that instinct trumps intellect. On the 10th Mar *Dad showed me a super chess trap which I must use on Fox.* The record shows that I was losing more games than I won and *got licked twice by Kirsch* on the 12th… and that *at the chess club there was a new chap there. I got licked easily* in two games but I actually won the third and that *made me as pleased as Punch.* I also record defeats on the 12th by Snorter, on the 19th by Rudd, *not easily,* and on the 20th by Fox though I did manage wins against Rudd and Fox and in one game with Rudd *brilliantly forced a stalemate.* But the victory I have treasured in my memory all my life was on 24th March when *I played Dad who was blindfold and actually beat him. He resigned after about the 25th move.* Truly Oedipal; the son who could only overcome the father when blind and emasculated.

The end of the spring term was upon us; there were more pressing preoccupations and the chess soap disappears from the journal with slight variations in the last two entries. The first sees Jack and me collaborating on a humorous book on chess which fizzles out after one page and the second in which Jack and I pay our last visit to the chess club. *Jack played Snorter and we almost killed ourselves laughing about him "losing tempo" and the way he looks at the board.* He would short-sightedly lower his head over the board and swoop and circle as he surveyed the position. What I find striking about my younger self is how I seem to take defeats in my stride, and my acceptance of the reality of my being a mediocre player.

It seems that for me the enjoyment was in the game itself. Also I was proud of my chess savvy father and how admiring of him Jack and other friends were, pleased that he was once again in the family fold and his presence was incarnated both for me and the rest of the world. At this time, he was still in the Army and was not demobbed until a few months after the journal comes to an end. He would spend his leaves and most weekends with us but during the week my mother and I were together alone and although the journal notes many excursions to the cinema, chats and domestic tasks performed by me, our relationship had developed into a volatile one and arguments were frequent. The 12th Jan: *Mum rowed at me for not having helped her,* 19th Jan: *I had a terrific row with Mum over nothing as usual even though I had got up at 9am and went and did her shopping*, 25th Jan: *I met Mum to go to the pictures but she got in a furious temper with me because I wanted to see another picture, so we came home,* 12th Mar: *Mum beat me home and was very annoyed in consequence*, 17th Mar: *In the evening I had a bit of a bust up because I had not finished my prep and I sat up late doing it,* 20th Mar: *I got a terrific sermonising letter from Dad all about my behavior to Mum, etc., etc.* followed by reparative actions on my part. *Helped mum do some work in the evening and the next day did some errands in the morning.* On the 10th May *I had an argument with mum as I didn't want to go to London, but of course I had to go.*

Ailments and health were concerns during the first three months of the year. 10th Jan: *Mum made me go to the doctor about some spots on my tongue. He said, "Stomatitis" or something, not serious.* 14th Jan: *Tongue is the same.* 15th Jan: *I went to the doctor again and he was puzzled over my tongue; he had to consult a book. Anyway he gave me some vitamin tablets.* 16th Jan: *Tongue no better.* 21st Jan: *Went and saw* Dr.*Vanderbort who said I have got 'locoprasia' due to a condition. He gave me some more tablets.* 23rd Jan: *My tongue is no better and I have developed a bad cough. Bad coughs seem pretty prevalent at our school now anyway.* 24th Jan: *I have a bad cough and cold and my tongue is no better.* 25th Jan: *My cough and cold were very bad so I went to bed at 9pm.* 26th Jan: *I woke up very early having sweated all night.* 1st Feb: *I had a bad attack of asthma at 3am but luckily this soon passed.* On the 6th Feb my anxious grandmother had arranged for me to be examined by Sir Adolphe Abrahams, medical officer in charge of the British teams in the Olympics from 1912 to 1948. *He was a queer, thin, hunched up sort of bloke but quite nice. After examining me he said he would write to mum* but no follow-up appears in the journal.

Money was another preoccupation during these months. Weekly pocket money helped but was inadequate for a boy who when in London was an avid attender of concerts, the theatre and the cinema, diner at Lyons

Corner Houses and buyer of books and gramophone records. I have described how I criminally supplemented my income at the expense of the Jewish National Fund; the journal contains no mention of this but records faithfully all the monetary gifts I received during this period. 2nd Jan: *The day had left me very short of money but Uncle Percy stepped into the breach and tipped me 10/-.* And so on: *received 7/6d postal order from Mum: Grandpa gave me £1, Percy tipped me 5/-, Grandpa gave me a pound tip.* But on the debit side on 11th Mar: *the Boss* [headmaster] *is starting a Good Causes Fund. That means forking out more dough!*

School holidays were the time when I saw my London uncles and aunts: Alf and Rosa, Jack and Ray, David and Zephyr and Percy and Ruby. Percy in particular I saw nearly every day as he called for my grandfather on his way to their factory which was then in Richmond Road, Hackney and would drop him home after work. On the 7th Jan I report that *I was woken early in the morning by shouting from Uncle Percy. I immediately guessed and got dressed as quickly as possible. Yes, it was a girl to be named Barbara. Uncle Percy was very happy and he scrounged £10 from Grandpa to open a £50 savings account for her.* There was death as well as new life. 2nd May: *Dad had to go up to Leeds as Zaida had died. The news did not affect me very much as I did not know the old chap very well but it is very sad all the same.* Nowhere near as sad as I would have been if it has been the death of Grandpa Simon which I thought was the case when Dad came home and announced 'Your grandfather has died' and I was briefly in a state of shock and grief until a minute or so later I twigged the actual identity of the deceased. It was an ill wind; a week later *I heard that Zaida's gold watch was to be given to me .On the 11th May I went to Ray's and saw Bubba but she didn't talk to me much.* This was not surprising as she was in a catatonic state, induced presumably by the trauma of Aaron's death. Esther had been brought to London to live with her daughter, Ray who could not cope and it was her daughter-in-law, Zephyr, who took on the task for the few remaining months of Esther's life.

On the16th Apr *I went to see David and Zephyr at their home in Watford. David joined us for lunch then disappeared. I did not talk to him much, he is studying psychiatry and is swotting like mad for the exam.* I think that David's choice of career combined with my own contemporaneous reading about the theories of Sigmund Freud implanted the germ of the idea which impelled me to join the Science 6th group at the beginning of the following academic year. I returned from Watford to Clapton *in time for the second Seder* [Passover] *night which was very lonely with only Grandma, Grandpa and myself.* The previous night's Seder was a different kettle offish; my mother and father were present and *we had a jolly old Seder night (the wine was lovely, also the grub) except* for the *'fier kashers'* which I had been swotting up all afternoon.

Post-barmitzvah, I ceased going to synagogue but was attending a Sunday morning mixed class on Judaism. On the 20th Jan *I called for Jack and we went to old Dr Jaffrey's Hebrew lesson*. I mention a few absentees and ended: *we had a jolly fierce discussion on Materialism*. But that was my only attendance. Reasons (or excuses) given were *because of cough, owing to rain, my birthday, bike puncture and finally, just the day I do go, Dr Jaffrey has to be ill.*

There are no further references to Dr Jaffrey's class and I made no further effort to attend the class. Whether this was due to his illness, my inertia, lack of interest, absences in London or the more pressing task of revising for exams I cannot say.

Apart from chess my main interests outside school were in the process of developing into lifelong loves. Hardly a day passed without my going to the cinema, listening to music, plays and comedy shows (Tommy Handley's *Itma* being consistently the most praised) on the radio and reading, mainly middle-of-the-road novels. During visits to London, I went to the theatre, concerts at the Albert Hall and the cinema almost daily, sometimes twice daily. During these months I was building up my knowledge of classical music.

I cycled a great deal but had persistent problems with my ancient second-hand bike which restricted my ability to get out and about. 16th Feb: *I spent the afternoon mending a puncture* but the next day, recording why I could not go to Dr Jaffrey, *I found that I had not mended the puncture at all*. On the 23rd Mar I started *a new bike campaign* for all the good it did me because a week later a*t long last I mended my puncture but immediately took it to Sudbury's to have a really good job made of it. It will cost £2 or more but there are a lot of things to have done to it; new brakes, chain, mudguards etc.* A further week on *I got my bike, it cost £1.13 and they had made quite a good job of it.* The next day, celebrating the return of a functioning bike, *Dennis and I went for a cycle ride through Sandon, Kelsall, Therfield, Littlington and Steeple Morden. We got a marvellous view of the surrounding country from Therfield and saw an old deserted aerodrome near Steeple Morden. Felt very stiff in the evening.*

At this time clothes rationing was still in force. On the whole I was interested in clothes only to conform to what my peers were wearing. My family, being in the *schmutter business* [rag trade] were hypercritical on the subject and I suppose some of that might have rubbed off on me. 5th Feb: *Mum bought me a scarf, navy blue, and I didn't like it but still...* 11th Feb: *A rotten day. I went to school in Dad's grey jacket as my blue one is so shabby.* 25th Feb: *I went with Grandma to get a pair of gloves. At Dudley's in Dalston I got a lovely pair of gauntlets.* I had always coveted gauntlets. 23rd Apr: *Uncle Percy gave me a very nice coat of his but a few days later I got a new overcoat from him.* On the 30th Apr I accompanied my grandmother first to Gamages [a department store in High Holborn long since demolished], then Selfridge's *to try and get a blazer but we could not get one.*

My main pre-occupation on returning to school in January was rehearsing the school production of *Macbeth*. I was cast as the Old Man who appears only in one short scene in Act II. The teachers responsible for the casting of the annual Shakespeare production seem to have discerned in me a talent for older male roles in our all-male casts: 1947, Sir Toby Belch in *Twelfth Night* and 1948, Capulet in *Romeo and Juliet*. Four years short of even one score, my first lines were:

> *Three score and ten can I remember well*
> *Within the volume of which time I have seen*
> *Hours dreadful and things strange*

Now four score plus, I can heartily endorse those words but at sixteen what did I know? 14th Jan: *We had a rehearsal of Macbeth but I went for nothing; I didn't come into it.* 15th Jan: *Had a rehearsal and said my little piece but as they started Act III I buzzed off.* 29th Jan: *I was measured for my Old Man costume.* 16th Feb, a Saturday: *I got up early to go to school for a rehearsal; this ruined my plan for going to London. I discovered that my part of Old Man is not all that easy but needs a bit of acting.* It seems as though on that day my inner luvvie was constellated. 28th Feb: *I turned up for rehearsal but all for nowt.* 14th Mar: *There was a rehearsal watched over by the Boss.* Disappointing news on the 18th Mar: *The Boss decided to call off the play to the public but to do one performance only for the school. Everyone thought this very unfair and that they might have told us earlier.* The reality was that we had not reached a standard fit for public performance, mainly because Mr Whitworth, a talented and experienced director of our school plays had only just been released from military service and had rejoined the school too late to squeeze a coherent performance out of us.

I was also a devoted attender of the Debating Society. 25th Jan: *After prayers the Head for some reason went on against boys talking to girls in the street. He had seen them in the street outside the Bancroft entrance on Wednesday and objected to them standing in 'groups'. After school there was a special 'surprise' meeting of the Debating Society. The 'surprise' was that they called a subject out of the box and also a name of a person present and that person had to spout on that subject for three minutes. Dennis had 'Homes', I had 'Evolution', Bert Reid had one on 'Protection' and he twisted it beautifully into a satire of what the Head had said in the* morning. *Shapira did a very good one on 'Heavenly Bodies'. Kirsch told me that if he had drawn 'Homes' he would have started off by saying "Elementary my dear Watson".* On 30th Jan, I report that much against my will I had *to oppose that cinema was worse than theatres in Friday's debate, but as no one else will do it I was a sport!?!* A few days later we had the debate. *Not many people came and we lost by thirteen votes to two.* On the 1st March, there was a *new racket in the Debating Society. The best papers on certain subjects were to be broadcast to USA and to get a representative opinion we discussed three of the subjects. These were 'What Youth Expects from UNO', 'What an International Youth Organisation could do', 'Who should control the Atom Bomb?' It was all quite good fun.* At one meeting *Mr Whitworth gave an interesting talk on Russia. He had gone there in 1931 during the 1st five-year plan.*

I was even more passionate about games which were compulsory as was gym which returned to the school during this period after the wartime absence of our gym master. In the journal I say how much I enjoyed the exercise and the games, hard work though they were. The record speaks for itself as to my talent for games. In the spring term the prescribed game was hockey. On 17th Jan *I played in a rather scrappy game but I enjoyed it.* I played again the next day and a month later *I watched the school play the Royal Masonic School, Watford; they were a super team and we did very well to lose 5-1.* On 11th Mar to *my surprise I was in the house trials for hockey. I played after school but I don't suppose I'll get in.* Two days later and again to my surprise, *I was in Pierson's 2nd XI as right back and without swanking I played quite a good game. We played Skynner and beat them 1-0. We won in the 1sts 5-2.* But the following week *we lost to Radcliffe 4-0 and two days later we played our last match and won 1-0.*

So much for hockey, cricket was the Summer Term game. On 12th Apr *Dennis and I played cricket all afternoon*, a mere hors d'oeuvre to 9th May when *I found out to my great joy that I was in Pierson's house cricket trials. Yippee!* The next day the trials took place. *I did lousily at batting and didn't even get a chance to bowl.* The following Monday *we played a very scrappy game; it must have been if they let me bowl.* Nevertheless, the next day *to my great astonishment I found I was in Pierson's 2nd XI. Fair gives me the willies, it does.* Prophetic words: on 17th May *I was in the house match against Mattocke. We lost 31-40. I made a superb duck, but did heroic work as long stop and only let a couple of byes. Still it was a good game and we won in the 1st XI.* My poor form continued and I tersely report on 19th May: *Usual routine day. I played games, batted and got a duck and bowled and got no wickets.*

The core of school life was of course academic work and this is faithfully represented in the journal. Everything was geared to the O level exams (then called School Certificate) we were taking later that year and as I describe the difficulties of and increasing amount of time spent doing homework, it is clear the pressures are mounting. For example, on 15th Feb: *School and prep is now one constant sweat. Prep 6-30 to 9-30pm.* 14th Mar: *We heard today that exams [mocks] are imminent.* 27th Mar: *First exams today, Geography, Maths and English Composition. I did not feel that I did very well. The next day History, Physics and French. The Physics exam was the worst exam I have ever done – and Latin and Maths, I did lousily.* But on the 1st, 2nd and 3rd Apr most results came through, not too bad considering my pessimistic forecasts: *1st in Geography, 4th in French, 4th in English Literature, 10th in Maths, 3rd in History, 1st in Latin and English Language* but prophetically in the case of *Physics, 21st and 13%.* Reality kicked in on the first day of the summer term. *Usual routine except that we filled in our School Certificate entry forms.*

Looking at the journal as a whole, I see my sixteen-year-old self as solipsistic and the centre of his own universe with immature opinions and undeveloped emotions though the fact that they were there in potential is amply demonstrated by the hurt, tender and vengeful feelings I express in relation to Beryl. But there are seeds of empathy and gratitude to be found in the entry of 3rd May: *In chatting to Bowyer I found out that his mother is dead and he, himself, has TB. Poor chap!* I had known Bowyer as a classmate for four years but had known nothing about him, just as I knew nothing about my other peers' families, backgrounds or personal circumstances. I thought my own were tragic and shameful enough and kept very quiet about them. This however was the first time I had been forced to confront real tragedy in a contemporary. Also in May I note that I wrote a letter to my grandmother thanking her for her hospitality and I have the sense that this sprang from genuine gratitude.

It was at this time that feelings were beginning to be opened up in me and, up to a point, I could bring myself to express them. On 11th May *I met Jack and Dennis and had a terrific row with Jack about old Jaffrey's Hebrew lessons. Jack has a very uncomfortable habit of hurting one's feelings. He said that he only went out with me for something to do. However, we didn't have an actual break.* Later that day all seem to be well; *Jack, Dennis and I played cricket and then went to a local fair, met other friends and had the most terrific fun in consequence. In fact, we had a smashing evening.* However, on Tuesday 21st May: *In the dinner hour I broke with Jack. He has...* And there it ends as does the Journal.

I have no idea what caused the break nor what *He has*. But the facts that we broke, that I did not, could not continue to record whatever it was '*He has*' and that I abruptly terminated the journal at that point, suggest that it was too painful for me to re-enact the event, let alone find the words to do so. Diverting my attention and energies to revising for O levels is an inadequate explanation for this total and final cut-off. Sad though it is, the eruption of feelings of rejection, betrayal and loss was a salutary experience and may have contributed to my fascination with the theories of Freud, particularly those relating to the existence of an unconscious mind.

There is a note I added beneath the final entry at the end of 1947.

> *'I am writing this two days before I start to keep a 1948 diary and am pleased to say that my style has improved or at least I hope so, for if it has not, it seems as if my '48 will be as boring as my '46. I have just read through the '46 and the monotonous recitation of facts and names appalls me. I therefore, start with a clean sheet in '48 and hope to make the most of it. Instead of bald narrative, I propose to write about people; surely the most interesting reading on which to look back in future years.'*

I find this note more than a little pompous and arrogant. Not surprisingly my 18-year-old was anxious to distance himself from his younger self but I think he underestimated the energy, enthusiasm, self-deprecating humour and honest reportage of that younger self, which can be more clearly and objectively apperceived by my present octogenarian self.

23. SIXTH FORM (1946-47)

Autumn sunshine bathed the courtyard of the old school buildings. It was the first day of term and we hung about, chatting, catching up, and waiting for instructions. I felt that I was on the verge of a new life. No more Master Boris Rumney. More Master of the Universe. Good School Certificate results. No more school uniform. We could enter and leave by the front door of the school. Grown-up at last, with our honours and achievements ahead of us. All things were possible.

The headmaster, Mr Jones, cropped grey hair and dapper in his double-breasted grey suit, called for silence.

"Welcome to the sixth form. If you haven't made up your mind what subjects you want to take for Higher School Certificate, have a word with Mr Miles. Those of you who have, Arts to the lower sixth room, Science to the physics lab."

Jack and I made our way towards the science block. We had already decided on our future careers; we both going to become doctors and that required passes in four science subjects to exempt ourselves from 1st MB.

I had recently discovered the theories of Sigmund Freud. It was an intellectual liberation. Or more accurately, a liberation from the intellect. My father and his family revered and celebrated above all, intellectual prowess, sharpness of mind, rigorous rationality and academic success, and I was at best a moderate scholar. My father excelled at mathematics, chess and rhetoric; he was a remorseless debater. I could never beat him by the strength of my arguments, but as an adult I browbeat him by mobilising my inner fascist and shouting him down. So the revelation and relief for me in psychoanalytic theory was that we were more than our conscious minds, that we were directed by mental processes of which we were unaware and that our dreams were not random mental events but had meaning which could be decoded. I decided that this was the world for me, that I wanted to be a psychoanalyst or psychotherapist or psychiatrist or psychologist; I wasn't at all sure of the nomenclature. There was no one who knew anything about the subject to guide me and based on the examples of Dr. Freud and Dr. Jung, I assumed that the way forward was through a qualification in medicine, so in the physics lab that morning I opted for four science subjects. Within weeks I was in desperate trouble.

Mr Webb, the chemistry master, had returned from the forces but was a boring and uninspired teacher. His first act was to give us long lists of chemical formulae to learn. I didn't understand them. I couldn't grasp them. I lost concentration and became miserable and frustrated.

Zoology initially seemed more fun. The sun shone on us as, armed with shrimp nets and buckets, we made our way to the stream at the edge of the school grounds. It was easy and enjoyable catching the frogs and horrifying (but fascinating) to watch them anaesthetised to death. But there the entertainment ended. The task was to dissect a frog and this I could not do. I couldn't follow the textbook anatomical diagram, wielded my scalpel clumsily and succeeded in puncturing several major blood vessels and severing ligaments and muscles all over the place. Jack and his frog were on the next bench to mine; he worked calmly with great delicacy and precision, creating a perfect representation of the diagram. I was full of admiration.

"Fox, you're a budding brain surgeon" I said.

Perhaps I should have persevered with these subjects, but my friends in the Arts Sixth were doing *Hamlet* and the *Romantic Poets* and I yearned to give up learning formulae by rote and to join them in subjects to which I was far better suited. So I asked for permission to switch from my course and in doing so gave up my plan to go to medical school as well as postponing for forty years my desire to become a psychotherapist.

There was a bit of catching up to do but I was much happier in my new subjects, especially English and Latin. Mr. Thomas, the English teacher, was also the director of the school play which that term was *Twelfth Night*. I was given the part of Sir Toby Belch. What with learning the lines, regular rehearsals and four main subjects to keep up with, the pressures began to mount and I could well have done without the headmaster's compulsory French class. His teaching technique was simple; we were given a French text and he would pick one of us to translate at sight. Halfway through the term he called on me.

"Rumney, top of page 26!"

"Monsieur Courbet ne pouvait trouver nulle part. Il s'était enfui." I then translated, "Mr Courbet was nowhere to be found; he had just done a bunk."

Whatever possessed me? Wanting to be clever? Wanting to be different? The illusion that I would be applauded for my adventurous use of the vernacular?

"How dare you, boy? Intolerable insolence! How dare you insult your headmaster. Get out! Get out of here! Leave the school immediately! I'll deal with you tomorrow."

I was in a state of shock. I left the room. I had rashly believed that my newly acquired sixth form status liberated me from the stultifying hierarchies. That teachers were now benign older brothers, not authoritarian fathers. That adventurous and creative work would be welcomed, not punished. And that an appropriate plunge into the demotic *done a bunk* instead of *had fled* would receive plaudits not wrath. But I had misjudged Mr Jones. No jumped-up whippersnapper like me would be allowed to affront the dignity of the headmaster.

Abashed and bewildered, I wandered the school corridors. What to do? Surely Jonesy was not serious about me going home for the day? At the end of his period it was time for lunch, a lunch I had already paid for. He had no right to deprive me of that. So when the dinner bell rang, I took my usual place at the sixth form table and had barely started on the dish of the day, Irish stew with mashed potatoes, when Mr Jones entered the dining hall. It was his habit to wander between the tables, holding a dish of say, watery cabbage, and ladling it out onto boys' plates, saying as he did so,

"It's good for you, boy. Eat it up."

And he would return later to ensure that every scrap had been consumed.

That day, the moment he came in, he spotted me. Already a ruddy complexioned man, he turned bright scarlet. He launched into a crescendoing tirade.

"What are you doing here, boy? I told you to go home. Not content with insolence, it's disobedience now, is it? I will not have it. You dare to defy me? I've met boys of your kidney before. Leave at once! Get out!"

My eyes pricked with tears. It was the humiliation of being harangued in this way, not just in front of masters and my peers, but also all the younger boys. I crept out of the school accompanied by Jack who walked to the bus stop with me. A good friend, he consoled me and said,

"I always knew the swine was an anti-Semite."

"Why, because of the *boys of your kidney* stuff?"

"Well, he obviously meant Jews. What else could it mean?"

What else indeed? My parents agreed. Now more than sixty-five years on, I'm not so sure. The Shorter Oxford Dictionary shows as a figurative meaning for kidney, *temperament, nature; hence, class, stamp,* and quotes *from The Merry Wives of Windsor' (III.v.116), "Think of that, a man of my kidney, that am as subject to heat as butter"*. Also Fielding, *"This fellow is not quite of a right kidney"*, the first meaning temperament, the second, class. No mention of Jews in either of these quotations. Mr Jones might only have meant boys of my nature or type.

At a time when anti-Semitism was still pervasive and could strike at any time from any quarter, the tendency of Jews to paranoia was common, so the case of Mr. Jones as Jew-hater is not proved. If a rush to judgment, it was understandable; even now the phrase is so visceral, so Antonio-addressing-Shylock. But I still wonder why Jack and I, the only sixth form

Jews, were the only boys not to have been made prefects – the appointment of whom was in the gift of Mr Jones.

The next morning, I was called to the headmaster's study.

"Well, boy, what have you got to say for yourself?"

"Nothing, sir".

His voice rose.

"Nothing? Nothing? At the least I would have expected an apology."

I reflected a moment before replying.

"I can't apologise sir. I don't think I've done anything wrong."

"Nothing wrong? Insolence to your headmaster, Rumney. Apologise and I may find it possible to be lenient."

"It would be hypocritical for me to apologise sir. I didn't mean to be insolent. I was just trying to translate, sir"

"You obstinate boy. Think over what I've said and come and see me after school."

I spent the rest of the day trying to rustle up support from the masters with whom I got on well. I even threatened Mr. Thomas that I would withdraw from the play because I was too upset to continue. Though sympathetic to me they couldn't oppose the headmaster; they too suffered from his rages and volatility. They counselled a strategic apology on my part. They were right of course.

After school, I presented myself to the headmaster.

"Well, boy?" he barked.

"It would be hypocritical for me to apologise, sir," I said, proud of my use of 'hypocritical' and of standing up for what I perceived as my integrity of self. Mr. Jones shook his head in disbelief.

"You disappoint me, Rumney. I won't forget this in a hurry. Now get out of my sight!"

Looking back now I can see how a diplomatic 'Sorry Sir' would have saved me a lot of grief.

A profile of Mr. Jones in a history of the school, *The John Mattocke Boys*, published in 1990, describes him as *a harsh unbending man who wielded the cane with great frequency and apparent pleasure... he ruled the School with a rod of iron... teachers as well as pupils were likely to be carpeted for their shortcomings... even to his staff he was very much a dictator and a bully.*

This episode marked the beginning of a collapse of morale from which I did not recover for the rest of my time at school. The bright hopes and exhilaration of the sunny courtyard only a few weeks before had evaporated. My brush with Mr Jones was not the only cause. Sex in the head and girls on the brain took up much of my thought and energy at the cost of concentration on my studies. Girls, girls, girls. Falling in love with nearly every one I met from the girls' high school. Trying desperately to impress them with my intellectual prowess. Some hope! Jack and John had girlfriends, as did all the elite members of my year. I had to make do with having a greater theoretical knowledge of sex than my peers and a wider range of correct technical terms.

Hard facts were hard to come by in those days, as was really graphic sexual writing. I had a good nose for snuffling out what was available: my research sources included a Sigmund Freud primer, bought second hand in Charing Cross Road, *Married Love*, which I discovered in my aunt Rosa's bookcase, explicit physiological diagrams in a medical encyclopaedia in Letchworth Public Library and Krafft-Ebing's pioneering work on sexual perversions and deviations, *Psychopathia Sexualis*, borrowed from the same library. I quote from Wikipedia: '*Krafft-Ebing's book became his best-known work. He intended it as a forensic reference for doctors and judges and wrote in a high academic tone, noting in the introduction that he had deliberately chosen a scientific term for the name of the book to discourage lay readers. He also wrote sections of the book in Latin for the same purpose. Despite this, the book was highly popular with lay readers*'. Well, the book was certainly popular with this lay reader. And it improved my Latin more than Virgil's *Aeneid*, Book VI or *Cicero's De Republica*, my set books for the year.

More general reading included *The Rape of Lucretia, Venus and Adonis* (thank God for the Bard), Chaucer, Henry Miller and *A Glastonbury Romance* by John Cowper Powys.

All of this was not bad for 1947 in deepest rural Hertfordshire, but no substitute for the real McCoy. It was all very well having the reputation of being the sixth form sexual *eminence grise* but no consolation when the elite group by which I was tolerated as some kind of court jester, all had girlfriends. I would accompany them to the Broadway Cinema on Saturday nights: Jack with Pat Woolley John Goodwin with Pat Luckhurst, Norman Knight with Elizabeth McDonald and me, unpartnered. In the back row, snogging started the moment the lights were dimmed and I, full of envy, tried to ignore the slurping sounds and intimate whispers by focusing on the movie.

For me, like most other young teenagers, film stars such as Cary Grant, Fredric March and Humphrey Bogart were the models of the looks, dress and cool behaviour to which I aspired. Looks particularly; I would spend hours in front of the mirror, squeezing my spots and blackheads, pushing up my nose in the hope of remodelling it from Semitic curve to Nordic straight and rehearsing expressions of contempt, indifference and sangfroid.

Jack had started to go out with Pat early that term. She had a round, pretty face, china blue eyes and was blonde, petite and plumpish. After lunch Jack and I would sit in the lower sixth classroom talking about their relationship. Prurient, I was avid for every detail. Initially, Jack, perhaps fearful of gossip or out of a chivalrous desire to protect Pat's reputation, was not very forthcoming and for some weeks admitted to nothing more than passionate necking. He even preached on the moral and practical dangers of *going the whole way*. Taking him at face value, I enthusiastically joined the debate in an effort to help him discover what it was that was stopping them, and what stratagems he could employ to break down whatever barriers or resistance there were. He finally admitted that they had been having sex for some time. Though hurt by his deception, I was too keen to hear the full story to make an issue of it. Logistics were a problem. They couldn't go to each other's bedrooms and winter weather made it impracticable to do it in the open air. But John Goodwin played cricket for Letchworth and, having a key to the pavilion, used to take Pat Luckhurst there. Jack's solution was ingenious. He pitched a tent out of sight behind the pavilion and furnished it with groundsheet, blankets, primus stove and a small cupboard containing tea things, biscuits and packets of condoms.

Jack explained that the actual acquisition of condoms was the second problem. They weren't hard to come by. But he was too embarrassed to buy them at a chemist in case the assistant was a woman or he was within earshot of one.

"At least at the barbers' they whisper, *Anything for the weekend sir?*" he added.

"So that's where you get them?" I asked.

"It's still embarrassing. I often came away empty-handed, well not empty-handed, but with jars of Brylcreem or packets of razorblades I didn't want or having a haircut I didn't need."

I was curious about Pat.

"Does she enjoy it?" I asked.

"Pat's a really goodhearted girl. She says she's in love with me and she lets me do it whenever I want. But she doesn't enjoy it in the way I do. I asked her if she was frigid or if I was doing it wrong and she said, 'No, I'm saving myself for that until I get married'."

"*That*, meaning?"

"Oh, sharpen up, Boris! You know: coming."

Jack and Pat were together for two years. He was very fond of her but not in love and broke it off when he started dental school. I was deeply envious of him. Not so much for the sex (enviable enough) but for the relationship. I pined for a steady girlfriend of my own to assuage the loneliness I often felt and with whom I could share my deepest dissatisfactions.

Jack's parents were hospitable and kept an open house for all his friends. His father owned and ran a grocery store in the Arcade, Hitchin, so the Foxes were largely unaffected by rationing and any food available from the shop was in plentiful supply. I was a regular guest at Sunday tea; the whole of Jack's family would be there, including Jack's older brother, Harold, recently demobbed from the RAF and John Goodwin. We played table tennis, gossiped, impending boredom staved off by the arrival of Mrs. Fox with plates of egg, tinned salmon and jam sandwiches, large quantities of golden, perfectly crisped chips, cakes, biscuits and cups of milky tea, spreads the size and opulence of which I rarely saw in the still meagrely rationed days of 1946. Mrs. Fox, once her job as provider of food was done, departed for the kitchen but Mr. Fox would remain, taking his habitual seat by the fireside, and would soon be immersed in an ill-tempered political argument with me, idealistically left wing at the time and still revelling in the Labour landslide of the previous year. Our voices rose but his was louder than mine and he had all the authority of age, as well as of volume, neither of which he hesitated to use to shout me down and shut me up.

One Sunday in late October I arrived to find the wreck of an ancient Austin 7 in Jack's drive with Harold, Jack and John busily dismantling bits from under the bonnet. I didn't like the look of this activity at all.

"What's going on?" I asked.

"Harold's just bought it. For £5. We're going to restore it," Jack replied.

"When?"

"Now. We've started taking it to bits. We're going to work on it every weekend until we've finished it."

My heart sank. What of Sunday afternoons now? I was no mechanic. I couldn't spend all afternoon engaged in shouting matches with Mr Fox.

"Can I help?" I asked.

Harold and Jack looked at each other

"Too many cooks." said Harold "But let me and Jack have a think about it. It's very skilled work but we'll see if there's anything you can do."

Until teatime I watched the three of them wrestling with recalcitrant engine parts. Harold and Jack were both born with mechanical genes but John had been given a subsidiary role, holding engine parts steady while the other two worked with spanners and other tools I couldn't identify, cleaning dirt-encrusted and oil-smeared bits of machinery and generally fetching and carrying. If the godlike Goodwin had been allotted such servile tasks what would they find for me?

The next Sunday I turned up wearing my oldest clothes, ready to have a go at anything they threw at me.

"We've got a really important job for you", Harold announced as soon as I had joined the working party in the drive. "Trouble is, it can only be done in the shed. Come, I'll show you."

He took me to the shed at the side of the back garden and pointed to a large rectangular piece of metal clamped in a vice, attached to a workbench. It was at least two inches thick.

"See the diagonal line I've marked across it?"

"Yes" I said.

So far so good. He thrust a tool into my hands.

"Look, we need a triangular piece of that metal to change the angle of the steering column. That's a hacksaw. Your job is to cut along the diagonal line absolutely straight and absolutely smooth. Got it?"

I nodded. With my woodworking experience at Calday Grammar School, it would be a piece of cake. I set to work and was soon dispirited to discover how slow progress was. It was also a solitary task. I missed the fun and comradeship of working with my friends, particularly as the rhythmic throat-clearing noises of my sawing was punctuated by the sound of frequent roars of laughter from the drive. I realised later that they had been laughing at me. Following my volunteering to help, Harold and Jack had conferred.

Jack was against my recruitment on the ground that I'd be hopeless and a liability. Harold added that I would never stop talking and agreed that I'd get in the way of the project. But he didn't want to hurt my feelings and planned a job for me which, whilst useful, would both take forever and keep me apart from the main working party. I worked on the metal for several Sundays When I finally presented the finished product to Harold, he ran his fingers over it and said,

"The edges are too rough. Rub them down until they're perfectly smooth."

That job took me three more weeks. I was glad to have made a contribution to the enterprise but I didn't want to be consigned to the isolation of the shed again, pleaded excessive homework and revision and listened to the Sunday afternoon classical music concerts on the Home Service instead. Harold and Jack worked on the car for about a year, finally producing a mint Austin 7, capable of doing 65mph and with new, rakish steering. Jack ran the car for several years, commuting daily from Letchworth to London, parking free and legally outside the Royal Dental Hospital in Leicester Square where he was a student.

24. NAOMI

I met my first girlfriend, Naomi, in what is now the Serpentine Gallery in Hyde Park but in 1947 was a huge cafeteria with a wide swathe of tables stretching all the way down to West Carriage Drive. At that time, it must have been the largest open air cafe in London and on the fine summer's day of my first encounter with Naomi it was packed. I had already spotted her slightly ahead of me in the queue for the Prom since early that morning as being a pretty, petite, vivacious girl, full breasted and with long, wavy, auburn hair. In the afternoon I bumped into her in the cafeteria. I was bold.

"I saw you in the Prom queue".

This was enough to get us started and we stayed together talking all afternoon and stood together body-to-body during the concert. When we came to part we exchanged addresses – I still remember hers: 44 Gilda Court, Edgware.

The bliss of that summer; the sun never ceased to shine both on the land and in my heart. I had a girlfriend. I was in love. We were besotted with music and with each other. During the school holidays, I stayed with my grandparents in London and saw Naomi nearly every night at the Proms. Afterwards we walked to Hyde Park Corner through the park, hand in hand, singing Sibelius, Schubert or whatever we had just heard until we went our separate ways home. I did not kiss her goodnight. I did not know how.

I spent most of the school summer holiday at the Proms, with or without Naomi. Not so much just at the Proms as queueing for them. The object was to secure a place right at the front, best of all by the rail separating audience and platform. To make certain of my place I would arrive at Door 11, the prommers' entrance, no later than mid-morning and always in time to find a place on the entrance's steps to sit on. I soon got to know other regulars as intent on obtaining a pole position as I. We began to look on ourselves as an elite group, the *Door 11 Gang*. Romances formed and dissolved, lifelong friendships were made. The ticket office opened at 7pm, we paid our 2/- (10p today) and sprinted for the coveted positions in front. The arena quickly filled up and back then 65 years ago, management allowed in many more promenaders than they do today. We were a youthful crowd, mainly teenagers or in our early twenties, who owe it to the Proms for our introduction to the repertoire as well as to new, contemporary music. Now when I see the Proms on television, I am amazed to see how old the prommers are; middle-aged and elderly, men seem to predominate and I wonder where all the young music lovers have disappeared to. The BBC Symphony Orchestra conducted by Adrian Boult (as he then was) bore the brunt of the season but in 1947 Basil Cameron and John Barbirolli also lent their batons and Ralph Vaughan Williams conducted one of his symphonies.

In mid-August Naomi went on holiday with her parents and I disconsolately returned home to Hertfordshire, bereft and bored. Luckily John Goodwin was around and we used to go up to the Letchworth cricket ground every day and bat and bowl to each other in the nets. I was passionate about cricket, a mediocre player, but John as well as captaining the school 1st XI was already playing for Letchworth and had been described in the local paper, *The Citizen*, as *six foot tall and powerfully built. A man's man and a woman's dream*. So for him to practise with me in the nets was a real act of friendship. He was a good friend and mentor in other ways too. I confided in him about Naomi.

"Have you snogged her yet?"
"No, I haven't even kissed her"
"Why not?"
"I don't know how"
"What the hell do you mean, you don't know how? You just do it"
"Yes, but don't your noses get in the way?"
"No, you silly bugger, of course they don't!".
"Well, I don't understand. How do…?"
"Look, I'll show you!"
And with that he showed me. It seemed simple enough.

A week later Naomi returned to London and so did I. Ray Waterman and my father were first cousins. I had first met her at a family party earlier that year and she invited me to spend a couple of weeks in the summer at her family home in Chesterford Gardens, Hampstead. I took the invitation for granted, but I can now see the generosity of spirit it represented. I am not sure that I would welcome the irruption into my house of a callow youth of 17!

> *My heart aches and a drowsy numbness pains my sense*
> *As if of hemlock I had drunk...*

It may be a false memory that this couplet flooded into my mind on the still, hot afternoon as I walked down Church Row on my way to Chesterford Gardens. I had never been to Hampstead before and it then possessed a peace, stillness and calm which must have been much closer to the Hampstead of Keats and Constable than it does today. I could scarcely believe that I was in London. My heart did ache with the beauty of the place and carrying my suitcase in the midday heat, a drowsy numbness did pain my sense, so with my head stuffed full of romantic notions derived from Keats et al., it is possible that the poem flickered through my mind as I made my way along Hampstead's bosky lanes.

Ray was different from any other adult I had ever encountered. Accessible and benign, she had a great talent for relating to young people. I chattered to her about anything that came into my head and was always responded to with tact and sympathy. Brash and opinionated, I would often engage in political debate with Ray and Alec, who were both Communists. Despite my naiveté and gauche views, I was never treated with scorn. Rather than demolishing me (as my father did), they listened with courtesy and respect.

I met David, Ray's younger brother. He was holed up in his room, never venturing out, suffering as I now know from some kind of mental breakdown. We talked together at length but the troubled things he had to say were beyond my understanding. He played his guitar and again and again his records of Shostakovich symphonies, the turbulence of which must have matched his own mood.

I played cricket with Ray's young sons, David and Peter, on Hampstead Heath and took them to London Zoo. As an only child, I revelled in the role of surrogate older brother, still young enough to enjoy their childish games but using my greater age and authority to lord it over them and basking in their admiration, an unaccustomed experience for me.

Sometimes during the day, I had the run of the house. I had brought with me numerous books, prescribed reading for the exams to come. In particular I investigated the treasures of Ray's study with awe. It was a real writer's study with a typewriter (I tapped away for hours on end) and a desk heaped with typescripts and articles by her, published in the *Manchester Guardian*.

Alec, Ray's husband, died of a heart condition in his fifties but Ray lived on to publish two novels based on characters drawn from my father's family. She died in 2001, a few days after my own mother.

On the last day of my stay I brought Naomi to lunch at Chesterford Gardens. I was full of pride in having a girlfriend and showing her off to Ray and Alec but I wasn't sure that they completely approved of her because she was defiantly uninterested in politics. Music was her whole life.

After lunch, Naomi and I went for walk on Hampstead Heath and lay down together in a secluded corner of Kenwood. I kissed her. She responded warmly and with great sweetness. Our noses did not get in the way. I was both moonstruck and over the moon. If it been something which was done then, I would have roared a mighty "Yeahhh!" and punched the air in triumph.

I kissed Naomi many more times that summer. But she was seventeen, attractive and much courted by young male Prommers. She found it all irresistible: she played the field and she played fast and loose. When we arranged to sleep on the steps of Door 11 so as to be among the first in the queue for the *Last Night of the Proms*, I thought she was my girlfriend. But it was the arm of another man which encircled her in the photograph of the *Door 11 Gang* which appeared on the front page of the *News Chronicle* the next morning.

We kept in touch for the next three years and when I came out of the Army in 1950 we went to a concert together. She wanted us to continue to see each other but I was on the point of starting university and said that I would be too inundated with work to go out with her on a regular basis. I'm not sure why I did that. There may be a kernel of truth in my excuse but I think that the main reason was that there was still a residue of hurt in my heart and that I felt I couldn't trust her. Perhaps also there was tit for tat pleasure in rejecting her. Soon after our last date she had a long relationship with a violinist, a well-known London busker, dark and romantic-looking, whom I had often seen playing Hungarian Rhapsodies and other virtuoso pieces in the West End.

The last time I saw her was in 1972 in the Scilly Isles. I was with my family in the Beach Cafe on Porthcressa, tucking into fish and chips when she came in with a man (not the violinist) and a boy of about seven and sat down at a nearby table. "That's my first girlfriend, Naomi". I whispered. "Don't be absurd!" said Rex who was with us at the time. I whistled the first few bars of Sibelius' Third Symphony, a favourite piece of ours, back in 1947. Her head swivelled round. I went over to her. 'You're Naomi Epps, aren't you? I'm Boris.' She introduced her partner, an ordinary-looking guy called Brian Chipps. They were living in Dartford but I'm not sure whether they were married; if they were, she would have gone from Epps to Chipps.

The most recent news I had of Naomi was from her brother – how he had my phone number I have no idea. After a long period in a North London nursing home in an advanced state of Alzheimer's disease, she had died. I meant to go to her funeral but somehow I didn't get round to it.

25. SIXTH FORM (1947-8)

The summer of music and love was over; the Autumn Term had begun and I was a second-year sixth-former in my last year of school. The auspices were not good. I had not opened any of the books I had intended to read during the summer in preparation for taking a Cambridge entrance exam. Cambridge was only 18 miles from Letchworth and I had cycled there many times, rowed on the River Cam and explored the colleges which were then accessible to the public without payment. I was besotted by the beauty of the place and could imagine nothing sweeter than spending three years there, reading English.

I don't know whether I was depressed or just not up to it, but during that term and for the rest of the year I couldn't settle down to work in a rigorous, tear-the-guts-out-of-it, kind of way. By then my main Higher School Certificate subjects were English, Latin and Geography, with French subsidiary. I became a master of distraction. Free periods, and there were many of them, were intended for study, but I couldn't settle down, attended Bert Reid's French classes even though I wasn't doing French literature but because he was such an inspiring teacher, doodled, daydreamed and engaged in chat with any other free-perioder who was around, who soon tiring of the interruption would say,

'For God's sake, Rumney, shut up. I've got a bloody essay to finish by tomorrow.'

In the first weeks of term, auditions took place for *Romeo and Juliet*, for which I was cast as old Capulet, Juliet's father. Lines to learn, not easy for me, and rehearsals after school were burdens I cheerfully bore. Acting not only mobilised my inner luvvie but provided a legitimate distraction from my other concerns.

Apart from schoolwork there were girls continually on my mind, not any girl in particular, but girls as a category. Forty miles separated Naomi and me and our initial flurry of letters soon petered out. She was clearly immersed in a busy musical and social life of her own and had no time for a gauche schoolboy like me.

I was assiduous in pursuing activities that interested me: listening to music and enlarging my repertoire, Chairman of the Music Society, Secretary of the Debating Society and above all the cinema. I joined the

Letchworth Film Society where I saw the Raimu trilogy, early Russian films directed by Eisenstein and the fantastical, existentialist films of Jean Cocteau.

Culpin was a first-year sixth-former whose father was the licensee of The Sun Hotel in Tile-house Street, a former coaching inn, originally built in the 16th century. Adjacent to the main building was a large detached outhouse, the first floor of which was used for private functions and dances. Culpin was allowed the use of this room on Friday nights and he invited elite sixth-formers from both the boys' and girls' schools to informal dances. I'm not sure how I qualified for an invitation. A number of 'nesses' come to mind: cockiness, chirpiness and eagerness, combined with verbal skills and an ability to make people laugh. But I never considered myself one of the truly elite, those confident, mature and well established sports jocks, the solid bourgeoisie of the future, not like me, a Jew and edgy outsider, yearning to be one of them and yet at the same time, snobbishly contemptuous of all they seemed to stand for, their total lack of cultural interests and their *Young Farmers'*, *Crusaders'* and *Young Conservative* badges. However as is the way with ambivalence I also wanted to be accepted by and admitted to the Gentile heart of the group. If I had been sharp enough I would have noticed that Gentile nearly spells elite backwards.

None of these thoughts prevented me from throwing myself enthusiastically into this end-of-school-week activity. It was not so much terpsichorean as erotic; a goddess leading a god on. The Victor Sylvester record would start up, you scrambled for a partner, danced chastely until Culpin turned the lights off and you were entitled to kiss your partner. Not just permitted but actually required by the law of the lads. The wonder was how expertly the girls kissed. How did they know? Instinct or experience? And all so different. But queen of them all was lovely Madge Farrow, full breasted, black hair and green eyes. So warm and sweetly welcoming. I imagine that at some deeply unconscious level they were testing for potential partners and at the same time practising for future ones. I certainly was. Many relationships were established at these dances but not by me. Although I learned much, I obviously still had to improve my osculatory skills.

It was during this period that I fell in love with Madeleine Ruzius. I met her on the coach taking a group of older boys and girls to an orchestral concert at the Vauxhall Motors works canteen in Luton. She was a slim, fair girl with sharp, intelligent features and a pellucidly clear voice. She was a quick, bright speaker, initially as interested in me as I was in her, and she engaged in the kind of flirtatious, sparring banter which now makes me think of Degas' painting *Spartan Girls Challenging Boys* at the London National Gallery. I organised and was in charge of the outing, so perhaps she gravitated towards me as a leader. I was captivated by her repartee and combativeness; qualities I was familiar with in my mother. It turned out that her parents were licensees of *The Unicorn*, a pub in the centre of Stevenage, telephone no. 345. I phoned her often from my local phone box, two old pence and no time limit. We spoke for hours but I think she had lost all interest in me and was intent on keeping me talking, the better to evoke the stream of my vapidities and inanities with which to regale her friends the next day. But love is blind and I was blinded. I planned our first date, bought tickets for the Sadlers Wells Ballet and asked her to come with me. Bizarrely, I could not bring myself to admit that I bought the tickets myself, out of my own money, perhaps on the ground that that would have made me appear too eager. I concocted a story that they had been given to me by an uncle.

I arrived absurdly early and an hour into the performance I gave up waiting and took the next train from Kings Cross back to Letchworth. I heard later that she had been out with Stuart Robertson that afternoon and had not bothered to meet me on the ground that *'after all he didn't pay for the tickets'*. As if that excused her, but lovesick fool that I was, I invited her to the school Christmas dance and presumably because Stuart, or indeed anyone else, had not invited her, faut de mieux she accepted me. At the dance she was preoccupied, her eyes darted all over the place and her conversation with me was strained and stilted. I assumed that she was ashamed to be seen with me, rather than with Stuart or some other popular young blood. At all costs, she needed to communicate this publicly by her demeanour: *Look, I'm here with Boris, but don't think for one moment that I'm enjoying myself.* I felt angry and humiliated and after the dance my pride kicked in and I stopped pursuing the delectable ice maiden.

About this time, we put on two performances of *Romeo and Juliet*. After the previous year's *Twelfth Night*, I felt an old hand, a seasoned actor. I did well enough, although on the second night I fluffed my lines in the scene over Juliet's grave. We had no Renaissance music for the ball scene, so I provided a record of one of Corelli's concerti grossi, written in the 18th century. No one seemed to notice this anachronism and we received good reviews in the local papers.

In the spring term I started to train after school for the annual cross-country race. I had high hopes of doing well, having trained hard and got my time down to one which would have taken me into the first three. My tactics were a failure, but they were self-invented; no advice or mentoring was available. From the start I ran at my own pace with the ruck, confident that the front-runners who shot off from the start would come back to me. False reasoning; I should have joined the leading party. I overtook many runners but only came seventh. It would have been sixth had not Woodhead overtaken me during the short time I was slowed down by a severe stitch.

I had recovered by the last mile and was running well and easily. The road leading to the finishing line at the school was thronged with spectators including my unrequited inamorata, Madeleine, animated, lithe and at her most beautiful, cheering us all on. How I would have loved to have been first just for her.

Higher School Certificate loomed. A constant pall of anxiety hung over me. But instead of it acting as a spur to action, I worked and revised in a desultory kind of way, unable to summon up the kind of will and concentration which had not been a problem in earlier years. I mooned about, went for long walks, listened to music, frittered time away. Now I re-experience the feeling whenever I vow to settle down to writing. A crossword puzzle, coffee, admin, a quick trip to Sainsbury, a friend I just have to phone, anything rather than put my mind to the task and pen to paper.

There were genuine issues with which I could justifiably distract myself from the tedium of Cicero's speeches and Walter Scott's *Guy Mannering*. The drama of the ending of the British mandate in Palestine: the atrocities committed by Jewish terrorist organisations, the Stern Gang and Irgun Zvai Leumi, in particular the blowing up of the King David Hotel in Jerusalem and the brutal murder by hanging, of two British servicemen. The turning back from Haifa of rust bucket ships crammed with survivors of the Nazi extermination camps whom the British authorities then dealt with by interning them in Cyprus. These events triggered a resurgence of anti-Semitism in England and as a Zionist and therefore passionate supporter of the creation of a Jewish state, I was involved in continuous heated discussions with my classmates about the rights and wrongs of Jewish/British/Arab actions. On 14th May 1948 the independence of Israel was declared, followed by the immediate military action by five Arab countries to crush the infant state, the survival of which was for several weeks on a knife edge.

By the end of the autumn term most of my contemporaries had been made prefects. Jack and I were not. Although I affected an insouciance, a devil-may-care attitude befitting the bohemian, anti-establishment outsider I believed myself to be, I felt deeply hurt and humiliated. At some level, I wanted to belong. I took to wandering into the Prefects' Room. Tommy Hall, for years the class sissy, then Head Boy, with whom I had been on good terms throughout the whole of our school life, we, being the only two in our class who shared a love of classical music, confronted me there one evening after school.

"Rumney, you shouldn't be here!"

"What do you mean, I shouldn't be here?"

"You're being deliberately obtuse. You know this room is for prefects only."

"But all my friends are here!"
"That's irrelevant. I must ask you to leave."
"Don't be ridiculous Tommy. I just came in for a chat."
"Chat elsewhere. Leave now or I'll be forced to call a master."
I was beaten. I left the Prefects' Room, never to return.

What with my lethargy and indifferent academic performance, I had long given up any grandiose ideas of applying for a place at Cambridge to read English Literature. My uncle Jay, then a Professor of Sociology at Rutgers University in America, sent me a copy of his introduction to sociology, *The Science of Society*, for my birthday. I was enraptured. This was the subject for me! Jay had studied at the LSE and had gone on to do his doctorate there, so I decided to follow in his footsteps and go there too. I submitted an application form and took an entrance exam which I passed, but because of the pressure on places from returning servicemen, I had to wait to take up my place until after I had completed my National Service.

I so wanted to shine at sport. In the spring term, the term for hockey, I played at left back in the first XI trials, but was not selected. I became a spectator instead at all the home games and house matches. I made sure that I was seen as no ordinary supporter by the creativity of my vocal support.

"Get that ball in, Rawlin!"
"We should win, Goodwin!"
"Pitch in, Hitchin!"

At the beginning of summer term, I turned up at nets for the start of the selection process for the cricket first XI, determined to demonstrate my skill as fast bowler. In my efforts to gain pace I sacrificed both length and direction. But that term I discovered that I could run fast and worked my way into the finals of the annual Sports Day 100 and 220 yards' races. I was also selected to run the first leg in my house 4x100 yards relay. I trained as best I could without proper running shoes and managed to borrow some from another competitor only on the day itself. I was up against my nemesis. Woodhead, county runner, who beat me by a head in both races, though up against him in the relay I handed the baton over first and my house, Pierson, was the winner. I had just received from aunt Rivka in America a multi-coloured sweater which in its peacocky garishness stood out against the drabness of postwar Hertfordshire. I wore it between races, preening myself like some Regency beau, as I strutted amongst the spectators and past the gaggle of Hitchin Girls' School groupies which included the celestial Madeleine on whom my unique garment had no effect whatsoever.

Thinking now about my efforts to attain distinction as well as distinctiveness and to be noticed, I am convinced that unconsciously I was yearning for a male adult to take me in hand, take an interest and show me how to do things, inclinations which my own frequently absent, laissez-faire father lacked.

The term wore on, exams drew closer. The Sunday before they started, Alf and Rosa drove down from Enfield to visit us and we went for a long walk in the country. I should have been revising.

The next day Jack and I went to the cinema are to see what turned out to be the Marx Brothers' last and weakest film, *The Big Store*. It was a brilliant, sunny evening and the two of us constituted the entire audience. I should have been revising.

During the exam weeks themselves, Jack, I and a few other boys spent every available moment when we weren't taking exams, playing cricket, so there were times when I entered the examination hall tired, hot and sweaty. I should have been revising.

The questions on Virgil's *Aeneid* were all on Book VI. My Latin master, Mr Monk, had conscientiously spent the year taking me through Book IV. I reported the error to the invigilator and arrangements were made for a week's moratorium during which a special paper on Book IV was prepared. I won the school Latin prize, the honour of which, in my mind, was greatly diminished by the fact that I was the only Latin scholar that year.

Term puttered to an end. At the precise time the service celebrating those pupils leaving the school was taking place, I was on a bus to London. My feelings were complex, a confused mixture of shame, anger, failure and freedom. My school life was over and I was off to my first promenade concert of the 1948 season.

26. WAITING FOR THE CALL TO ARMS

I stayed with my grandparents for most of the next few months, resolving to lead a rich cultural life until the start of my National Service. I was determined to have a go at reading the canon. I took Proust's *Swann's Way* out of the library but could not get beyond the first twenty pages and never have since. I read Thackeray's *Vanity Fair* and JB Priestley's *The Good Companions*. I enjoyed both but was mocked by intellectual relatives for the frivolity of my choices. I worked in my father's office; no pay, but he treated me to delicious lunches at Bloom's famous Jewish restaurant, next door to the Whitechapel Art Gallery.

A letter arrived from the War Office informing me that because I had dual Polish and British nationality, I was ineligible to join the British Army unless I renounced the Polish part of me. This had arisen because when I was born my father had Polish nationality only and therefore so had I, and it was not until I was four years old that he became naturalised and I automatically acquired British nationality as well. A form of renunciation was enclosed. For me the decision was clear-cut. I was proud to be British and by 1948 Poland had become a communist, satellite state of Soviet Russia. I wanted no formal juridical connection with it, with its unknown practical consequences, even though by refusing to sign I could have escaped National Service.

At the Proms I picked up with Jane Alderson, a tall, striking brunette with dark brown hair and long, curly lashed eyes, olive skin and a full mouth. I had met her at the Albert Hall the previous year. She was then the girlfriend of a Charing Cross Hospital medical student, a tall handsome man, and although at the time in love with Naomi I fancied her for the statuesque assurance conferred by her good looks and envied John his apparent dominion over her.

We hit it off and spent the summer together. I was housesitting for aunt Ray and uncle Jack, off on a long holiday, so means and opportunity conveniently coincided with desire. For both of us there was double desire: the desire to have sex and the desire to rid ourselves of our virginity. In Ray's house in suburban Whetstone, we achieved both objectives; Karma Sutra it wasn't, but it was a start.

The Higher School Certificate results were published in mid-August.

As I was in London, I phoned the school for news. Expected, but nonetheless disappointing, I had not done well. But at least I had done enough to pass and so satisfy the LSE entry requirements.

Early in October I received my calling up papers summoning me to present myself at the 64th Training Regiment, Royal Artillery, Oswestry on Thursday, 4th November 1948. A travel warrant was enclosed. I spent the intervening weeks saying goodbye to friends and relatives and cramming in films and concerts as if filling myself up against an anticipated cultural famine. I had my hair cut reasonably short in the hope that the Army barber would consider no further scissoring was necessary. I wanted to start my service fresh and free from encumbrances. I was not in love with Jane but sensed that she was becoming strongly attached to me. Cowardly and craven, I wrote her a Dear Jane letter, pleading the fact of my leaving London for an unknown future and destination as the excuse for ending our relationship.

And so early on the morning of the 4th November, I carried my battered brown suitcase to Stoke Newington Common and boarded the number 73 bus to Euston station.

27. OLD FRIEND

We've known each other, Jack and I, for seventy years and during the whole of that time have always been the best of friends. He is also the person who has known me longest; everyone else is dead. That makes him especially precious to me, but for Jack that position is reserved for Harold, his older brother. Still Jack and I, as contemporaries, share a past, nostalgic memories of school and a passion for Letchworth Garden City in which we both grew up. We meet about once a month for a chat and a rant. He waits for me in his car in Manchester Square; we drive to the cafeteria/restaurant in Regents Park. Not the greatest cuisine, but within a few yards of a number of disabled parking bays. Jack's lower discs are shot to pieces from thirty years of practising dentistry and he can only walk short distances without pain.

It's a warm, sunny day and we take a table in the shady, dappled courtyard and order drinks. We exchange family news and move on to the big political issues of the day. Jack has become as right-wing as his father, when as a sixteen-year-old I did battle with him. For him Israel can do no wrong. But we go back too far for any differences between us to matter; despite his age and disabilities his spirit shines out, he twinkles and is funny and responsive. He glides and holds a pilot's licence. Hungry for what life can offer, the question he still asks himself every morning upon waking is 'What shall I do today?'.

We finish our drinks and order food and wine: Jack, courgette soup and steak and me, smoked salmon with granary bread and risotto

This time we each have business with the other. Jack has borrowed books about Letchworth from Harold's wife, Nancy, a Letchworth girl born and bred. Knowing that I am in writing about my life in Letchworth, he thought I might find the books useful, crammed as they are with photographs of the city as we knew it in the 1940s. They are a great resource but I'm a little worried.

"Will that be okay with Nancy?" I ask.

"Nancy won't even remember that I borrowed them"

Silly me, forgetting. Nancy is dementing; she can still complete *The Times* cryptic crossword but can't remember what happened five minutes ago. I thought yes, well, we memoirists don't remember either - not what people looked like, what they wore or said; it all vanishes leaving only me, me, me.

Jack and I riffle through the books together, exchanging memories as we go. "There's the record shop we listened to the latest jazz in."... "That's the newsagent I did my paper round for. 7/6d a week I got."

Our starters arrive. We put the books away. I make a start on my smoked salmon and say:

"Listen, Jack, I'm writing about my time at Hitchin Grammar School. People have commented that I haven't got inside characters other than me. But for the life of me I haven't a clue what was going on inside anyone else's head. Or how others experienced me."

"Oh well, you were an intellectual."

"To you maybe I was an intellectual. To an intellectual I wasn't an intellectual."

"Yes you were. You listened to classical music, you went to the theatre, you read books."

And he emphasises the words music and theatre and books by elongating them, particularly the first syllables or in the case of books, the first three letters, so that something of the scorn he felt for my interests all those years ago becomes reactivated in the telling. He continues:

"You were in the Arts Sixth. You read literature. You knew about poetry. And you were Bert Reid's pet."

Mr Reid's pet! This really surprises me. Mr Reid was the French master, tall, thin, aquiline nose, severe and ascetic in manner. He was the school's unquestioned scholar and intellectual. Even though not taking the full French course, I attended his classes on Racine's *Phèdre* and the poetry of Baudelaire, de Musset, Verlaine and other Symbolist poets. In his exposition of the set books he generated a sense of something important and exciting. He had that gift of opening our eyes to the power of fine writing. I had no feeling that I was in any way his pet but it was on his recommendation that I went to the first English production of Sartre's *Les Mains Sales* (then called *Crime Passionel*) and read the novels of Camus.

I lay the last of the salmon on bread and wash it down with some wine before continuing.

"So how did this belief in my being an intellectual affect you all?"

"Well, you were ostracised."

This is also a revelation to me. To be ostracised is to be shunned, treated like a pariah. Surely I would have noticed. Perhaps I was cold shouldered because I was a bore – a musical proselytiser. I had all the fervour of the newly converted. It was beyond my comprehension that once my friends' ears were opened to Beethoven and Brahms, their hearts and minds would not be opened too. I spoke about music incessantly, reminded my friends of impending broadcasts and devised a plan to stimulate interest as if I were some primitive, one-man Classic FM. Often when with a group of boys, I would whistle or hum the first few bars of the last movement of Beethoven's 2nd piano Concerto:

"Da-dah da-dah da-da-da-da – Da-dah da-dah da-da-da-da."

In my fantasy the boys in their curiosity about such a jolly, rhythmic tune, would say:

'Nice music, Rumney! What is it?'

Of course nobody did.

Perhaps it was not so much that I wanted converts as yearned for soulmates. But the things that were beginning to matter to me were in short supply. There was very little cultural activity in Hitchin at that time. Jack had told me that they didn't have any music in his house so he didn't get to know any. And this was probably the same for most of the boys. If it had not been for the war I would have gone to school in Hackney and my friends would have included Harold Pinter, Arnold Wesker, Maurice Peston and Barry Supple. When I returned to live in London, all but Pinter became my friends. Until then I experienced only loneliness and longing.

Within a quarter of a mile from my house there was a field which sloped down to a small copse. When I was in the sixth form, on summer evenings after I had done, or as a respite from, my homework, I would walk down to this copse and fantasise that I would meet there a young Hungarian gypsy type of girl, dark and vivacious, in colourful bohemian clothes. A girl with whom I could share the feelings which I kept locked away, not out of inclination but because there was no one to share them with. While I was mooning about in the copse, Jack was out there shagging Pat Woolley.

Our waitress clears our dirty plates and brings us our main courses. We continue to talk between mouthfuls.

"You know all about Pat," Jack says as though something had been triggered off in him by my investigation and it is now his turn to tell me his story. "John Goodwin was with Pat Luckhurst so we went out as a foursome. You obviously couldn't be part of that."

"You were a lucky sod having a girlfriend like that at sixteen."

"I suppose so, but it was a mixed blessing."

"How do you mean?"

"When Harold got engaged to Nancy, all hell broke loose between him and my parents."

"Because she wasn't Jewish?"

"That's right. So starting with Pat I had to keep all my relationships secret for ten years until I met Judy (his wife). That's a lot of girls I could never take home. But my parents never suspected a thing. I'd tell them I was out seeing John or at swimming practice."

"It's funny, it was never a problem for me, bringing girlfriends home, Jewish or not. That included Jessie; she was black, from Trinidad, which was a big deal sixty years ago."

"God, I could never have done that. I could never have taken Ilse home. It was bad enough that she wasn't Jewish, but German, just ten years after the war, can you imagine?"

Coffee arrives and Jack continues reminiscing about Ilse, his dental nurse when he was stationed in Hamburg, Major Fox of the Royal Army Dental Corps. A woman he had loved. I've heard the story before and go off into a little reverie of my own. On our second date, in a salt beef bar in Windmill Street, Soho, it emerged that my wife's Christian mother had converted to Judaism in order to marry her Jewish father. Would I have married her if she had been non-Jewish? I'm sure I would, but the fact that she was not, certainly eased things as far as my family was concerned.

"So yes" he says, going back to our time at school. "I went through the Science Sixth in a fog. I was completely lost."

"Well, not all the science teachers were back from the war."

"No, I can't blame that. Others managed to keep up."

"Yeah, me too. I also went to pieces in the Sixth form. It still hurts. But at least you made your mark as a swimmer."

"Second." Jack says. "To Stuart Robertson. He was junior county champion. I never even made it to county standard. That's how much of a mark I made. I did train but he had a trainer. I reckon that if I had pushed myself more, I'd have done better."

I think to myself how closely his sporting experiences mirrored mine. I came second in the 100 and 220 yard sprints to David Woodhead, also a county champion. I didn't train much; I didn't know how. Unlike Woodhead, but like Jack, I had no trainer or teacher to take me in hand. I just ran as fast as I could and it wasn't fast enough.

"These things still rankle don't they?" I say.

"Yes they do. Though for me things changed for the better after school. And I've had a very fortunate life. But I can still jump back into that painful pool of memories in a flash."

The surprise is that Jack is as deprecating as I am about himself as a sixth former. I search for something positive to console him with.

"At least you were the best-looking boy in the school. A cross between James Dean and Steve McQueen."

"I didn't think so."

"So what did you see when you looked in the mirror?"

"Just an ordinary boy, clear skin, clean, neat."

The pretty Polish waitress arrives with the bill and as usual we chip in equally.

"So, Boris, what do you make of it all?"

"Well, I think that back then we were so self-absorbed that others were of importance only to the extent that they gratified our own desires and needs."

"You speak for yourself." Jack says mock-reproachfully. "No, you're right. We were obsessed with girls and struggling to keep up at school. And I was crazy about cars."

"Music was my obsession. And trying to get noticed in a couldn't-care-less world."

Jack reflects for a moment then says,

"We didn't think much of ourselves, did we?"

"No. We only felt second-best."

We leave the restaurant and Jack gives me a lift to Warren Street Station.

28. ARMY LIFE: TRAINING

Urgent shouting. Loud clanging. The lights went on. The booming voice of Bombardier Matthews, beating two saucepans together. "Wakey wakey! Rise and shine! Move, you idle lot. Hands off cocks; into socks." He crashed his swagger stick on the metallic end of every bed in the hut. It was 6am. I awoke, fully alert, even though I had only had four hours' sleep. This was my first reveille as 22078494, Gunner Rumney. B, 64th Training Regiment, Royal Artillery.

From Oswestry station Army trucks had taken us to the camp where sandwiches, tea and cakes and a welcoming speech from a senior officer awaited us. That was the last time we were at leisure for ten hours. There were a multitude of transformations and new ways of comporting ourselves to learn.

First we undressed for a cursory medical examination which involved coughing and testicles. We were given our army numbers, rushed through a store room to be kitted out with uniform, boots, gaiters, a brass buckled belt, a metal dish with a handle for soup and tea, and a knife, fork and spoon. An NCO with two stripes strode in. In his early twenties, he was tall, lithe and smartly turned out. He had the lean, mean, good looks of Clint Eastwood in his Spaghetti Western days. He looked as svelte in his uniform as if he were wearing a DJ. He called us to silence.

"Right, you bunch of ninnies. You're in the Army now and don't forget it. I'm Bombardier Matthews and you will always address me as Bombardier. Got it?"

"Yes Bombardier", we shouted back

"You're in C squad, my squad, and while you're here I'm the one in charge. I'm responsible for every aspect of your miserable little lives. I give the orders. I'm here to make soldiers out of you. And I'll make your lives a living hell until you are. Got it?"

"Yes Bombardier."

"Right squad, get fell in and I'll take you to your hotel – I mean hut – you lucky lads."

The hut was a long room, heated by a central stove, each bed space provided with an overhead locker. There were toilets and washing facilities at the far end. Bombardier Matthews proceeded to instruct us in the arts of making our bed in the morning and cleaning our boots, belt and gaiters.

"Right squad, I want to see you all smartly turned out tomorrow morning or you'll be in the shit. Reveille at 6am. Parade outside the hut for breakfast at 6-30, room and personal inspection at 8. Understood?"

"Yes Bombardier", this time rather more uncertainly.

We worked until the early hours. Unpacking and stowing our Army stuff in our lockers in the prescribed form. Cleaning our boots. Being new, they were already clean by any civilian standard but not by the standards of bullshit. First the stippling on the toecaps had to be smoothed out with a hot iron. I discovered that *spit and polish* was literal in its operation. With a clean cloth you smeared boot polish on to the toecap, mixed it with a gobbet of spittle and gently rubbed it in until absorbed. The process was repeated numerous times until you obtained a mirror-like surface. The belts and gaiters had to be cleaned by blancoing them. You spread evenly on the belt a khaki coloured mud substance and left it to dry. The belt buckle being tarnished, was rubbed with Duraglit, a metal polish wadding, until it gleamed. As I performed these laborious tasks, I was struck by how absurd they were, but what was heartening was the sense of communal endeavour and getting to know the other squaddies with whom I would be sharing all my days and nights for the next twelve weeks.

I leapt out of bed at reveille amid the clangour made by Bombardier Matthews; half an hour for *a shit, a shower and a shave* and a struggle into my strange khaki uniform, belt and unbroken-in boots. Outside the hut, the Bombardier marshalled us into three rows and ordered us to hold our eating utensils in our left-hand behind our backs. He bellowed,

"Right turn. By the right, quick march."

There was immediate confusion as we all had it in our minds that you commenced marching with your left foot, but here we were being commanded to step off with our right. The Bombardier soon corrected us. Our original assumption had been correct; the order was to do with *dressing*, into the mysteries of which we had not yet been initiated. On that cold, bright November dawn it felt bizarre marching to the cookhouse, holding our primitive eating utensils behind our backs. I couldn't help laughing at the inanity of it but fortunately Bombardier Matthews did not hear me.

After breakfast the hut became a frenzy of activity as we made our beds, folding and squaring off the blankets and sheets, tidying and sweeping our bed spaces and readjusting our dress. Bombardier Matthews swept in.

"Stand by your beds... Attennnnnshun!."

Major Lucas and the Battery Sergeant Major entered and inspected each bed space and its occupant intently. The sergeant-major addressed my immediate neighbour.

"Have you shaved, Gunner?"

"Yes sar'major!"

"Then stand closer to your razor next time."

He pointed out dirty boots, that is boots whose reflections were less than dazzling, imperfectly squared off bedding, locker contents not arranged precisely in accordance with regulations and specks of dust under the bed. The major and his BSM departed leaving the Bombardier to pick up the pieces.

He screamed "You idle sods! The place is a shithouse. I'll have your guts for garters! You'd better pass muster tomorrow or I'll put you all on a charge", and with that he pulled apart offenders' bedclothes, and scattered the contents of their lockers onto their beds. He ordered us to parade outside the hut and so began several days of drill instruction, gym sessions, intelligence and practical tests, visits to the tailors' shop to refine the fit of our best uniform and to the barber for a close-cropping. I did well in the intelligence test but in the practical we were each confronted by the constituent parts of a bicycle pump to re-assemble. I could not make head nor tail of it and was the only one in my squad to fail the test.

During the first few weeks what struck me most about army life was its sheer strangeness, being sealed off from ordinary life, the bleakness of the camp environment with its concrete roads and parade grounds, drab, functional buildings and everywhere khaki: khaki men, khaki trucks, khaki 25 pounder guns, the lack of interest in cultural or aesthetic values, in fact anything irrelevant or counter-productive to moulding young men into efficient fighting machines. I was bemused by the emphasis on bullshit and the pettifogging details of dress and discipline by which you were bound every moment of the day. Even receiving your weekly pay of £1.40 involved a parade and a ritual march to the pay desk, halting, saluting and identifying yourself.

'22078494, Gunner Rumney B, Sir!'

You were handed your pay, signed for it, saluted again, executed a smart about turn and off you marched.

I marvelled at the NCOs love of hyperbole and gallows humour;

"You're a useless shower of shit, Gunner! What are you?"

"A useless shower, Bombardier."

"Shower of what, Gunner?"

"Of shit, Bombardier."

Or, on inspection parade,

"Am I hurting you son?"

"No sir."

"Well I should be. I'm standing on your hair. Get it cut."

The main line to London ran by the edge of the camp. On my third day

The Splits

I saw an express train streaming past, London bound, and I felt an intense longing to be on it, away from that mad place.

On our first Sunday there were no duties except compulsory church parade from which, being Jewish, I was exempt. I bought an *Observer* from the camp NAAFI and settled for the day in the recreation hut where there were easy chairs and a radio. Reading the news and reviews and listening to Brahms 4th Symphony in that oasis of calm, I re-experienced for a few hours something of my old civilian self, no longer just a number.

As the days passed and we became more habituated to the routine and what was required of us, there were aspects of the training I enjoyed. The physicality of it. I threw myself into the marching and rifle drill and the gym. I became a moderately smart soldier. I liked the camaraderie of the squad and getting to know young men from other places and backgrounds: Scousers, Geordies, Brummies, Glaswegians and public schoolboys. Gunner Horrigan, Port of London Docker in civvie life, was the only one I did not get on with. I did not understand his hostility towards me until one evening in our hut we were all talking football. I said I was a Tottenham supporter and Horrigan burst out

"Course you are! You're a fucking Jew aren't you? All you fucking Yids support Spurs."

I went for him. He boxed for the Regiment, welterweight, but although he landed some heavy blows, so did I, and when we were eventually separated, it was by general agreement adjudged a draw. I think Horrigan respected me for standing up to him and although we didn't go as far as becoming boon pals, he was always civil to me for the remainder of our training.

Our basic training was for four weeks, at the end of which all the squads in the regiment, several hundred men, were put through their paces at a ceremonial passing out parade. Some RA top brass took the salute. We marched to the accompaniment of one of the Royal Artillery bands. Some years later I wrote a poem based on the exhilaration evoked by this experience:

> *Extraordinary! Joy and exultation!*
> *Quite against my principles,*
> *Eighteen, against almost everything,*
> *The old regime, regimentation.*
> *More specifically the Regiment,*
> *64th Training Regiment, RA.*
> *Passing-out parade, marching*
> *To a military band, to martial music.*
> *Performing drill with perfect precision.*
> *Present arms, slope arms,*

Right turn, quick march.
Ceasing to exist in your own skin,
Submerged in the corporate whole.
No wonder my heart beats faster
When I see old footage of Nuremberg rallies,
Leni Riefenstahl's 'Triumph of the Will'.

In the NAAFI, after we had been dismissed, Bdr Matthews came up to us. "Well done lads! I was really proud of you. Tea and cakes are on me."

Basic training over, we moved on to eight weeks of artillery training on the classic medium range field gun, the 25 pounder. I am not sure how I got through that period. I was baffled by its mechanism, range and direction finding and how to load and fire it. I was a useless shower of shit. What was I? Hopeless. There were strange, archaic commands such as *'Cease firing.Rear. Limber up'*. Nothing made sense to me. The limit of my ability was to pass shells from one person to another.

The culmination of our training, in our final week, was a trip to the RA's firing range at Trawsfynnydd. I did not see this just as a relief from the monotony of camp life for two days. I was eager for new experience and responded with open-mouthed awe and incredulity to it. Despite the tales of the privations we would suffer circulating in the squad, the excursion felt like a treat. After lunch we boarded the army truck waiting for us on the parade ground and set off in bright December sunshine. I was filled with wonder at the endless moors, the feeling of vast space, the sheep-filled hillsides enclosed by drystone walls: a landscape virtually empty of habitation. We followed the road along the edge of Lake Bala and soon reached camp. It was dusk; cold and drizzling. The camp itself was unmanned; military stays were brief, so our hut was unheated and our bedding damp. We sat disconsolately on our beds, eating the meagre iron rations with which we had been issued. Still hungry, wrapped in our greatcoats and waterproof capes, we set off to the nearby village where to our astonishment we found a cafe open. The owner, a jovial plump lady, was not at all fazed by the sudden arrival of thirty famished young soldiers and we were soon tucking into huge plates of double eggs and chips and mugs of fresh tea.

By the next morning the mist had lifted and it was bright and sharp. We set off to the firing range and manhandled our 25 Pounders so that they faced west towards the distant high hills of Moel Ysgfarnogod and Rhinog Fawr. We were given a range and direction and fired off five rounds during which I remained on the periphery of the gun emplacement in the prescribed kneeling position, arms straight down by my side, motionless, taking no part in the exercise and relieved to hear the final command *'Cease firing.Rear. Limber up'*, whatever it meant.

I ended my eight weeks of artillery training with deeply ambivalent feelings. There was much that I liked and I wanted to do well and be accepted, especially by the public schoolboys, Willis, Robbens and Tumin (in later life a High Court Judge). It wasn't only that I wished to be liked by them, I wanted to be like them. In their competence and confidence, they seemed much more mature and worldly than I. They had all been in their schools' Officer Training Corps, so it was a natural step for them to apply for WOSB, the War Office Selection Board, responsible for selecting suitable candidates for officer training. Not to be left behind I applied too.

I was split between my desire for acceptance and ambition to get on and my feeling that I was living in a parallel absurdist world of pointless bull and petty regulation. No *why* was permitted. We could not question any order, rule or punishment however unreasonable or unjust. You weren't expected to understand, only blindly obey.

"Listen squad, we've got a divisional HQ inspection of the camp on Friday. Our job is to paint all the stones at the side of camp roads white."

"Why white, Bombardier? And why paint them at all?"

"Because I say so, Gunner Rumney. It's an order. Any more and I'll have you up on a charge for insubordination, so button your lip. Do you follow me, Gunner Rumney?"

"Yes, Bombardier."

WOSB took place in a large country house near Trowbridge. It was as though I had an unconscious wish to fail. Civilian shoes were allowed so I turned up in my scuffed, crepe soled, brothel creepers. Bad impression, Gunner Rumney. Immediately after a very good dinner we were shepherded into a beautifully furnished drawing room where the invigilating officer threw a copy of Hansard on to the coffee table. He remained silent, leaving us to initiate a discussion. I don't know what possessed me. This was just after the Soviet attempt to blockade the NATO allies out of Berlin. The beginning of the Cold War. But there was I singing the praises of the Soviet system, instancing the Moscow Metro system and the large number of gifted chess players in the Soviet Union as evidence of the superiority of communism to the decadent capitalist societies of the West.

The next morning, we were split into groups of four and took it in turns to take the others safely across an imaginary river or ravine, using only a variety of ropes and planks (always too short), grappling hooks and other simple items of equipment. The tasks were varied so each leader had to start afresh. My three team mates each took immediate command and the problem by the scruff of the neck and successfully delivered us all to the other side. When it was my turn to be leader my mind froze and in my state of paralysis I could see no way to bridge the gap. I dithered and waffled and my time was up. My chances were up too, and later that day I was told (very charmingly) that they had concluded that I wasn't officer material. The next morning, I was on a train back to Oswestry.

Needless to say, Willis, Robbens and Tumin were selected. I had the heartbreak of seeing them preparing to leave for Mons, the officer training barracks, while I waited for my transfer to Woolwich to train as a clerk, generally reckoned to be a cushy number and a large part of me pined for an easy life with lots of time for reading and listening to music. But my pang at the officer cadets' departure was to do with my loss of them, not only as friends and companions but also as comrades in arms in the rigours and challenges of officer training. And of coming through it, an officer, like them, bound for life in blood brotherhood. It felt as though by inexplicable acts of self-sabotage I had let an important rite of passage slip through my fingers.

As we marched from the station to Woolwich Barracks we passed a contingent marching in the opposite direction and I spotted my anti-Semitic hut mate, Horrigan, on the start of his journey to a posting in Germany. We waved and never saw each other again. At the barracks I felt as though I had arrived on a film set. They were built in Georgian style between the end of the 18th and the beginning of the 19th centuries. The south side constitutes one of the longest facades in Britain. The rest of the garrison was like a small, enclosed town, a mixture of grand buildings, cobbled streets and passageways and little squares in one of which was our barrack room. I quickly made friends with Tony Denning, off to the Chelsea School of Art after military service, and Bernard Chernoff, later Bernard Sheridan, the founder of a firm of solicitors famous for its entertainment and human rights practice.

After Oswestry, Woolwich had an almost louche feel to it. We weren't hounded by NCOs and bull was at a minimum. We could wear civvies when off duty. The Army Catering Corps trained at the barracks and provided our mess with consistently delicious meals. The Royal Artillery band frequently played for us during lunch. And most importantly we were in London with the West End only half an hour away. Tony Denning and I were off *up West* in our civvies nearly every evening, making straight for the Union Jack Club for free theatre and opera tickets. There always seemed to be seats available at Sadlers Wells. For Johann Strauss's *Die Fledermaus* we found ourselves, two private soldiers, sitting in the second row of the stalls. That night, wandering through Soho on our way back to Charing Cross station, we were accosted by prostitutes offering us the *full Monty* for thirty bob. "Can't afford it, we're soldiers", we called back. "Rub your jack for half a crown, then." No deal – we had a train to catch.

Tony was also on the clerks course, held in a dreary building on the periphery of the garrison. We were a class of about thirty, led by two

Sergeant Instructors. One room contained the ancient Imperial typewriters on which we practised two finger typing. No help or training was given. But then not much was expected from us; achieve thirty words a minute and we passed. In the adjoining classroom the two instructors alternated in delivering boring monologues on Kings Regulations, Army Procedures and Regimental Orders. Tedium and lack of sleep caused me to lose concentration as well as interest. I was too busy rushing up to London to revise and I failed the end of course test. Tony passed, but despite my failure, within a week we were both posted as clerks to the 31st TRRA, Kinmel Park Camp, three miles inland from Rhyl, North Wales.

29. KINMEL PARK

It stands on my desk, a framed black and white studio photograph of me at the age of nineteen. I'm not even sure why it's there. Not, I think, out of any particular vanity on my part. It wasn't even mine. It was my mother's, one of the numerous family photos which filled the sideboard, mantelpiece, nest of tables and every other available surface in her living room. I appropriated it when she died. Perhaps the reason it's on display is born of my mourning, the passing of what that young man once was, full of wonder and excitement.

So perhaps I am writing about this time to reconnect with the young me, so avid to embrace and enjoy whatever new experiences came my way. I had the photo taken soon after I arrived in Rhyl. There I pose, bright eyed, eager, full of myself in my best uniform, looking very smart. Blue beret with Royal Artillery badge, polished and gleaming, khaki tie, shirt and tunic sharply pressed. White blancoed lanyard on my left shoulder. I look proud. So I should. I was a man at his peak in that magical year in the Arcadia that was North Wales.

The weather was at its peak too as Tony Denning and I arrived at Rhyl Station immediately after Easter on the 19th April 1949. It was unusually hot and the sun continued to shine, almost unbroken, until mid-October. A truck was waiting to take us across the Vale of Clwyd to Kinmel Park Camp. A few hundred yards short of the camp entrance, we caught sight of Bodelwydden Marble Church, with its spire, 200 feet high, iridescent in the sunlight.

Our regiment trained drivers, but as staff, we had special accommodation and were billeted in a hut with partitioned bed spaces which allowed us a modicum of privacy. As senior clerks were already in place, Tony and I were just general office dogsbodies. I was mainly tied to a typewriter, responsible for correspondence, charge sheets, travel warrants and, most important, the daily regimental orders. These consisted of instructions about who was to do what, when and where, the next day as well as news of postings, awards, sports fixtures and so on.

I typed these onto a paperbacked waxy surface, punctured by the typeface and so ink-permeable and duplicatable on a special machine. Individual items started to arrive on my desk after midday, building up as the afternoon wore on. Ill-trained two finger typist that I was, I was hard put to it to keep up and in my haste made many typing errors which I corrected by the use of a fast hardening, nail polish-like substance; it may even have been nail polish. Once printed out, a messenger distributed copies of the orders to all officers, NCOs and barrack rooms. Every member of the regiment was expected to have familiarised himself with their contents.

Working hours were 8:30am to 5:30pm and only to 12:30pm on Saturdays, so there was plenty of time for off duty living. Initially Tony and I would go to Rhyl which was just beginning to warm up for the summer season and its influx of holidaymakers. There were numerous cafes, several cinemas and a dance hall to keep us fed and entertained.

One evening we went for a walk in the hills behind the camp. I already had the urge to write and on my return I wrote a piece called the *The Valley of Frustration*. Here's a sample:

> *What a sensuous harmony of sight, sound and smell, enhanced by the rich and subtle detail of the orchestration, the whole, a magnificent score by Master Composer. After the eye had ceased to be dazzled and the ear to be deafened by the sudden splendour of the scene, the mind unconsciously tried to classify and catalogue the various and abundant impressions which it could not help but receive. The nose lingeringly savoured the sweet, fresh smell of new mown hay, the ear picked out in turn the despondent contra-bassoons of the cattle, the gay flutes and piccolos of the birds and the querulous oboes of the sheep – a quartet of sublime improvisations.*

I ended by regretting my mediocrity, my inability to adequately transcribe into poetry what I saw and felt... '*Let higher, nobler mortals than us, create.*' I was in a state of heightened feeling and wrote with the utmost sincerity but now can hardly bear to read it for embarrassment.

So many of us late teenagers seemed to overwrite in those days. My archive of that period is stuffed with such specimens of friends' writing. Who were we trying to impress? All my early writing shouts *Pseud!* My heart was in the right place but I substituted overblown images and overheated metaphors for a straightforward description of the land falling away from where we were standing, the clear light and the foothills of Snowdonia on the distant horizon. But I could not do that now, even with my improved writing skills because I have lost the desire and sense of wonder I once had.

A few weeks later Tony and I were sitting on a bench outside *The*

Plough Inn in St. Asaph, a tiny city, barely two miles from the camp, sipping our half pints of beer. I was moaning about how I had signed up for an English literature correspondence course and had received my first reading list: Laurence Sterne, Henry Fielding, Tobias Smollett and Samuel Richardson. I had already bought *Humphrey Clinker* and *Tristram Shandy* and found them forbiddingly long. I felt overwhelmed.

"And the other problem", I was telling Tony, "Is that there is nowhere to work or to keep my books. The barrack room's out of the question, too noisy, blokes taking the piss. I can't concentrate for more than five minutes."

"You can talk! It's much worse for me. I'd like to paint, get my materials sent down. Where could I do it? I need a studio."

As we continued to grumble, a young man cantered up on his horse and began a conversation with a young woman leaning out of a first-floor window of the pub. They chatted away about friends in common and what they were all going to do during *the long vac.* then he raised his arm in farewell and trotted off. The girl disappeared from sight but a couple of minutes later emerged from the pub entrance and I, always the opportunist, called out, "Come and have a drink with us."

She looked us over and said,

"I'm just off on an errand. I'll be back in a tick."

And she was. She introduced herself, Barbara Cooper, the innkeeper's daughter. We quickly established our credentials, Tony to Chelsea Art School once demobbed and I to the LSE to read Sociology. Barbara had just left school with a good Higher School Certificate and like me, a wannabe writer, no plans as yet but 'hoping to get into journalism for starters'.

"So how are you enjoying life at Kinmel Park?" she asked. One thing led to another and we were soon describing to her the frustrations of being an artist or student in an army environment.

"Do you know Leslie Ellis?" she asked.

"We don't know anyone here. Why do you ask?"

"He may be able to help. I'll ask him."

When we phoned her the next day for news, she told us that we had been invited to his regular musical soirée the following week. We were to call for her and she would take us to his house.

The best word in all its senses to describe Leslie was *exquisite*: cultivated, charming,, polished, precious, mannered and effete. His furnishings were refined and fastidious: Chinese carpets, brocade curtains and early 19th century furniture. In fact, Leslie, although about forty, at every opportunity would adopt the manner and mannerisms of a Regency buck.

He greeted Barbara that evening with: "Ah, here comes my Lady

Caroline. What sweet fortune, to favour us with your presence. I brook no further delay; tell me, I pray, who are these two handsome blades who attend upon you?"

We were ushered into the drawing-room where his sister Phoebe and her fiancé were already seated. Leslie handed us glasses of Tio Pepe. I had never had sherry before except in trifle. There were nuts and canapés. The gramophone was of the highest fidelity of its day. The first piece Leslie played was Benjamin Britten's *Serenade for Tenor, Horn and Strings*. I was dazzled by all these manifestations of refined living and felt enormously lucky and honoured to be admitted into such a cultivated milieu. After the Britten, Leslie said, "We need something a little more cheerful. What does my assembled company say to Beethoven's Seventh Symphony?" There was a general murmur of assent.

"Wagner called it the apotheosis of the dance", I ventured.

Phoebe looked at me blankly. Leslie said that he had come across it somewhere and put on the first side of the symphony.

I felt chastened by the failure of my attempt to impress and show that I was more than just a *handsome blade*, which in fact I wasn't; the *handsome blade* was Tony. Leslie had noticed. Then and throughout the year of our friendship I was completely oblivious of his sexual orientation and his infatuation for Tony. I knew all about homosexuality. I knew in what direction homosexual libido lay and what they did. After all I was the maestro of sexual theory. I had a copy of the Kinsey report, *Sexual Behaviour in the Human Male*, only recently published in England and had gained considerable popularity from my readings of selected passages in the barrack room. But I had no actual experience as such. I had never come across a gay boy or man or, if I had, had failed to recognise him as such. It wasn't that I felt any distaste or disgust about homosexuality; it was just that I had no gay antennae. So although I experienced Leslie as *exquisitely* affected, it never occurred to me that he was actually gay. Tony was discreet; he didn't reveal until after we had left North Wales that Leslie had made several passes at him which he had warded off by asserting forcibly that he was 'not that way inclined'.

The 4th movement Allegro con brio brought the Beethoven to a thunderous end. Phoebe brought in coffee and sandwiches. Leslie said,

"Barbara informs me that you cannot pursue your literary and artistic studies surrounded by the brouhaha of barrack life."

We confirmed this to be the case.

"Oh dear! I did not study much at Oxford, too busy gallivanting around. But I would have done even less without the Bodleian and a room of my own. Now, I have a proposal for you. There's an empty store room above my garage. I have no use for it. You can have it for a peppercorn rent."

It was still light and he took us to a large, raftered room with its own entrance. It was cobwebbed, the accumulated dust and dirt of the ages lying everywhere. There were a few discarded chairs and an ancient wooden table. We took the room on the spot, thanking Leslie profusely for his generosity, said our goodbyes to everyone and returned to camp, the key to our studio already in our possession.

We spent the next few weekends cleaning the place up, scouring the Rhyl off-licences for empty Cointreau, Benedictine, Drambuie and other liqueur bottles and picking up bargain items from second-hand shops. We used the bottles as candleholders, placing them on horizontal beams and any other usable surfaces. Tony used a 48 hour leave to bring back from home, art materials and some of his paintings which we hung on the studio walls. By June we had finished the job of rehabilitating our loft and celebrated by giving a party. Apart from Leslie and Phoebe we invited friends we had met through Barbara: Michael Stevenson, tall, slim and fair, Cambridge cricketing blue, Adrian Stocks, short stout and dark, son of Dr Stocks, St. Asaph Cathedral organist and Gillian Slee, blonde, beautiful and formidably bright who reduced both Tony and me to a state of besottedness, but ended up marrying Jonathan Cohen, philosopher and as a Professor of Cognitive Psychology in her own right. We, two lowly ranked artillerymen, had within two months inveigled ourselves into the cream of St. Asaph society. But my attempt to impress Gillian and so secure her as a girlfriend failed. I made a good start with my talk of books and music and psychoanalysis, but I did not measure up to her intellectual standards. I soon ran out of steam and she, of interest.

Wine was little drunk in 1949. My only experience was of the intensely sweet Palestinian muscatel used at home on Sabbath eve and other high days and holy days, that of Tony, a Catholic, was of communion wine. My social drinking had involved, in pubs, small amounts of beer, preferably diluted into shandy and at parties, gin and orange. Tony and I decided to provide Tio Pepe and gin with lime juice which he assured me was a more sophisticated mixer than orange. Party snacks were primitive; we just emptied a few packets of Smith's crisps into a bowl.

Our party was a success. We were delighted to have entered St. Asaph society with a splash and proud of our achievement in creating a study/studio. But we didn't use it very much. A few days later Tony received bad news from home; his father had fallen ill and Tony was needed to keep the family farm going. He was given two months' compassionate leave and left Rhyl right away. Losing my friend made me restless.

I had no desire to use the studio on my own and threw myself into a variety of other activities. Another split. I had a strong yearning to lead a life of study and contemplation but my drives were elsewhere and I surrendered to my stronger extrovert side and the distractions of the pleasure principle. I was brash and bumptious with bags of energy to discharge.

While Tony was away, I was the beneficiary of an extraordinary skive, a week in London at the Army's expense, a good hotel, superb Jewish cuisine and a visit to Bevis Marks, the gem of London synagogues. They called it a Moral Leadership Course. It was open to all Jewish national serviceman, irrespective of their morals (of which I had few) or of their potential for leadership for which, as WASB had proved, I had none.

As we gathered for our first seminar, I met Michael Goldman who became a lifelong friend and who ten years later was to be best man at my wedding. I claimed that I intended to become a jazz critic. Where that came from I have no idea. Apart from liking jazz and a few visits to the London Jazz Club in Oxford Street, the previous year, I knew little about it. Like father, like son. I obviously had a strong urge to impress, to aggrandise myself as a way of dealing with my envy of Michael's sharp wit, the depth of his reading, his reserved place at Oxford, and, especially galling, his greater knowledge of classical music, an area in which I considered myself something of an expert. One thing we did share equally was an enthusiasm for and dedication to pursuing girls. Michael was an attractive man, a bit like a good-looking young Henry Kissinger, tall, Semitic features, black wavy hair and even, white teeth. We were not totally dissimilar; me, tallish, Semitic features, dark wavy hair (but prematurely balding), uneven, yellowish teeth.

It was at a lecture given to us course-members by an Israeli embassy official that I first learnt about Habonim, a left-wing organisation devoted to youth *aliyah*, preparing and training young people for emigration to Israel, specifically to kibbutzim. The notion of a new kind of Jew, liberated from the *shtetl*, unafraid of bearing and using arms, working on the land, living communally, sharing goods and property and making decisions democratically, was very appealing but for as long as I was stuck in North Wales there was no way I could pursue my new enthusiasm.

My job as clerk was cushy and weekends from midday Saturday were always free. On Sundays, Leslie often took us to Liverpool in his Daimler limousine, first to Gilbert Scott's great Anglican Cathedral for morning service, then on to Chinatown for a Chinese meal and finally to the Philharmonic Hall for a concert. These were new and heady experiences for me. Being billeted in camp felt progressively more irrelevant and irksome.

"Why don't we apply to live out?" I asked Tony.

"You're crazy! We've got no grounds."

"Study." I said. "I've got to prepare for the LSE and you're, well, you've got to show Chelsea that you're a serious painter. We can't do it in camp, there are no facilities, no privacy."

Tony was sceptical. "Ingenious, but we'll never get permission."

"Let's try anyway."

We did get permission. Later Tony discovered that this was given by the Battery Commander on a misunderstanding of Kings Regulations, as the right to live out of did not apply to National Servicemen. We found a large furnished room with its own entrance and kitchenette in the centre of St. Asaph at a ridiculously low rent which was paid by the Army. In addition, we were allowed a weekly allocation of rations from the quartermaster's stores to cover us for meals when we were not at camp. There was a local bus to get us to work on time.

This move considerably facilitated our social lives in St. Asaph. We were far too busy to study. We gave frequent tea parties for our friends for which I prepared one or other of my two signature dishes.

~ Eggs Rumney ~

Heat butter in frying pan until sizzling.
Crack in required number of eggs and, while frying,
mix yokes and whites together; when marbled
and firm, serve and add salt to taste.

~ Sardine Mush ~

Bone and degut two or more tins of sardines in oil.
Add chopped onion, cucumber, tomatoes and Heinz
salad cream to taste. Mash thoroughly with fork
and serve as sandwiches or on toast.

Barbara too kept open house most evenings. I would frequently pop down to *The Plough Inn* and sit with her in the restaurant kitchen finishing the remains of the lunch soup – Brown Windsor or Mulligatawny – talking, baring our souls, until the early hours, about politics, books, local gossip and our hopes for the future, hers to be a writer, mine to be a somebody. I last saw her at a party in London and then we disappeared from each other's lives. Too late now, but when I think of her, I miss her friendship.

But in addition to my high life, lofty thoughts and aspirant ideals, I also had a hankering for Army low life. I wrote a poem dedicated to the clerks of Kinmel Park, *sensual scribes despised by all,* who released from duty at the weekend, would *descend on Rhyl to make a new Parnassus. Wine women and song? Nay, a new cry is heard – beer, bint and croon.* Well, I was one of the sensual scribes. And a group of us would descend on Rhyl, first for a couple of fortifying pints and then on to the Queens Palace ballroom in the hope of picking up a girl. A predatory lot, we lined up against the wall, appraising the talent. I never failed to find a girl to dance with provided the tempo was within my limited repertoire of quickstep, foxtrot or slow waltz. The trick was to ensure you had the last waltz with the girl of your choice whom you could then ask to escort home. I was singularly unsuccessful at this endgame until I met and danced with Noreen, Irish, long, jet black hair, green eyes, olive skin, she had something of the looks of Lauren Bacall. She reminded me of my first adolescent love, Beryl Green. We walked along the promenade. It was a perfect summer night, a full moon shining on a calm sea.

"Just look at that sea," I said

"Milky," she added.

Milky! Music to my ears. I was in love. We arranged to meet the following week.

But there was Peter Price. In the Darwinian world I inhabited in those early adult years, there was always a Peter Price. This Peter Price was a friend, a fellow clerk, tall, auburn curly hair and large pale eyes, always beautifully turned out and most potent of all, a smooth, persuasive manner and line of chat. He too had spotted Noreen at a dance, set his cap at her and that was my hopes dashed.

It was Peter Price with whom I went to a dance in Abergele. We picked up a couple of Welsh nurses and took them back to their workplace, a sanatorium in the hills, inland from the coast. In the sanatorium grounds I kissed the nurse, Gwynneth, to whom I had attached myself and she responded with great warmth. We continued in this fashion for a while and when I thought the moment was ripe, I put my tongue in her mouth. She tore herself out of my arms. She was angry and upset. She may even have said "How dare you? I'm not that type of girl."

I defended myself: "That's French kissing. We all do it in London", as if London was le denier cri on matters of modish erotic practice.

Gwyneth was neither impressed nor mollified and without even a goodbye, stormed off to the nurses' home. Peter was some yards away, busily encoiled with his nurse. There was nothing for it but to walk back the two miles to Abergele. At least it was downhill but the last bus to St. Asaph had long since departed and I had no alternative but to hike the further five miles' home along the A55. Such long night walks home were a common occurrence during this period of my life when my fealty, that is my felt rather than imposed fealty, was due, not to King and Country, but to Eros. I would walk a girl home however far, whatever the weather, in the hope of amorous reward and the long trudge back home was the price I was prepared to pay.

One morning I was summoned to the Battery Commander's office.

"Rumney, you've got Higher School Certificate, haven't you?"

"Yes sir."

"Good. The Education Corps wallahs are a man short. I'd like to put you up for it. You will be in charge of chaps so you'll be made up to acting Lance bombardier. Well?"

"I'll take it sir"

I was overwhelmed. Promotion to NCO. Consorting with the bright lads of the Education Corps. Getting away from the tedium of typing Regimental Orders. My creativity in that area was not appreciated. Some months before this job offer, the news came through that a Bombardier Bryson was to be transferred to our unit. I was instructed to include this news in the daily Orders: *'Bombardier Bryson WG has with effect from 14th of December 1949 been transferred to 31st TRRA'*. This was the standard form. But Bombardier Bryson was a celebrity. He was a talented footballer. So I added the words: *'Welcome to the Regiment, Bombardier Bryson!'*

This unauthorised addendum caused a stir and much amusement throughout the camp. It was also deemed to be an act of insolence on my part and it was this offence under Kings Regulations with which I was charged. In full battle dress uniform, I was marched into Major Singleton's office. The charge was read out, the offending sentence produced.

"Anything to say, Gunner?"

I had learnt my lesson.

"I wish to apologise Sir. I don't know what came over me. I was excited because Bombardier Bryson would be eligible to play for the Regiment, Sir."

"Understandable Gunner, but you must not, repeat not, ever tamper with Regimental Orders. Is that clear?"

"Yes Sir"

"Very well. On this occasion I'll let you off with a caution. Dismissed."

I thought education would be worthwhile and creative and with my gift of the gab, a doddle. I met with the team, mature men in their early twenties, trained teachers, all sergeants, impeccably turned out. Smartness was not my strong point and I felt like a slovenly schoolboy in their presence. After a brief interrogation about my qualifications and background, the senior Sergeant handed me a pile of books and pamphlets and said,

"You'll be teaching classes of ignorant oiks. Some of them can't even write their own name. Civics, that's your subject. But don't expect them to be interested. Your main job will be to keep them in order."

I was both intimidated and disbelieving. Keep them in order? Me, one of the only boys is in the sixth form not appointed prefect? But I would show them. With my enthusiasm, I would break through their apathy. I studied hard, prepared well. I described our electoral system, explained how our government worked, invited questions and attempted to initiate discussion. But I failed completely to engage them. It was not indiscipline but lack of response that was the problem. I just could not get through. Boredom permeated the room. The class, all trainee drivers, looked at me with incomprehension or contempt. I think that the truth was that I was not a very inspiring teacher.

Walking to the education centre one morning my progress was blocked by the Regimental Sergeant Major.

"Name and number, Lance bombardier."

"22078494, Rumney B, Sar'major"

"Well, Lance bombardier Rumney you're a disgrace to the Regiment. Dirty boots, dirty belt. You're an NCO. Supposed to be an example. I'm putting you on a charge."

And the next day I was up before the Major again, stripped of my stripe and sentenced to five days confined to barracks.

CB meant that I had to sleep and stay within the confines of the Camp. It was an unwelcome interruption to my social and cultural life especially since Leslie had arranged one of his Liverpool trips. It also involved fatigues, additional duties such as cookhouse tasks, peeling mountains of potatoes, unloading stores, cleaning and polishing kitchen floors and equipment. These jobs carried out in collaboration with other miscreant detainees were quite relaxing and matey as we sat around an immense cauldron, yarning and gossiping as we peeled. I was relaxed and free from the anxieties and humiliations of teaching men who would rather be driving army trucks than listening to me chuntering on.

The first four months of 1950 and my last as a soldier, glided pleasantly by. Two weeks before I was due to complete my service, I received a written summons from the Regimental Commander requiring me to present myself at Headquarters for the purpose of giving evidence at a Court of Enquiry convened for the purpose of investigating the disappearance of a pair of boots. In my best uniform and highly polished boots and brasses, I entered the Commander's room which had been rearranged to serve as a courtroom. The Commander, as President of the Enquiry, sat at a long table, flanked by two officers acting as assessors. The Adjutant's role was to examine the witnesses and establish a trail of the missing boots in order to determine whether anyone was to blame for their loss. The boots, valued at two pounds ten shillings, had been ordered for a Gunner Lewis whose own boots had been irreparably damaged in training. I had received and signed for the boots when delivered and had taken them to the Quartermaster's Stores where I obtained a signature in turn. And so the Enquiry ground on. Four more witnesses testified, the

Adjutant reviewed the evidence and the Enquiry adjourned for lunch. After the recess the President read the findings of the Court:

> *'The boots were duly received by the Regiment and in particular by the Quartermaster and thereafter went missing for reasons this Court has been unable to ascertain. No fault can be laid at the door of any individual charged with the carriage of the said boots. A copy of these findings will be sent to North West Regional Command HQ'.*

We were dismissed. Ten grown men had spent several hours attempting to track down a pair of boots. But I did not sneer. I had been totally engrossed by the forensic methods of patiently trying to arrive at the truth. 'I'd quite like to do this,' I thought.

Tony was the clerk responsible for the preparation of my release documents. The COs testimonial included the following:

'Clean and well turned out at all times, Gunner Rumney's conduct throughout has been exemplary. He served as a clerk/typist and was diligent and conscientious in the discharge of his duties.'

Was he describing the right Gunner? I learned many years later that Tony had carte blanche in the writing of all discharge testimonials.

Armed with my release papers which were effective from 15th May 1950, I said my farewells to all my friends and au revoir to Tony who was coming to London soon after his own demob. I headed straight back to London; my parents had moved from Letchworth some weeks earlier and we were now sharing my grandparents' house in Clapton. The next morning, I made the short journey to Aldershot where the formalities of the release process were completed. These included choosing a demob suit, overcoat and other basic articles of clothing and saluting the officer who was handing out final payments of money due on release. I selected a single breasted, three-piece, dark grey, tweedy suit. Sturdily made, it served me well for the six years of my impecunious student/trainee days.

As I travelled back to London, I felt neither depression nor exultation. I was journeying into the unknown. I had nearly five months before starting at the LSE and I did not have the faintest idea of what I was going to do until then.

On the first day of my renewed life as a civilian I had a row with my father. He had enthusiastically embraced the wartime word blitz to mean a ruthless attack on and destruction of unwanted papers. documents, bills and letters. How he must have enjoyed the move from Letchworth. In his mind it would have legitimated the massive assault he made in my absence, on my books, letters, writings and most precious of all, my 1948 journal.

30. STRIFE AND STRIVING

Released from the Army, there was not much going on for me in London. I found it hard to re-establish myself in civilian life. My friends were all in Letchworth or North Wales and being back in the bosom of a now extended family was no comfort. I was used to an independent life, so to maintain that independence, I got a clerical job in a pharmaceutical factory manufacturing Kolynos toothpaste, just by Clapton Common, about five minutes' walk from my house. My wages were £5 per week, a lot of money in those days. I quickly mastered my duties – they were simple and repetitive – and I completed all that was required of me with time to spare. Working in the same room as my manager frustrated any possibility of reading, chatting with colleagues or going for a wander.

Evenings and weekends were almost as dreary. Springfield Park was just a few hundred yards from my house where I played putting with my grandfather. At the bottom of the park by the River Lea there were tennis courts where I watched with envy, a group of young tennis players. The two who stood out were a beautiful, full bosomed and vivacious redhead, Trudy Greenfield and her boyfriend, Emil Landis, a dental student who looked like a young Cary Grant. In their tennis whites and with their racquet skills, they seemed to have attained a combination of maturity and gaiety to which I yearned to aspire. Many months later I got to know several members of this group and Trudy, also known as MTB because her mother always referred to her as 'My Trudy Bless her', became a good friend.

I rowed on the Lea or took long walks over the Walthamstow and Hackney Marshes. Movies were some solace; there were ten cinemas within a mile of where I lived. Two of them, the Vogue, where I had seen 3-D films as early as 1938, and the Classic were repertory cinemas. I caught up with Chaplin, the Marx Brothers, and many others from the canon. But the biggest and most popular cinema was the Regent at the top of Stamford Hill. There was a large, piazza-like space opposite where early on Saturday evenings, post-Sabbath, multitudes of young Jewish men and women would congregate, the already partnered to show off their coupledom and to enjoy a gossip before the film, the singletons hopeful of bagging a date in time for the beginning of the show. I had no entrée into this throng and watched their antics with longing as I queued for a seat.

I was separated from all my old friends. Jack Fox was still in Letchworth, busy living a triple life: a student at the Royal Dental Hospital with a whole new circle of friends, an entirely separate social life in Letchworth where he was now installed as guitarist in Seamus O'Brien's jazz band and secretly dating a non-Jewish girl. He did once drive to Clapton in his Austin 7. With pride I took him on a tour of the Park, the River and the Marshes but he wasn't very impressed. The only person I knew locally was Bernard Chernoff from Army days. We met in Clapton and I also took him on my local tour. The thing that sticks in my mind was my humiliation in being corrected by him when I said *renumeration* instead of *remuneration* Very similar to my feelings on misspelling *express* when I was six. We met, usually by chance, many times over the years, and we would chat for a few minutes then I would say something and Bernard would exclaim 'Boris, you're incorrigible!'. Incorrigible? I thought he was using the word endearingly, acknowledging me as lively, full of fun and beans. There was something in me, if not incorrigible, then bumptious or irrepressible, a desire to shock or more precisely to impress, to make others sit up and take notice. It also included elements of indiscretion, tactlessness and at worst, self-destructiveness.

Soon after my meeting with Bernard, a perfect example of my *incorrigibility* occurred at the toothpaste factory. I had only been working there for a month when, on the 25th June, North Korea invaded South Korea. The US obtained a Security Council resolution entitling it to intervene. A serious conflict with the Soviet Union and China was on the cards. Nearer home, all those in National Service, due to be released, had their period of service extended by one year. For me it had been a close thing. North Korea claimed that South Korea had attacked first. In spite of all the evidence to the contrary, particularly the Soviet blockade of Berlin in 1948, I still had great admiration for Soviet achievements and by extension for other communist countries. It wasn't that I adopted the North's version of events and rejected the South's; my point then was that in the absence of absolute proof, either version could be true, and therefore there should be no rush to judgment. Even now I can see that my argument was not without merit. It would have been fine to have argued these matters with family and friends, but no, I couldn't be satisfied with that. I trailed round the factory, a forbidden act in itself, buttonholing perfectly innocent workers and forcing them to engage in discussion of the Korean crisis. They were more embarrassed than scandalised but I was reported to management and sacked for misconduct. I had only been there for six weeks. It was early July and there were still three months to go before the start of the University year.

Returning to London and living in a predominantly Jewish

neighbourhood, with my Zionist parents and my traditionalist grandparents who were Yiddish to the core, I felt a strong urge to explore my own Jewishness and Jewish history. With savings from my job, augmented by the Army final payout, I had sufficient funds to take a break from paid work and decided to spend a few weeks studying. Borrowing from the well-stocked Hackney Central Library, I made efforts to relearn Hebrew and read books on the development of Judaism, Jewish history, the diaspora, the causes and growth of anti-Semitism, the origins of Zionism and the events leading up to the creation of the State of Israel.

Now that I was in London, I could also pursue my interest in Habonim. I found out from their London office that there was to be a six-week *hachshara* course – preparation and training for emigration to Israel – in August at one of their training farms, Hurst Grange, near Twyford in Berkshire. They were also looking for a volunteer to spend a week prior to the course to help prepare for the forty course members and I was happy to sign up for the task.

While waiting to go to Twyford, as a respite from my Jewish studies and following in my father's footsteps, I wrote a cod academic lecture, *Shakespeare Was a Jew*. Relying less on quotations from Shakespeare's plays than my father, I concocted a fictional extension of some of my recent historical research. My starting off point was Edward 1's expulsion of the Jews from England in 1290, following which many remained by converting to Christianity while staying true to their old faith. One such family, that of Chaim Sac Shafir, fled from Warwick to Stratford on Avon and were baptised at the Parish Church. Chaim changed his name to Henry Shakespeare and thereafter the family clandestinely practised Judaism right down to and including William. The Hathaways (formerly Hattenweg) were part of that small community and William's marriage to Anne was an arranged one. The fact that Anne was some years older than William was irrelevant; it wasn't just that she was a nice Jewish girl; more to the point, she was the only Jewish girl. From the markings on my manuscript copy it would seem that it was published but I have no recollection where or by whom.

I arrived at Hurst Grange to a most friendly and hospitable reception from the residents who were already living there as a community in training for emigration to a kibbutz, and struck up a friendship with a Scottish girl called Zena who had given up completing her English literature degree to go on *hachshara*. We would take evening walks together, talking books and exchanging confidences about our lives and hopes, so much so that the community assumed that we had become an item. This was not the case; we enjoyed the same sort of friendship that I had had with Barbara Cooper.

I started work the next day. My task was to clean the barn and the stables, both long disused, and prepare them as sleeping accommodation for course members. This was as tough as anything I had ever done in the Army and as a first stage involved swilling and scouring and scrubbing and sweeping the accumulated muck and dirt, dung, droppings and cobwebs of many years. I helped with the heavy iron bedsteads, mattresses and bedding which had to be humped from the attics in the main house to the sparkling, cleaned up outbuildings. Finally, I compiled lists of who was to sleep where, boys and girls in separate rooms, Habonim being a prudish organisation.

The next day, course participants started to trickle in. I was allocated a place in the barn with seven others; we bonded immediately and gossiped, told jokes and exchanged personal histories and ambitions for our futures until the early hours. One of my barn mates was Bryan Lipson who was to play a pivotal role in my life.

From the start I threw myself into all the course activities. We operated as a community and shared in the daily kitchen, cleaning and laundry duties. There were seminars on a variety of subjects relating to Israel and kibbutz life.

Hebrew was taught and because at that time, kibbutz economy was primarily agricultural and Hurst Grange had its own farmland, we were expected to devote several hours a week assisting the residents in hoeing, digging, pulling up produce and picking fruit. I found this work not only physically uncomfortable but also extremely boring and slacked or sloped off whenever the coast was clear.

I had not done this kind of work since the age of fourteen at the School Agricultural Camp. At Hurst Grange I liked it even less than then. The sun was too hot, my back ached and my hands soon became scratched and raw. My whole being felt prickly. I didn't even try to reconcile my work-shy symptoms with my kibbutz ideals; at some level I knew that this was not a career for me.

There were vast expanses of time for socialising, reading and playing table tennis and cricket on the spacious lawns. In the evenings, residents and course members joined forces for discussions or entertainment: singing, revues and play readings, always ending with the dizzying dance, the whirling circle of the traditional hora which like a treadmill had no formal end and so went on for hours, gathering in speed and intensity.

I had a part in *The Dybbuk*, a seminal play in Jewish theatre about a young bride possessed by a malign spirit. In my high piping tenor, I sang a sweetly mournful Arabic folk song *Baladi, ya Baladi – Oh my Country, my Country* – and wrote a playlet in rhyming pentameters, based on a real incident involving a barn resident who had to rush out in the middle of the night for a pee and was spotted in the act by the girls in the stables, giving rise to much hysterical laughter and hilarity. In my dramatisation, two lovers enter, huggermugger, anxious that the crunching sounds underfoot would give them away:

> *Disturbéd gravel in Satanic spite*
> *Hurls violent curses through the moonlit night.*

I was finding my feet and was gratified to be making a contribution that was valued by the community.

But there was a downside to all this creative endeavour. First, and perhaps most naturally, the search for the someone to love remained an undercurrent throughout my time at Hurst Grange. Halfway through the first week, Stefa Tenby arrived. Tall and lithe, with short jet black hair, round faced with large, brooding dark eyes and a wide labile mouth, she had a look of intelligence and depth. I was immediately captivated. My first opportunity to captivate her arose a couple of days after her arrival when we were on kitchen duty together. She was easy to talk to and responsive to me. Being interested to hear about me, I inferred that she was interested in me. I regaled her with my stories of Army life, culminating in my welcoming of Lance Bombardier Bryson and its consequences. With that I really blew it. Her interest, if there ever was any, evaporated in a moment. Just like Gillian Slee in St. Asaph, Stefa was a serious person and what I had exhibited was a lack of gravitas and there is a sense in which she was right. *Habonim* was new to me and I had not grown up in its ideology and culture which was decidedly not flippant or frivolous but rigorous, highly principled and requiring the submission of the individual to the community. In *kibbutzim* at that time, personal possessions and wealth were kept to a minimum and decisions, for example, the allocation of funds to enable a member to visit his/her parents, were made by the governing committee.

Much as I was enjoying the course and admired the *kibbutznik* ideal, part of me felt rebellious against the subordination of the individual to the group, the puritanical disapproval of frivolity and what I saw as the suppression of the élan vital of the individual. This was, I recognise, due to my own massive egotism, the desire to make a mark, be admired and demonstrate my distinctiveness within the collective. As a further example of my incorrigibility, I invited everyone to a reading of Rabelais' *Gargantua and Pantagruel* as a celebration of the naturalness and joy of bodily functions and appetites. This attempt to bring lightheartedness and introduce instinctual life into the course met with bafflement and antipathy. I was too naive and myopic to realise that as a newcomer I should have kept my head down. But what had become plain to me by the end of the course was that I was not going to sign up for life on a kibbutz.

I also handled my rejection by Stefa very badly. In a novel by Peter de

Vries, the narrator copes with desirable but unattainable women by finding a flaw with which to justify dismissing them: ankles a little too thick, nose a trifle too retroussé. In my hurt, I used a similar tactic to erase Stefa from my consciousness. To my lifelong shame, in the barn, to much laughter and general agreement, I traduced her as snobbish and standoffish and described her looks as simian.

About a week before the end of the course, my mother phoned me. A letter had arrived from the London County Council, should she open it? The LCC at that time was the University grant-making authority. I had made an application and had had an interview just before coming on the course and was awaiting the result. I said yes, my heart pounding as she fumbled with the phone and the envelope. At last she extracted the letter. *'Dear Mr.Rumney, It is with regret that we write to inform you...'* I was distraught. The grant covered fees as well as cash for upkeep. I didn't see how my parents could afford it. For many years my life had been predicated on my going to university. Now that was out. What would I do? Get a job? What job? Become a resident at Hurst Grange and train as a kibbutznik perhaps. I felt unhinged, all at sea, the nearest to breakdown I had ever been.

I was due home for the weekend to attend my parents' house-warming party and there would be time to discuss my future. In the midst of the high decibel range of the Rumney clan coming together, I was in a state of utter misery, feeling a failure and futureless in the presence of all my bright and high-performing relatives. I spoke at length and in confidence to my uncle David, psychiatrist and psycho-analyst, uncharacteristically quiet and thoughtful for a Rumney. He listened carefully and said little but that very fact had the effect of calming me down and enabled me to become thoughtful in turn.

I spent a restless night rehearsing what to say to my parents. The LCC had given as its reason for refusing me a grant, my poor Higher School Certificate results. It was clear that I was not academic and if an academic career was unachievable then what future did a degree in sociology offer me? Probation officer? I knew with certainty that I did not want to be one of those.

In my ignorance I did not know that there were other possibilities; several sociologist friends at the LSE made very successful careers creating their own marketing and market research businesses. But I wouldn't have wanted to be one of those either. What I latched onto was law and becoming a lawyer. The officer conducting the Court of Enquiry concerning the missing pair of boots had at the end of the proceedings congratulated me on the way I had given my evidence and for my legal mind. Such throwaway remarks can lodge in the memory and have a powerful and permanent influence on the way you perceive yourself. I was

Boris, the man with *the legal mind*. I was therefore obviously destined to become a lawyer.

I put all that to my parents the next morning.

"Look, it means I'll have a profession and with luck a steady job. There's a chap on the course, Bryan Lipson, he's a law student. I'll talk to him, find out about the law course. I'll tell you what he says next week."

Bryan was about to enter his last year at UCL. He was my age but had been exempted from National Service due to poor eyesight. Olive-skinned, black hair and with neat, even features, he had spent his first fifteen years in Swansea before moving to North London and still had the vestiges of a Welsh accent which lent melodious tones to his mellifluous baritone voice. We became firm friends and eventually law partners for twenty-five years. In 1956 I was best man at his wedding.

I returned to Hurst Grange and after the first day's programme was over, I buttonholed Bryan and pacing round the garden we talked well into the night. I explained my predicament to him and that I was considering switching from sociology to law.

"It's hard work," he said, "But very interesting."

He got into his stride.

"It exercises the mind. Teaches you a very specific type of reasoning, how to make distinctions in law between differing sets of facts."

After he had expatiated on the human interest elements in criminal and divorce law and the arcane and archaic concepts to be studied in Land Law and Equity and Trusts, I asked him why he had become a lawyer.

"Because I worship at the shrine of the Great Goddess Fact," he replied.

Pompous? Grandiose? Both probably, but at the time I was greatly impressed. Fact. Not fiction, not fantasy. Something you could get your teeth into. Something to rely on. I had made up my mind. I was being sensible and realistic for once. The discipline of the law would steady me down, make a man of me, a serious man.

The course ended on Friday night with a hora which went on... and on... for several hours. Back in London I told my parents that I would like to switch to law as a prelude to training as a solicitor. If they could finance me for the first year, I could reapply for a grant for the last two. Though they had never interfered or tried to influence me in my choice of study or career, they were delighted; their son, the solicitor. They could manage the expense and my grandparents agreed to chip in.

Secure in parental backing, I arranged an interview with Professor Sir David Hughes Parry, the Director of the LSE Law Department. Though a rather stiff and formal man, slow and sparing of speech and with a strong Welsh accent, the interview went well and he offered me a place. Law was then an intercollegiate degree run in conjunction with Kings College

London and UCL and so three weeks later I set out for the welcoming lecture at UCL, to be given by Professor Georg Schwartzenberger, International Lawyer and refugee from Nazi Germany. As I sat on the 653 trolley bus on the way to Gower Street, I felt a mixture of excitement and trepidation. What would my fellow students be like? Would I like them? Would they like me? The lecture theatre was crowded with the new intake, mainly men, but I soon spotted beautiful Benita Cohen who sadly abandoned the law for marriage at the end of the first term. The Professor's analysis of the function and process of law in a democratic society was inspirational and I was moved by his argument that law, being based on an ever-changing system of social and political values, possessed its own dynamic for change. I felt that I had made the right decision and left the theatre with a sense of optimism.

31. MY FATHER – A CLEVER FOOL
Part 3

In November 1950 I had barely settled into my first term as a law student when disaster struck. My father had been up to his old tricks again, borrowing money from MLTO members and losing it gambling on God knows what: horses, dogs, cards - I never did find out. A meeting of the MLTO Board was convened to consider the matter. On the afternoon of that day I telephoned from a public phone kiosk in Kingsway "What news?"

"Dad's been sacked".

By the time I had got home that evening a massive depression had settled on everyone. My mother had given my father his marching orders.

"It's been once too often, Maxie, I've had enough, I've had it up to here. You can get out. I want you out of the house tomorrow."

Dad was in our tiny dining room, slumped on a hard chair, head in hands, immersed in sorrow. We sat together that last night in silence. I was appalled but couldn't find the words to tell him that I loved him whatever he had done and that I didn't want him to go. I couldn't find any words. Then, unaccountably, blood flowed from my nose. I couldn't staunch it. I fled the room. Finally, when it stopped flowing I went to bed and wept myself to sleep. My father left the next morning and I didn't see him again for more than two years.

I have no idea where or how my father lived during that time. He became something of a down-and-out and quite ill. He kept in touch with his sisters and it was they who let it be known to my mother that he was remorseful for all the hurt he had caused, had stopped gambling and was desperate to return to the wife he had never ceased loving.

All this mournful news and yearning was duly passed on to me by my mother and as I was by then a know-it-all, third-year student about to take my final exams, I offered myself as go-between. So it was that a few days later I met my father at Lyons Corner House in the Strand. I describe this meeting in Chapter 35. I reported back and a meeting was arranged between Mum and Dad at my aunt's house. What followed, yet again, was his courtship of her and within weeks, much to my relief, his reinstatement as husband. He was a much chastened man and from then on, until his death, completely under the thumb of my mother who held the purse strings and all the emotional cards. He owed her big time and in all their rows and arguments, she never hesitated to remind him of that. He had found work as an office manager from an old friend, Sam Wachsman, who had built up a successful business, manufacturing deodorants and deodorisers, and remained in employment until his retirement at the age of 70. He also found small satisfactions in tutoring young family members in maths and in his published mathematical papers, of which he distributed off-prints to all and sundry. But his theorems were so abstruse that they were incomprehensible to a layman and nobody could give him the pleasure and satisfaction of positive feedback. All I could offer was a lame "Well done Dad!"

There were further but less destructive lapses during his long period of reformation. In 1964 I was a solicitor practising in central London. He suddenly appeared at my office, unannounced, and quickly got down to business. A friend, so he claimed, was starting up a wholesale perfume business and he could have a share in it for an investment of £200. "I have to try something", he said. Would I lend him the money? Not a word to Mum. Mum's the word. Thus I became enmeshed in his web of deception. I'm not sure whether I was taken in, or if I wanted to bring an end to his entreaties and save his dignity, or if I needed to signal to him that I believed and trusted him. Anyway, mug that I was, I wrote out a cheque. It was a lot of money in those days. I never got it back or heard anything further about the perfume business. I didn't have the heart to confront him.

In 1974 my parents both retired and came to live near me in Blackheath. Shortly after they had settled in, my mother in some distress reported to me that she had over several weeks discovered money missing from her handbag as well as some betting slips from a local bookmaker. I asked her about their financial arrangements and she told me that she had maintained full control over all moneys. She dished out cash to my father (which he had to account for) as and when he needed it. I advised her to give him a weekly sum which was his to do as he liked with, no questions asked. She agreed to do this and I never heard a further word of complaint from her. I wonder if his thrill of gambling was in its transgressiveness and that once it became licit it lost its allure.

My father died in 1981. A few weeks before his death he said to my mother, "I hate Blackheath". Pure displacement; what he hated was what his life had come to and what he had done with it, the poor, sweet, brilliant, woebegone man. He was split between being a loving, companionable, stimulating father and an absent, neglectful, self-absorbed one, as I was (and still am) split in my feelings towards him, between love, gratitude and admiration and sadness, anguish and resentment.

32. LONDON SCHOOL OF ECONOMICS
Year 1

"Don'cher know the market fluctuates?"

This from a fruit and veg stallholder in Whitechapel Road opposite the entrance to the Royal London Hospital in reply to my question,

"Why have these grapes gone up a shilling a pound since last Friday?"

I had just been paid my wages for the vacation job at the Royal London Hospital that had come to an end. Grapes were a luxury in 1950 and I was buying a treat for the family's Sabbath eve meal. What the market trader said made a deep impression on me. If I had not, at the last minute switched my course to Law, I would then have been struggling with basic economics and it seemed to me that the whole of economic theory could be encapsulated in those three words: the market fluctuates. Their implication was of uncertainty and unpredictability, unlike the law which I then believed, incorrectly, was both certain and predictable. I was very taken with this conceit and wrote it up into a light-hearted essay which I submitted to Netta, a girl I rather fancied. She was part of a group of Bohemian literati and louche aesthetes which published an arty student magazine. I hoped that the piece might presage my entrée into this enviable group but having heard nothing from Netta for several weeks, I approached her for news.

"I'm really sorry Basil, I lost your manuscript. Do you have a copy?"

Of course I didn't. And she didn't even remember my name. So ended all hopes of getting acquainted with this bright eyed, dusky, forgetful, interesting, neglectful, gypsy clad young woman.

The truth was that I wanted to make my mark in some corner of the LSE and in the process find myself a girlfriend. During the first term I tried my luck in the Jewish Society's social for freshers. I met and attached myself to Pat Galinsky, a first-year sociology student who lived in Stamford Hill and who was plainly interested in me. She was a pleasant, friendly girl and I enjoyed her company. We had one date and I took her (that's what men did then, the taking) to a popular restaurant at 92 Fitzroy Street for their famous two shillings Spaghetti Bolognese. A nice evening but I wasn't attracted to her and I made no further move to take her out.

I went to an emergency meeting of the Labour Society called to discuss the war in Korea. I (once again) made the point from the floor that North

Korea contended that the initial acts of aggression had been committed by South Korea and that this should be investigated before any motion was passed condemning North Korea. My intervention was dismissed by the Chairman, Christopher Rowlands who later became MP for Meriden and was tipped for high office but died tragically young of an untreatable virus contracted on a foreign trip.

"There is no credible evidence of such aggression on the part of South Korea. Any further comments, anyone?"

I felt diminished and downcast. There was no future for me in the Labour Society. I never attended another meeting.

Although I failed to achieve any kind of celebrity in my first year, I did make a large number of enduring friendships, springing initially from my *Habonim* days but also through living in what was at that time a predominantly Jewish area: Clapton, Stamford Hill and Stoke Newington. Neighbourhood friendships formed at the LSE included Maurice Peston, Barry Supple, Martin Schwartz, Gerald de Groot, Warren Robin, Len Gatty, Brian Cookson and Lionel Gordon.

Bryan Lipson, although nominally a student of University College, spent most of his time at the LSE because there was a regular poker school in the JCR, but mainly because he fell in love with an LSE sociology student, Claudine Weisbort, a slim, shy girl with the demeanour of a startled gazelle.

Through Bryan, I met an ex-Habonimnik, Morris Kogan. He and I often met on Sunday evening for a snack at Lyons tea shop in Aldgate before walking to the Peoples Palace Theatre in Bow Road to see their Sunday night classic continental movie, price of admission one shilling. I did not see much of him during term time as he was an undergraduate at Christ's College, Cambridge, reading history.

Malcolm Lassman, in my year, and his older brother, Lionel, also a lawyer but a year ahead of us, were both good looking with olive skins and glossy black hair, invariably dressed smartly in navy blue double-breasted suits. They were both good bridge players and spent much of their time whiling the hours away in the JCR, surrounded by a crowd of admiring spectators. They were of a more affluent background than most of us. Lionel was the more confident of the two: brash and full of braggadocio. He would have made a good actor and became the nearest thing professionally: a successful criminal barrister. I preferred Malcolm who was quiet of voice, sensitive and gentle. He spent his working life as an in-house lawyer for a commercial organization.

There were four subjects set for this year: Roman law, the law of contract, constitutional law and the English legal system, the last being the history of the development of English law and its procedures from the time of Henry II. During my first term, I had some difficulty in adjusting to the first three of these subjects and the rote learning of legal principles and rules and the application of them to specific sets of facts. I was much more interested in the social and political forces which underlay and created the principles and rules. So during the constitutional law lectures being given by Professor de Smith I would be constantly piping up with such comments as,

"But surely, sir, you can't understand the relationship between the judiciary and Parliament without considering the political processes prevailing at the time, giving rise to such relationship."

But of course that was not the point; we were limited in our study to what was the bare law and Professor de Smith soon made it very clear that that was what he intended to stick to. Anything else, as far as he was concerned, were metaphysical embellishments. I was squashed for my bumptiousness, being too clever by half.

In a less obtrusive way, I introduced some lighter content into a paper on a contractual dispute involving three parties. I headed the paper *A Conflict of Marxists* and named the litigants Groucho, Chico and Harpo. My flights of fancy were ignored and no additional marks were awarded for humour or imagination.

By the end of term, I had the sense to calm down and conform. I worked every day in the Law Library, reading Law Reports, the verbatim, often very lengthy, judgements made in individual cases. I began to understand and admire the tortuous intellectual processes involved in considering the binding precedents set by earlier cases and analysing whether the current case should be followed or be distinguished from them and it was through this work, as well as wanting to graduate, that I dropped my rebellious facade and accepted that I was not special but just a run-of-the-mill law student.

My new-found serious approach to my studies if anything made life harder. I could no longer shelter behind broad concepts and generalisations. In the law, the devil is very much in the detail. And there was so much detail to memorise and my memory, adequate for most purposes, was not up to the retention of the names of leading cases, what they decided and why, and the content of statutes including relevant section numbers.

I hated Roman Law, taught to us by a tall, handsome but snooty Oxbridge barrister called Potter who reeled off by rote the laws applicable to commerce, slavery, civil and criminal wrongs and family law as well as court procedures and remedies and penalties available to the judges, all of which changed and developed over the course of the Roman Empire and culminated in the exhaustive codes created by the Emperor Justinian. Like Constitutional Law, this complex and ever changing legal system was taught without reference to the historical, social and political forces underpinning it and so made little sense to me and required only that it be learned by heart. The other subjects at least represented the law prevailing at the time and therefore I was able to relate to them and hold them in my head more easily.

I was confronted by intellectual challenges at the LSE and emotional ones at home. Since my father's departure and the loss of his salary, money was tight and for the first few months we survived only by the generosity of my grandparents. My mother's depression expressed itself in her increasing bitterness and irritability, particularly with me. One Saturday evening I was on the point of leaving to meet a friend when she said,

"You're never here, Boris! Why do you always have to go out?"

"It's my social life, Mum."

"Yes I know but it's not healthy."

"Not healthy? Of course it's healthy."

"Healthy? Always out, never at home! Healthy?"

"Look, Mum, don't take it out on me just because I have a life and you don't. You're jealous, that's the trouble."

She was silent for a moment, her face contorted with rage.

"How dare you speak to me like that? Jealous? Of you, my own son? It just shows how little you know me."

To avoid her fury, I quickly exited and ran for an approaching 653 trolley bus. It was not the end of the matter. My mother, deeply insulted, angry because there had been some truth in my cruel accusation of envy or, in her loneliness, resentful that I was not spending more time with her, resorted to her usual tactic, that of silence. For several days she did not address a single word to me and although this was not wholly comfortable, I managed to bear it with cheerful equanimity.

Things improved at least financially just before Christmas. The combined efforts of my uncle Percy and uncle Alf enabled my mother to open and run a stall at Watford Market; Percy supplied the product, women's' skirts and Alf, himself a long-standing stallholder at the market, provided the entrée when a stall became vacant. The product was a popular one at a good price and in catching the pre-Christmas period, my mother made a success of the venture from the start and money ceased to be a problem.

She very soon came to love the market: taking cash, the camaraderie of other stallholders, the dramas and the gossip. She even had a date. An old friend of my father, Bar Kochva, a well-known Zionist printer and publisher in Whitechapel, asked her out to dinner. On her return from her evening out:

"How did you get on, Mum?"

"Fine."

"Did you enjoy the meal?"
"Very nice."
I sensed that all had not been well.
"You seeing him again?"
"No, definitely not."
"Why? Didn't he ask you?"
"Don't be rude! No, he made a pass at me in the taxi home."
"So?"
"So I told him that I wasn't that sort of woman, that he was married and I was married and that whatever Max had done, he was still being disloyal to a friend."

Bar Kochva was an attractive man and something of a womaniser and I was sorry that my mother had passed up the chance of taking a lover. At least she wouldn't have had to rely on me emotionally and for company.

One evening, I went to meet my friend Michael Honey whom I had got to know through Don Roodyn. Michael was a student at Kings College, London, studying Civil Engineering. From Czechoslovakia, Jewish, yet with his round fleshy face, grey eyes and slightly puggy nose, he looked more Eastern European than Semitic. He spoke melodiously with a slight Czech accent. We met outside the Regent Cinema and saw some instantly forgettable film, then crossed the road to the crowded salt beef bar. We chatted, one thing led to another and then he began telling me the story of his life before he came to England. He lived with his parents and siblings in Prague. Somehow his father and a brother made it to London before Michael and other members of his family were rounded up by the SS with other Prague Jews and sent to the nearby old Austrian military town of Terezin. Held there until early 1944, he was with most of the other Terezin residents transported to Auschwitz where he remained until liberated by the Russians in 1945. After the war ended, he joined his father in Stamford Hill.

"What was life like in Auschwitz?" I asked.
"Unspeakable. Unimaginable."

He then proceeded to speak of the unimaginable, describing conditions and life in the camp, culminating for most of the inmates in the gas chambers.

"How on earth did you survive?"
"I was clever. I watched the Germans very carefully. I was a bright 16-year-old and I was given the job of servant batman to an SS officer. I clicked my heels and saluted, adopted at all times an efficient military demeanour, obeyed all orders meticulously and worked hard, never stopped. He often beat me just to show me who was Aryan and who was Jewish but I must have pleased him enough for him to make sure that I was not placed on one of the daily extermination lists."

It was a cold night but I was so enthralled by what Michael was telling me that I was aware of nothing other than the awfulness of his narrative. We walked the streets, sitting at times on a Clapton Common bench or popping along for a cup of tea at the all-night stall on Stamford Hill, Michael speaking of his experiences the whole time. We finally parted at five in the morning.

I got my first vacation job through the University of London Union: a two-week stint working on a time and motion study in the A&E Department of the Royal London Hospital. This involved me and several other students holding clipboards and timing patients as they arrived and progressed through waiting for treatment to when they left. Our research was done in the huge cavernous entrance hall which served as a waiting-room.

At that time the East End was still predominantly Jewish, bursting with Jewish clothing manufacturers, other businesses, shops and restaurants. Of the latter, Blooms, bustling with lunchtime customers was the best-known but I, although provisioned with sandwiches from home, supplemented these at a more modest establishment in Whitechapel Road where I lunched on a large bowl of their steaming, delicious, wholesome and *hamishe* [as cooked at home] barley soup, accompanied by a plate of fresh, crusty rye bread, all for the price of nine old pence. Once I had established myself as a regular, I even took to eating my sandwiches with a post-potage glass of lemon tea under the disapproving gaze of the portly waitress. She never said a word but she must have thought:

'What chutzpah! What a *shnorrer*!' [scrounger]

In the afternoon the number of patients dwindled and when they had all gone we reinvented the empty waiting-room into an arena in which we held wheelchair races and jousting bouts with the various walking sticks and umbrellas we found lying around.

Social life with my LSE colleagues started on the 653 trolleybus which stopped virtually outside my house in Upper Clapton Road and took me to Manor House station for the Piccadilly Line to Holborn. En route, the bus picked up Gerald, Martin, Warren and Lionel; we were all bound for our 10am lectures. Brenda Sands, an LSE sociology student, lived in a large house in Amherst Park, just next door to the Regent Cinema and that is where she joined us. She was one of those women who exert a strange fascination over men, even though not conventionally beautiful. Very petite and a little dumpy, she had a most beguiling face: large round dark eyes with long straight lashes, a small, 'butter-wouldn't-melt' mouth, topped by a mop of black curly hair, all of which gave her a doll-like look, rather like Giulietta Masina in the 1954 classic Italian film *La Strada*. She was part of the luvvie set, appearing alongside Ron Moody, Bernard Levin and Fenella Fielding in the annual students' review, one of a trio of high kicking girls belting out satirical songs, such as on the subject of the increase in the cost of calls from public telephone boxes from two to three old pence with the refrain of 'Honi soit qui pays three pence'.

In my years at the LSE, girls were in the minority and Brenda was very much in demand. She had several suitors by the time I started to take her out at the end of my first academic year, the most notable of whom was one of my ex-Grocers friends, Warren Robin. Who could have stood a chance against Warren? With blonde hair, pain-shot blue eyes and a film star smile, he was irresistible to women. A multitalented man: member of the local synagogue choir, he had a fine tenor voice and would, had it not be for family pressures, have pursued a musical career. He had been opening batsman for Grocers First XI and Mercutio to Harold Pinter's Romeo in Grocers' annual Shakespeare production. Allied to a photographic memory, he had a remarkable talent for mimicry; he could remember all the plays and operas he had ever seen, repeating or singing long stretches of dialogue or arias. If you missed *Bedtime with Braden* or *The Goon Show* the previous night, Warren would oblige with a complete reprise the next morning.

But I was not deterred. Being Warren's senior and having done my National Service, I felt more mature and in with a chance. The Festival of Britain had just started and my first date with Brenda was a concert at the newly opened Royal Festival Hall which in its originality, clarity and spaciousness filled us with awe. After a drink at the central Bar, we entered the auditorium. As the orchestra tuned up, I wondered at the overhanging boxes like open drawers which demanded to be shut and the organ pipes looking for all the world like a modernist perspective painting of New York.

Don and Michael had invited me to join them on their proposed trip to Italy in September. I was delighted. I had to get the money together so on the first day of the summer vacation, I went to my local Labour Exchange to find work. I was interviewed by a clerk there.

"What's your experience?"

"Not much. Clerk in the Army. I've been a law student since."

"Let's see! There's labouring and clerical vacancies."

It was a beautiful summer.

"Something out of doors?"

He riffled through his card index system.

"I've got a demolition job on the Woodberry Down Estate. £5 a week."

That sounded manly. Also door-to-door on the 653.

"I'll take it."

That day I went off to meet my future employer. The area looked as if it had just been heavily bombed. The grand houses had been either demolished or earmarked for demolition in readiness for the construction of an extensive London County Council housing estate. My interview with a huge Irish foreman was held outside one of those houses on which labourers, precariously balanced on walls, gables and windowsills, wielded sledgehammers, dismantling large chunks of wall and masonry with every blow. He looked me up and down.

"What can I do for you?"

"The Labour told me there's a job going here."

"Experience?"

"None. I'm a student."

"Look lad, this isn't a suitable job for you."

"Why not? I'm willing to learn."

"Take it from me, I know. Your hands would be plates of meat within a week."

Back at the Labour Exchange, the clerk found me a job in Homerton, at a small factory manufacturing caravan furniture. My only carpentry experience was in the woodwork class at Calday Grammar School. My story was that I had decided to leave college for the real world and learn a trade. They must have been desperate for labour because I was offered the job on the spot and started the next morning. I was allocated to a section on the second floor where four craftsmen who seemed decades older and more mature than I, were engaged in making cupboards and worktops. I was set to sweeping up sawdust and shavings every half hour or so and fetching tea and cheese rolls from a nearby cafe. I sandpapered and I varnished. I schlepped timber, paint, ironmongery and other raw materials from the store room and finished products down to the stockroom. General factotum, that was me. After a couple of weeks, I was let loose on screwing hinges onto cupboard doors. It was no wonder that 1951 marked the beginning of the decline in the quality of British manufactured goods.

The working days passed uneventfully, in the evenings, magically. In June and early July, Brenda and I went rowing on the River Lea and for long walks on Hackney and Walthamstow Marshes where we kissed for the first time, she, so sweetly and tenderly. We visited *Battersea Pleasure Gardens* designed by the artist John Piper, which with its bright colours and open-air cafes felt like I imagined the South of France to be. We experienced suspension of gravity on the Rotor which for me merely intensified my feelings of walking on air, of unnatural lightness whenever I was with Brenda. We danced smoochy, slow foxtrots under an immense marquee, one penny per set.

One Sunday in early July we went out into the country, walked and had lunch in an ancient market town pub. At dusk we caught a train to take us on the fifty-mile journey back to London. We had a compartment to ourselves and we kissed and talked.

Out of the blue she asked, "Why do you like me?"

"I don't like you. I love you."

"So you don't like me?"

"Don't be silly! Of course I like you. I like you and love you."

"Why do you like me?"

I thought for a few moments, trying to articulate the confused thoughts racing through my brain and to poeticize my infatuation. I finally replied,

"I feel as though I'm transported into a magical world when I'm with you. You have a fairylike quality, a lightness, an aura."

I don't think she wanted to be a fairy; I should have added - which was true – that she was beautiful but more than that, there was something deeply sensual about her and it was the the combination of the sensuality and the magic which made her so entrancingly, enchantingly seductive.

I saw her back to her house and we sat on the steps leading to the front door. We chatted for a while then she said,

"I'm sorry Boris but I can't go out with you anymore."

I had no inkling that this was coming. In an instant my most precious assumptions that I was making good progress in the courtship stakes, that Brenda really liked me, had turned out to be empty illusions. In a state of shock, I asked her why.

"Well, final year's coming up. Exams next May. Get thee to a nunnery Brenda!"

I nodded.

"It's Warren isn't it?" I said.

"Yes." she replied.

I left her house and ran the mile home as a way of fending off feelings I was not yet ready to confront. I undressed and went straight to bed. I was still functioning but my heart had died.

Once we had met by chance at Holborn Station on the way home from the LSE. As we were on the down escalator, I asked her,

"Why the deep sigh?"

"Not sighing, exhaling." she replied.

That night and for many nights thereafter it was I who did the sighing – and the crying.

Waking the next morning, my heart not so much dead as crushed, I felt limp and purposeless. I was incapable of going to work. I phoned in to claim illness which was true; I was sick at heart and drained of will and energy.

Within a couple of days, I had recovered sufficiently to want to find a new job. The clerk at the Labour Exchange looked at me wearily. I concocted some excuse about not being up to the furniture job which was true but not the reason for my leaving it. He said, "I think you'd be better suited to a desk job."

And that is what he found me, estimator with Steele's Glass in Dalston.

I sat in the same room as the chief estimator, Mr Randell, who provided me with a Ready Reckoner and a tariff of the firm's prices which depended on the type and size of glass purchased as well as the finish required. A customer would submit a specification and drawing of what was wanted and the estimator's job was to calculate the cost. I was fine until confronted by the method of calculating the many varieties of bevelled edging which I could not grasp despite Mr Randell's careful instructions. My increasing boredom and frustration were exacerbated by the fact that my desk was opposite Mr Randell so I was never out of his watchful gaze, no skive was possible and I was able to leave what began to feel like a prison cell only for short comfort breaks and my lunch hour. The firm was only a short walk from the centre of Dalston with its busy shopping streets and crowded Ridley Road market which I would prowl listlessly during my lunch break. The one consolation was that by some oversight the Labour government, led by Clement Attlee, had failed to include *halva* in the sweet ration so this middle-eastern delicacy became the daily dessert of my otherwise frugal midday meal.

By the end of August I had saved £40, out of which £19 went on the return fare from London to Rome. I said farewell to Mr Randell, having given my notice on the ground that I was resuming my law studies. Early one evening, in the first week of September, Don, Michael and I set off from Stoke Newington on the 76 bus to Victoria Station, steam train to Newhaven, ferry to Dieppe and an even more primitive steam train to Gare St. Lazare, Paris. We arrived early in the morning, all still quiet, first experience of café au lait, baguette and butter. First time abroad, and agog at everything, Life felt more intense as the city gradually came to life and we walked the streets and boulevards seeing sights and hearing sounds known of since childhood. From the moment of arrival until I left Paris for home four weeks later I was in a perpetual state of wonder and awe. In those days just being in France and Italy was so different from dreary, war-weary England. Heaving crowds of tourists were in the unimaginable future. In Italy, postage was cheaper if you limited your postcards to five words. To one friend I wrote '*Ecstasy verbally indescribable*'. Of course I was pleased with myself for my ingenuity but it did represent precisely what I felt at the time.

Loading up with baguettes, cheese, slices of saucisson and giant tomatoes (never seen in England) before boarding the train at Gare de Lyon. Cramming into a compartment with other students. Being woken at the Italian frontier by passport control officials. We broke our journey at Santa Margherita on the Ligurian coast and made our way down to the town in the silence of the hot afternoon sun. We found a cheap hotel a few yards from the sea, primitive by today's standards. Each morning we had to go to the kitchen for *l'acqua calda per radere* – hot water for shaving.

In the evening, we sat in the hotel's alfresco dining area with Ambrogio, a young Roman doctor and his voluptuous, overflowing, flame haired wife, Olympia. Discussing national types Ambrogio pronounced on the three of us.

"Donaldo, you like Italiano from Milano, Michele, you from l'Italia centrale, but you Boris, you, Inglese tipicale"

I put on a smile but was greatly affronted. This was a compliment? A typical Englishman was the very last way I would have wanted to describe myself. I was an Anglo-Jew, and in my own eyes, a rebellious, nonconforming citizen of the world. In my heart I felt infinitely more Italian than the other two.

Ambrogio and Olympia were certainly typical Italians as far as their gustatory capacities were concerned. Each evening they tucked into a robust four course meal before our very eyes, while we, impoverished students on an inferior tariff, satisfied our hunger with crusty rolls, a bowl of pasta and fruit.

One day we found a free beach between Santa Margherita and Portofino. I volunteered to get lunch for us all and as I strode along the coast road to Portofino in the blaze of the midday sun, in search of a general store, I thought life can't get any better than this. There was I, a man of twenty-one, at his peak, in a moment of joy and total well-being. There was a novel kind of pleasure in buying bread, tomatoes, salami, fruit and bottles of ice-cold beer, paying for them in a strange currency and carrying them back to my friends.

En route to Rome from Santa Margherita we stopped off at Pisa to see and climb to the top of the Leaning Tower. Donald, the scientist, distanced himself from this experience by saying, "So, an image of the Tower has struck my retina, sending a message to my brain which in turn has interpreted the image, identified it and given it language."

Michael and I sneered at Don's response to the visceral combination of beauty and oddness created by the world-famous campanile. But we were guilty of collecting and ticking off acknowledged masterpieces as we slavishly followed the guidebook's prescribed route.

"So that was the St. Peter's, eh? What a sight! Now, which way for the Sistine Chapel?"

We booked into the Rome youth hostel. The first thing I noticed about the Eternal City was not the wealth of antiquities or the grandeur of its piazzas but the beauty of the girls and in particular the ubiquitous Vespas and Lambrettas ridden by glossy haired, olive skinned young men and their pillion passenger girlfriends, waist-long, raven tresses, Botticelli features and brightly coloured, figure contouring dresses, sitting demurely sidesaddle. Perhaps Don's mind was on the same track; within hours of arriving, he insisted on phoning a *Habonim* contact and arranged for us to meet a number of Italian Jewish students on our very first evening. A mixed party of eight or so boys and girls turned up and took us on a walking tour of Rome's major sights. I teamed up with Debora, a law student at the University of Bologna and we compared notes on our respective courses as best we could with a mixture of English, French and Italian. I had picked up a few words in my first week in Italy and the rest I adapted from such Latin as I remembered from school. Our hosts looked and behaved more Italian than Jewish but then I had already observed that Italians looked and behaved like Jews but with better looks and style.

The next day we got down to the business of sightseeing. Baedeker was our taskmaster. Don had an old battered copy and we followed its directions slavishly. So many Roman ruins, churches, paintings, so much baroque. But also so few tourists; to experience the wonders of an unpeopled Sistine Chapel and Michelangelo's Pieta in situ in St Peter's, long before its removal from the threat of crazy iconoclasts; the Trevi fountain, illuminated at night, twenty or thirty young people singing, dancing, throwing in coins; wandering around the vast spaces of the Pantheon when without warning the organ burst into the great Bach toccata and fugue.

We had parted from our Jewish friends, having arranged to join them on a trip to Ostia Lido, a seaside town a few miles from Rome. On a crowded beach we created enough space to play volleyball. We three Englishmen, in the same team, were keen to show the Roman Jews who had won the war and saved their lives. We leapt and dived and punched the ball high into the azure sky. Don made a spectacular jump to volley out of our opponent's reach, fell awkwardly and lay moaning in the sand. He had damaged his right leg in a way undiagnosable by us. Our Jewish friends took no notice of Don's distress and continued the game. Abandoned by them, Michael and I left the beach supporting Don as best we could as he hopped along on his uninjured leg back to Rome and the youth hostel. The next morning, we took him to the A & E Department of a nearby hospital. It was packed with locals in varying degrees of misery: patients were lying in trolleys, screaming with pain, parents pacifying crying children. All this combined with a complete lack of orderly administration, created a scene of total chaos. How primitive, I thought. How different from the calm efficiency and orderliness of our National Health hospitals.

Don was eventually seen, a torn ligament diagnosed, the injured area was bound and he was provided with crutches. Back at the hostel we held a council of war. Obviously Don could not be left alone. There were two weeks of our holiday to go and Michael and I were too selfish to sacrifice them by doing what would have been best for Don – taking him back to London as quickly as possible. What we arranged was that I would go to

Florence for five days while Michael looked after Don in Rome in the hope that in that time he would at least be mobile enough to travel. Michael would then accompany him to Pisa on the Rome-Paris express, hop off and go on to Florence and I would hop on in his place. I felt very important and conspiratorial as the train steamed in and panted as if getting its breath back while Michael urgently briefed me on Don's condition and gave me instructions as where to take him on arrival at Paris. The journey was uneventful enough but on disembarking at Gare de Lyon, in grappling with and carrying two heavy rucksacks and helping Don onto the platform, I hurt my back and the milling passengers were treated to the comical sight of Don hobbling along on his crutches and me, my face contorted in agony, bent double, shuffling along the platform dragging two rucksacks behind me.

We took a taxi to a flat in a smart arrondissement where a relative of the Roodyns lived and who was to take responsibility for Don's safe passage home. So still in discomfort but with some relief, I made my farewells and took the Metro to Maison de Mines, a students' hostel in Rue St Jacques, south of Boulevard St Michel. Over the next few days I did the usual tourist things. How different it was then: no queues at the Louvre and standing alone gazing at an unprotected Mona Lisa; the impact of the Impressionists, then housed in the Jeu de Paumes; breakfasting at dawn on a bacon baguette and café au lait amidst the noise and bustle of Les Halles, the central market of Paris until it was closed down in 1971; the distinctive pungent smells of the Metro, garlic and Gauloises; walking through Montmartre in the bright autumn sunshine, the Place de Tertre deserted, not a street portrait artist to be seen.

I spent a day in Versailles. Such grandeur. Bated breath stuff. I took a break to eat my sandwich lunch on a bench overlooking an ornamental lake. Behind me was a private house, from whose radio suddenly came the strains of Mozart's 40th Symphony. Perfect for the period. I felt as though I bore a charmed life. Twice in one holiday. That exact fusion of music and architecture, coming out of the blue by pure chance, affected me more deeply than the grandiose buildings and their interiors.

On my last night I went to the Palais Garnier in Rue Scribe, the opulent opera house of Paris now superseded by the modern Bastille. I had a seat, high in the gods, to which I was escorted by an aged crone who demanded her customary ten francs. The opera was *Tristan and Isolde*, the stage reduced to postage stamp size, the seating uncomfortable and the libretto, before the advent of surtitles, incomprehensible. But the orgasmic love duet in Act Two and Isolde's *Liebestod* at the end of Act Three were heartbreaking. Wagner's wizardry at wrenching your heart opened up the grief from which I had for two months been in denial and exposed my feelings of woundedness which were still fresh and raw.

I left Paris the next day. The crossing was calm and the sun shone as it had for the whole month. Soon I was back home and the beginning of the new academic year was only days away.

33. LONDON SCHOOL OF ECONOMICS
Year 2

Back to the grind. Four new subjects: criminal law, tort, equity and trusts and land law. And an exam on each of them at the end of the year. I enjoyed criminal law and tort; they concerned people and events and therefore rules which I could relate to. I grappled with the concepts of intentionality, *mens rea* [guilty mind] and the defence of insanity based on the M'Naghten Rules because they were about states of mind which interested me, though nowhere near as much as depth psychology. Equity and Land Law were highly technical collections of rules about trusts and property, the preserve of the well off, and of which I had no experience, so the only course was to learn by rote and commit to memory.

Brenda was in her last year. It was very painful. I could not avoid her; she was around every day and everywhere: en route to and from the LSE, in its corridors and cafeterias and worst of all the Law Library in which she had taken to working. Sometimes I sat next to her; she offered me *Polos* but nothing else. She and Warren were now an established item but fortunately for my still hurting heart, I rarely saw them together.

At the end of October, Clement Attlee, barely surviving in Parliament with a majority severely reduced in the 1950 election, called a General Election. At that time, you were not eligible to vote until you were twenty-one, so this was the first time I had been able to exercise my democratic right. The result was still in doubt by the end of Election Day and the next morning we crammed into the Graham Wallas room at the LSE where a wireless had been rigged up so that we could listen to the remaining constituency results as they came in. As the morning progressed the outcome became clear and as most of us present were staunch Labour supporters, each new Conservative victory was greeted with cries and groans of disappointment.

By the end of the morning the Conservative majority had climbed into double figures and we knew that Winston Churchill was back to lead the country with what we felt was the same old gang of reactionaries: Anthony Eden as Foreign Secretary, Rab Butler, Home Office and Harold Macmillan, Housing Minister. Two Parliamentary Secretaries, unknown then but achieving notoriety in later years were Reginald Maudling and John Profumo. A new face was Edward Heath, Prime Minister to be, but then a lowly Economic Secretary to the Treasury.

We mourned the passing of the Labour government, which when first elected in 1945, gave us the hope of a bright and fair postwar future. They would not return to power for thirteen years. Meanwhile at a more parochial level, the Law Department was experiencing its own political upheaval. The LSE Law Society was dominated by the year ahead of us and was chaired by a very bright but rather pompous student called Gerald Butler, who at the AGM of the Society later that term, put himself and his acolytes up for re-election. We of the second year were appalled. The old guard had organised nothing the previous year and had no programme to propose for the next. We did, and on that basis received overwhelming support and ousted the old gang, replacing Gerald Butler with Cyril Goldberg and the entire committee (including me) were voted in from our year.

I was the creative spirit on the committee and came up with the ideas for the year ahead: the publication of a termly law magazine to be totally the work of students and to be called *Obiter* and a series of lectures to be given by teachers from other LSE disciplines along the lines of Psychology and the Law, Economic History and the Law, Sociology and the Law and so on. The latter programme arose out of my impatience with the way law was taught, as a set of rules, laws unto themselves, isolated from societal and political influences.

Organising and getting these activities off the ground was time-consuming but rewarding. I edited the first issue of *Obiter*, solicited contributions and arranged printing. I even wrote an article myself on what I thought was an outrageous law, just enacted, by which US troops stationed in the UK were made subject, not to UK criminal law, but to their own laws, court-martials and legal procedures.

As to the lecture series, I had to prepare a programme and meet with the speakers to explain what it was I wanted. Lunchtime lecture rooms had to be booked and the lectures publicised throughout the LSE. They were a great success, attended by teachers and students from other disciplines, and brought the Law Department which had tended to be isolated from the mainstream of the LSE, into the heart of its intellectual life.

Brenda came along to the Sociology and the Law lecture which I was chairing. As the room was filling up she approached me.

"Boris, could you come for a walk when this is finished?"

Although taken by surprise, I was quick enough to realise that she was not just seeking me out as a companion with whom to enjoy some exercise and a breath of fresh air. I said,

"Why, what's up?"

"I just need to talk to you".

I was so overcome by a tangle of confused thoughts and emotions that I was lucky to get through my functions as chairman and heard scarcely enough of the lecture to make the customary rounding up comments at the end. What was this about? What was she up to? Why single me out to share any confidences? Did she want us to get together, resume a friendship or even a relationship? Hope mingled with a determination not to be hurt again. Curiosity played a large part too, as well as a feeling of specialness in being the one she had chosen to talk to.

We walked down to the Embankment and along the river past the Houses of Parliament, on and on, past Dolphin Square right down to Chelsea Reach where we stopped for tea at *The Blue Cockatoo*. She talked, I listened. All was not well in her relationship with Warren. She couldn't explain, he was a nice, attractive man but there was something not right about him for her.

"What shall I do?" she asked, appealing to me guilessly with large, mournful eyes. Who was I to give relationship advice, emotionally invested as I was in any outcome? My nascent lawyerly skills kicked in and I delivered a dispassionate on the one hand, on the other hand, type of judgement. I hadn't the faintest idea how she wanted me to respond, why she had chosen me, whether she was using me as a sounding board or just considered me a sympathetic and mature sort of chap to confide in. After tea, I said that I had to get back to college for an Equity lecture. She did not want me to go.

"Let's go up West, see a film and have a bite to eat."

"I can't. Equity's my weak subject. I can't get behind."

She pleaded with me to stay. I was adamant. In my heart I knew it wasn't about the Equity lecture. I had been too hurt and was protecting myself from being sucked in and spat out again.

We parted at Earls Court Road Station. I scarcely saw her again. Exams were upon us; after she had taken them, she departed to New York where she met a wealthy car dealer to whom she became engaged by the end of the summer. Warren recovered quickly enough and within the first term of the next academic year was to be seen in the company of Beth (another sociology student), very pretty, slim, dark doe eyes and as shy as a startled fawn. Warren had met his true, lifelong love. They soon married and are still as active, full of fun and joie de vivre as ever. Brenda settled in America, married her car dealer and died in her fifties.

I was soon in a state of high anxiety. I had an ambitious programme of revision planned for the Easter vacation but my mind wandered, I couldn't concentrate and nothing seemed to stick in my memory. I thought that maybe there was some medicine, some magic potion which could transform my muddled, barely functioning mind into a clear thinking one. There was. My doctor, David Romney, prescribed amphetamine tablets. Their effect was instantaneous. I felt alert, energetic and omnipotent. I needed little sleep and bounded manically through my work, committing sufficient law to memory to get me through to the third and final year.

We celebrated the end of the academic year with a small party hosted by Valerie Mairants, an LSE law student, a year below us, who had become Cyril Goldberg's girlfriend. Valerie was petite, sharp featured, auburn haired, and also articulate and opinionated, not surprising, as her parents were members of the Communist Party. She was also a talented pianist. Musicality was in her genes, her father Ivan Mairants, was a distinguished guitarist of the time.

Valerie had invited her best friend, Beryl Cohen, to the party. I was immediately struck by her good looks; everything about her was soft, soft black hair, soft dark eyes, an all over soft rosiness; also soft of expression and voice. Very soon she was soft on me and I, on her. There was dancing and we danced close. *The Blue Tango* became our tune.

We met a couple of times before we left London, she for a holiday in Scotland, I to revisit my old North Wales haunts and find a job for the summer. I hitched my way along the coast from Chester to Llandudno and within a day of arriving there, I was installed as a porter at the palatial *Gogarth Abbey Hotel*, facing the sea on the north side of Great Ormes Head, a mile or so from Llandudno. Here I humped luggage, cleaned shoes, made and served teas and coffees as well as a variety of other menial tasks. The work wasn't onerous but I was bored and lonely. There were only so many times I could walk around Great Ormes Head or along the Llandudno front, envying what seemed a whole world full of laughing, self-absorbed, intertwined couples, a world from which I felt painfully excluded.

So after two weeks, having heard that jobs were available at Butlin's Holiday Camp near Pwllweli, I gave my notice and set off from Llandudno to the small station, right by the sea, serving the camp. I made my way up to the camp office and without fuss or formality was taken on as a kitchen porter in the Windsor Dining Hall and allocated a billet in one of the chalets dedicated to camp workers. My weekly wage was £4 plus board and lodging and the right to use all the camp facilities. What serendipity; I felt like the Marx Bros in *A Night at the Opera* when as stowaways on a transatlantic liner, famished from lack of food, they wander into the steerage cafeteria and are plied with huge plates of food. Before I even lifted a finger in labour, I enjoyed a three course dinner, a dance at the Camp ballroom, a good night's sleep and a large breakfast.

The kitchen was attached to the dining hall serving several hundred campers at a sitting of which there were two per meal. Redcoats, responsible for organising and running events and entertainments were the aristocrats of camp employees, top of the hierarchy, kitchen porters at the bottom. We were skivvies, maids-of-all-work. Humping supplies from delivery vans was heavy work. I developed muscles I didn't know I had. Swabbing and mopping. Eviscerating chickens. Keeping the enormous bubbling stockpot, (providing the basis for the daily soup) going by the constant addition of vegetable peelings, stale bread crusts, eggshells and anything else not actually putrid or mouldy. About two hours before the first sitting we helped serve up the menu du jour, hundreds of identical portions; the plates were then placed in the drawers of tall, electrically heated steel cabinets on wheels for efficient and speedy service by the waitresses on the arrival of the hordes of hungry campers.

Ah, the waitresses, they were so pretty and so friendly. We all went dancing most nights and I had brief attachments with several of them. But I only had eyes for Kay Bassano, a Redcoat with blonde hair cascading down to her waist. One night we danced and she invited me back to her chalet. I was twenty-two and had had two serious girlfriends. I should have known better. I do not know what came over me. Kay was lying on her bed, I too was on the bed, but sitting. We were chatting and it would have been the most natural thing for me to have attempted a trial kiss, instead of which I went into lecture mode, haranguing Kay with my half-baked version of Freud's theories, the centrality of the sexual instinct in the development of the human psyche, the importance of dreams and so on ad nauseam. I even got off the bed and paced the room, the better to gesture and inflect my monologue. All animation left Kay's face but I plodded on. Finally, she gave me my marching orders!

"I'm on early shift tomorrow. Must get my beauty sleep."

And off I crept, not even a good night kiss. What was I playing at? Even now, I'm not sure: too nervous to make a direct pass, fearing rejection or to make an impression, show that I was different, superior even to the male Redcoats and their relentless jollity? Seduction by psychoanalysis? Some hopes: it was a crass way to establish an erotic transference.

Not all my free time was spent in the pursuit of women. There were a number of students around, friendly members of the freemasonry of youth. We spent many evenings sharing our hopes for the future, gossiping and playing chess and cards. An older man, Haynes, was an elusive presence, flitting in and out, never participating in our social life. One day he rushed into the chalet, packed a bag, rushed out again and disappeared for good. It was rumoured that he was involved in some criminal activity and that the police were after him.

On my return to the LSE at the start of the autumn term I had an interview with Sir David Hughes Parry to discuss what optional subjects I should take that year. In his lilting Welsh accent, he asked

"So, Rumney, how was your vacation?"

"Spent part of it in Wales, sir. Working at Pwllweli Holiday Camp."

"Well, well! So was I. Not at the camp of course, I'm a magistrate at the Pwllweli Court."

"You didn't come across a man called Haynes, did you, sir? He left the camp in a hurry and we wondered..."

"Haynes, you say? He was up before me for theft from chalets. Record as long as your arm. I sentenced him to three months' imprisonment."

In my last weeks at Butlins I met a couple of French students, Nicole, writing a thesis on working-class holidays in the UK, France and Germany and was doing on the spot research in Butlins and Pierre, studying law in Lyon. Pierre and I hitchhiked to Stratford-upon-Avon where we saw Anthony Quayle play Coriolanus, then on to Exeter, Dartmouth and Salisbury from where we hitched a lift in a government minister's limousine back to London. Pierre stayed a couple of nights in Clapton before returning to France. For the last four weeks of the vacation I worked as a labourer at the art deco *Black Cat* factory in Camden Town, at the time owned by Carreras, manufacturers of Piccadilly and Dunhill cigarettes.

34. LONDON SCHOOL OF ECONOMICS
Year 3

At my interview with Professor Hughes Parry I chose as my three optional subjects, Wills and Probate, Industrial Law and Domestic Relations. The one compulsory subject was Jurisprudence, the philosophy of law. I particularly took to the American Realists and their human rather than abstract approach to law-making. The notion that a judge's decision-making might be influenced by his plus or minus reactions to blondes or by what he had for breakfast made good sense to me. I had no trouble understanding or retaining such material in my memory. Apart from Wills and Probate, highly complex and technical, like all subjects relating to property, I was much happier in this year. Jurisprudence satisfied the bit of me interested in legal theory and how it slotted into the broader philosophical picture and government and society generally. Similar considerations applied to Industrial Law and Domestic Relations, both of which were taught by Professor Otto Kahn-Freund who had been a judge in Germany, was stripped of his post when the Nazis came to power and fled to England. He was an inspiring teacher who always related the development of law to political and social forces. Industrial Law and Domestic Relations were ideal subjects for such treatment, the former involving work, the workplace and trade unions, the latter, marriage, divorce and the treatment of children.

I settled into something close to cosy domesticity that year. As soon as I returned from North Wales, I picked up with Beryl and we became steady boy and girl friend. I was over Brenda. She had left the LSE and I saw her for the last time when she came to meet a friend at the LSE. I was with Beryl and as Brenda passed she looked sharply at us both. The fact that she was at the least, curious enough to see who I was with was strangely reparative. I was announcing, 'See what a pretty girl I'm with. Life moves on, I'm no longer pining for you', and she couldn't resist taking a peep.

The LSE Law Library was open on Saturdays until 5pm. My mother was at Watford Market, so I had a lunch prepared by my master chef grandmother from her short but impeccable repertoire. Replete, stuffed even, I would make my way to Houghton Street and nod over text books and ancient Law Reports. At closing time I'd meet Beryl and Cyril and

Valerie and we'd go off to the Strand Palace Hotel for tea and Kunzle cakes.

Jack was by then a fourth-year student at the Royal Dental Hospital, leading his own social life, which I felt to be far more exciting than mine but he and I still kept in touch. He had made many friends at the Hospital, some of them lifelong. Whilst a student, he cared for my teeth in a large hall at RDH, containing about twenty or so dental chairs where he carried out fillings using a noisy, slowly rotating drill, without anaesthetic, treatment I submitted to stoically. Dental students were far more larky then we at the LSE. At that time, all four sides of Leicester Square were vehicular thoroughfares and one day Jack and his joker friends put up signs at all four corners prohibiting left turns and commanding *Turn Right*. Cars and taxis kept going round and round the square until, having first ensured that there was no policeman in sight, they surreptitiously turned left.

I spent weekends with him at Letchworth where he had a separate social life, mainly centred around Seamus O'Brien and his jazz band. Seamus was a brilliant pianist with a voice like Fats Waller and had been described in a national music magazine as *'gravel throated Seamus O'Brien'*. Other talented musicians made up the band which also included self-taught Jack on guitar. He was quite frank about his motives,

'I wasn't particularly good, I only learnt a few basic chords to get into the band and the social life that went with it. And it attracted lots of girls.'

True, during this period Jack had many girlfriends.

At the LSE some of my friends were already entering into long-term attachments. Apart from Cyril and myself, there were Warren and Beth, Gerald and Ida and Martin and Sheila. Bryan Lipson had been dumped by Claudine Weisport with whom he was deeply in love, in favour of a member of the Rimmel cosmetics family but was soon snapped up by Hannah Schindler whose family had emigrated to the UK from Israel in 1948 (an unusual way round for Jews at that time) because her father had worked for the British military authorities during the mandate and was therefore persona non grata following independence. All these couplings (save mine) led to marriages.

It was obvious that Beryl was in love with me but although I was attracted to and felt great warmth for her, I did not experience her as a soulmate. There was a lack of physical robustness in her but that was not the main drawback. I was four years her senior and twenty-two to eighteen felt like a big gap. She was an only child and had lived a sheltered life. There was something timid about her. She had a passivity, a lack of combativeness which I found dull and irritating. I took to playing bridge in the Junior Common Room every lunchtime with Cyril, Harry Futerman and Brian Cookson, the last two also being good friends from my year.

Beryl and Valerie sat together in attendance. I was not a good player but what I loved about the game was its total absorption, the complete shutting out of everything else in the external world, including any compulsion to relate or make conversation with, our girlfriends. It was a mechanism of escape, time passed seamlessly, unnoticed and the lure of the game held me in thrall ('Another rubber, gentlemen?') much to the cost of my studies and eventual class of degree.

One Saturday afternoon I was on the upper deck of a 73 bus on the way to meet Beryl at Oxford Circus. As we stop-started along Tottenham Court Road, I spotted a mixed group of whom I imagined to be St Martins' art students. The girls were attractive, animated and laughing without inhibition; all were obviously delighted to be with each other and having great fun. I felt almost sick with envy. I made a vow. I would not be the initiator, would not speak first. I would leave it to Beryl to open a conversation. We met, said hello and walked down Regent Street. There was utter silence between us. See, I was right, she was incapable of getting anything going. She always wanted to leave it to me. Did I intimidate her? I didn't want a girl friend who felt intimidated by me. Eventually we got to Piccadilly Circus.

"Is there something wrong Boris?"

At last she had spoken, "No, why do you ask?"

She looked upset, near to tears.

"You seem strange. Are you angry with me?"

"I was testing you."

"Testing me? Why? What for?"

"To see what would happen if I left it to you to speak."

And then it all came out. I always seemed to take command. She always felt nervous about introducing a topic or telling me something or expressing an opinion in case I rubbished her. The truth was that she often felt inadequate when she was with me and no one had ever made her feel like that before. I was astonished. I had no idea that I was experienced by her or indeed by anyone else as so powerful or critical. I thought I was a kind, open-minded, easy-going kind of chap. But her revelation led to a softening of both my feelings towards and treatment of her. Her admission of diffidence and vulnerability in my presence saddened me. It was the last thing I desired in any relationship with a woman and I was filled with remorse and a determination to cosset and protect her from hurt.

There was however one area of my life in which the rule *Noli me tangere* [do not touch me] applied and if transgressed, the new gentle me crumbled into a cold rage. One fine summer day after lunch at the LSE, Beryl and I strolled down to the Embankment Gardens and sat on a bench, chatting about our friends and the ups and downs of their loves. Out of the blue she asked the forbidden question.

"You talk about everything and everyone but you never mention your father. Is he dead or something?"

These women, I thought, they always want to know. Am I not good enough, respectable enough, in the eyes of right-thinking Jewish parents to court or even marry their daughter, with that gaping hole, a missing, disreputable father.

I replied coldly, enunciating every syllable with preternatural clarity, "Did it not occur to you that if I had wanted to talk about my father I would have done so?"

And with that I left her sitting on the bench and walked back to the LSE, angry with her for daring to trespass on that secret, wounded part of myself.

We kissed and made up of course and resumed our busy life together (parties, friends, cinema) and apart (work, bridge, family). But something was missing. Love. I longed to love. I was attracted. I liked. I was faithful. She was clearly in love with me but I was only nearly-in-love with her. Love had never been declared or spoken of. I became impatient with the status quo. One evening we were in a seedy cafe in Dalston, drinking cups of tepid, stewed tea, waiting to go to the cinema. Over the teacups I reached out for her hand, clasped it with both of mine and said, "I love you."

"I love you too."

I had hoped to make the desire a reality through the power of language. I did love her, but not enough, not without reservation and my saying that I was, did not make it any truer or transform her from a good mate to a soulmate. My heart was in the right place but it was a cruel, thoughtless thing to do: to lead a genuine, loving girl on so and give her false hopes of a future together.

A few days before the final examinations, Dad's cousin, David, once again prescribed amphetamine, which apart from its physiological effects also turned out to be a mood enhancer and whether or not there was an element of placebo, the little white pills boosted my confidence that I would pass the forthcoming exams.

35. MY FATHER – A CLEVER FOOL
Part 4

I have no idea where or how my father lived during the time since he had been ejected from Upper Clapton Road. He became something of a down-and-out and quite ill.

In that summer of 1953 there was another issue to distract me both from revision for the final exams and my relationship with Beryl. My father had been visiting his sister, my aunt Rosa, and reports were coming back to my mother that he had been seriously ill and was still looking unwell, thin and down at heel. Above all he wanted to return home to my mother. He had had an offer of a job from an old friend, Sam Wachsman. I sat with my mother in our living room and asked,

"How do you feel about getting back together again?"

"I really don't know. I hate Max for what he's done but I still miss him. You know, when he wasn't being a naughty boy, he was very good company."

"So why not give it a try?"

"But how would I ever trust him again?"

"Look, I've got an idea. Let me go and meet him and feel out the lie of the land."

"Are you sure you're happy to do that?"

"Mum, I'd really like to see you back together again but not at any price. I'm twenty-three with three years of law studies behind me. You'll just have to trust me."

And with that my mother gave me permission to go ahead.

I got in touch with my father and arranged to meet at the Lyons Corner House in the Strand, just by Trafalgar Square. I thought he'd need a good meal and took him to the eat-as-much-as-you-like Salad Bar so beloved of Jack and me in our teen trips to London. It was the first time I had seen him for nearly three years and I scrutinized him carefully as he tucked into a plate piled high with roast chicken legs, sliced ham and a portion from every other dish at the counter. He looked pale and drawn, there were several shaving nicks on his face and throat, the penalty of using a blunt razor blade.

Despite Rosa's report, he wasn't exactly down at heel. He had dressed carefully but his suit was shiny with wear and his shirt collar and cuffs were frayed. He had lost his bouncy self-confidence, his enfant terrible charm and was embarrassingly deferential and grateful for my kindness and consideration. He asked me how things were and I gave him a brief summary of my time at the LSE.

"What about you, Dad?"

"Not so good. It's been hard. I've tried but nothing has turned out well."

"And now? What about now?"

"I'm nearly over the gastric problems I've been suffering from. I'm a bit short of cash but I'm starting a job with Sam Wachsman in a couple of weeks' time. Office manager, book-keeping, that sort of thing."

He was beginning to regain his old self-assurance.

"And what about the gambling?"

"Finished with. It's all behind me, a mug's game."

Was it? He had declared that he had kicked his habit many times in the past and promised that he would never place a bet again. We went up to the counter to choose our dessert. Back at our table, Dad asked, "How's Sophie?"

I knew that he'd been kept up to date by Rosa.

"She's fine, keeps going, all things considered."

"Good, good! Give her my love."

The time had come. I steeled myself and plunged in.

"I will. Look Dad, would you like to see her?"

He leaned towards me, his face a mixture of hope and longing.

"More than anything in the world, my boy. But I'm not sure she'd want to see me."

I played it diplomatically.

"I've no idea. But I'll put it to her and if she would, I'll get Rosa to fix up something at her house."

We chatted on for a while, I paid the bill and on parting we shook hands warmly.

I reported to Mum, she met Dad at Rosa's and before I could turn round and much to my relief, he was reinstalled as husband to my mother. I welcomed his return and was glad that my mission of reconnaissance had contributed in a small way to their reconciliation but was in too preoccupied about the upcoming finals to pay much heed to their fourth honeymoon.

36. GAP MONTHS

The exams were over and our time at the LSE was done. There was no marking of the occasion, no goodbyes or parties or balls. Out into Houghton Street one last time and that was that. I had no feelings of sadness or gratitude. I was onto the next thing, fixing up a three-year training contract, then known as articles. The solicitor trainer was known as the principal and the trainee as an articled clerk. It was not easy. Many solicitors still demanded a hefty capital sum by way of premium from their articled clerks-to-be. It was not just that my parents could scarcely afford such an outlay, but my own feelings of self-worth would not allow it. I believed that with the Army and a law degree behind me, I was worth at least a small salary, so many of the interviews I had with rapacious solicitors ended in disappointment for us both.

Until I found suitable articles I needed to earn money and went back to Carreras. Because of my previous experience I was put in charge of feeding a huge shredding machine with tobacco leaf. In my dung-brown overalls, I revelled in the physical and rhythmic nature of the work as I pitchforked quantities of leaf into the mouth of my insatiable machine. It was mindless but after a year of abstract thinking and rote learning, I loved it. It took up all my energy and by the end of my three-month stint I was leaner and fitter than I had ever been. Add the joshing camaraderie and I could understand the pride and communal bonding enjoyed by coal miners.

Working in the leaf department required a greater amount of sheer physical effort than any other job in the factory and those who worked there considered themselves the *crème de la crème* of the entire labour force. There were plenty of opportunities for getting to know my fellow workers as we were allowed a ten minute break every hour, for which a special enclosure was roped off with seating on the factory floor. Free cigarettes were provided; during the time I was there they were promoting a new brand, *Dunhill's*. In addition, we could take two packs of twenty home for the weekend. Occasionally groups of market researchers, clipboards in hand, would descend on the smokers in the enclosure to record our views on the new cigarette. To most of us it was no different, better or worse than any other British brand. Based on my observation that we had to stub out a half finished cigarette on returning to work, I produced a short paper proposing the manufacture of a new small sized cigarette, to be called *Breaks* which would last about five minutes and so minimise waste and smokers' frustration. I received a polite letter from management rejecting my idea on the ground that there was no market for such a product in the foreseeable future. So much for my attempt to distinguish myself from the ruck and attract the attention of the Directors.

Stimulated by my Industrial Law studies, I was interested in how the factory functioned in its management and labour relations. In the vast cafeteria which served plentiful, tasty and cheap lunches of which I took full advantage, the factory chapter of the Transport and General Workers Union held after-work meetings which I sneaked into. During lunch breaks I would sit in the library, (Carreras were enlightened employers) reading up on the history of Trade Unionism in Great Britain.

I took time off to attend interviews with solicitors seeking articled clerks and was eventually accepted by a smooth, Oxford accented, sole practitioner, Mr JK Edmondson of 20 Bunhill Row EC2 whose offices occupied a four-storey terraced house. His own office had a floor-to-ceiling bay window overlooking the parade ground and 18th-century headquarters of the Honourable Artillery Company in City Road. No premium, but no salary either. It was the best deal on offer, at least for a non-Oxbridge graduate who had recently heard that he had been awarded a Lower Second degree. I was bitterly disappointed, had done well in the subjects I enjoyed but had been brought down badly by those of a technical, property-based nature which I could not fully grasp until I had practical experience of them.

JK as I learned to call him, but not to his face, wanted me to start in the middle of September in time for the Courts' awakening from their lengthy summer slumber. That gave me four weeks to give my notice to Carreras and squeeze in a short holiday by taking advantage of a spare seat in uncle Alf's car. He, Rosa and my father's cousin Judd, his wife, Fay and their sixteen-year-old daughter, Gillian, were off to St. Ives and I, short of money, cut off from my friends and desperate for a break, would have accompanied him or, come to that, anyone else, to Southend-on-Sea if that had been all that was on offer.

Alf had recently acquired a new Ford Consul, a boxy but roomy car, with front bench seating, which comfortably accommodated the six of us. There was then a camaraderie amongst drivers: whenever a Consul appeared in the opposite direction both Alf and the other driver would sound their horns and flash their lights.

My sense of wonder had returned as we left London behind and I was entranced by the new places at which we stopped en route: Bath, Babbacombe Bay, arriving at Polperro at sunset where we stayed overnight. We reached St. Ives in the late afternoon of the second day and booked into the Carbis Bay Hotel. There was no room for me in the main building and I was billeted in an annexe with a motherly lady to look after me and provide breakfast which I took all on my own. I ate main meals with my party and after the first dinner discovered that there were others in the hotel of my own age and lost no time getting to know them. There was James, a tall handsome Scot, studying law at Edinburgh University and two pretty secretaries from Birmingham, with Brummie accents to prove it, Beryl and Carol. Beryl was blonde, slim with long slender legs and whose sharp features were expressive of her sharp intelligence, Carol, taller, rounder, fuller figure, a rosy open face, a generous mouth and large brown eyes and dark hair. It was Carol who was my type and the one I instantly fancied. So why was it that when all the guests had gone to bed and we had pushed all the chairs back to create space for dancing and found some dance records and how to work the radiogram, I asked Beryl and not Carol to dance? Fear of rejection, if I showed that I was interested? Starting slowly and letting the others come back to me, my futile strategy in the school cross-country race? I have no idea but the ways of wooing and winning were obviously beyond me.

That misplaced initiative of mine settled the pairing for the rest of the holiday: James and Carol, me and Beryl. In retrospect no complaint; Beryl was a bright, affectionate companion and the four of us had a fine time, spending our days on the beach and the evenings in The Sloop Inn where an enthusiastic crowd gathered to listen to whatever live music was on offer. I felt on top form, soaking in the sun, slim and muscular from my weeks of hard physical labour. On our last night, Beryl confided in me that Carol was not at all interested in James but tagged along so as to keep our little party going. On hearing that, a little worm of discontent bored its way into my mind. But I rationalised: even if I had approached Carol first she might have fancied me no more than James. And maybe Beryl didn't really fancy me either. Or James. I kissed these insoluble saboteurs out of my mind. Then returning from the beach to the hotel, we kissed again and promised to keep in touch. I wrote but she never replied.

The family were most displeased with me. My desertion was felt as a betrayal. I suspect that one of the reasons I had been welcomed as one of their party was as a companion for Gillian. But I never saw myself in that role, only in a vaguely avuncular one. Gillian was a petite, slightly dumpy girl, very shy and probably overawed by my brash, cocky 23-year-old self. There was however one respect in which I had a profound influence on her. I had been telling her about my Jurisprudence course and in particular the philosophical precept that you couldn't derive a value judgement from a fact or set of facts. This revelation triggered in her such an interest in philosophy that she ended up as a philosophy don at Oxford.

37. ARTICLES – PART 1

Back from St Ives, I prepared for my entrance into the practice of law by buying a bowler hat, the sine qua non of City workers, as well as an elegant rolled umbrella. So one fine Monday morning, wearing my waistcoated army demob suit and my pristine bowler and carrying my briefcase containing *The Times* and an omelette sandwich prepared by my mother, I set off down Cazenove Road to Stoke Newington High Street to catch a trolley bus to Finsbury Square. I cut through the Bunhill Fields Cemetery, passing the graves of Daniel Defoe, William Blake and John Bunyan and arrived at JK Edmonson and Co in good time.

JK summoned me to his room and called down the executive staff to meet me: John Dee, tall, thin, dark and saturnine, thick rimmed glasses and a sepulchral voice, the managing clerk who dealt with the firms conveyancing and probate, and Roy Hallel, a five-year articled clerk with one year yet to go, tall, well built, aquiline nose, also bespectacled. In his habitual mode of speech, JK introduced me as *'Boris Rumney the Red: read law at the LSE and our new resident brainbox'.* I was the only member of the firm with a degree. Mr Wright arrived, a little late and flustered. Apart from three secretaries the five of us constituted the firm. Kenneth Wright was a litigation managing clerk – he would now be called a paralegal – unqualified but the most experienced litigator in the firm in matters of practice, procedure and general know-how. It was he who would initiate me into the world of the courts and show me the ropes. For the first few days I was to shadow him before being entrusted with any work of my own.

"What have you got on today, Wright?" JK asked.

"Lots of work at the High Court, sir. Appointment before the Master at 10.30."

He looked at his watch.

"It's 9:45 now. I must run."

"Right, off you go. And take Rumney with you."

We walked to Moorgate to take the train to the Temple. What was a Master? It sounded even grander than a Judge. There was the Master of the Rolls, chief judge of the Court of Appeal but I couldn't imagine a mere managing clerk having a right of audience before him. I had just read CP

Snow's novel *The Masters* but ruled out the possibility of the Master of an Oxbridge college having any judicial function. *Master of Ceremonies,* something to do with High Court protocol perhaps?

"What's a Master?" I asked as we waited for a train.

"He's a sort of minor judge. Deals with interlocutory matters."

"What are interlocutory matters?"

"Things that have to be decided before the case can come on to trial. A Summons for Directions, for Instance."

"What's a Summons for...?"

"All in good time, Rumney. You'll find out; I've got one before Master Grundy this morning."

Time was pressing and we sped up from Temple Station to the majestic Royal Courts of Justice in the Strand, rushed up the stairs to the Bear Garden and into Master Grundy's room where Mr Wright's opposite number was already waiting. Master Grundy opened the proceedings and I learnt by experiencing the process itself, that a Summons for Directions was an application to have a timetable set for all the steps preceding the actual trial of a case.

After a quick cup of tea in the court cafeteria, Mr Wright took me back to the Bear Garden, so named by Queen Victoria because of the hubbub made by the crowds of lawyers, clients and their adversaries who gathered there to sort out pre-trial issues. Nothing had changed since her Majesty's visit in 1882. There was a social element too. As we pushed our way through the throng, Mr Wright paused to greet and catch up with many other paralegals with whom he had had legal business over the years. Once through the Bear Garden, we called in at neighbouring rooms to issue writs, file documents, fix dates for trials and many other routine tasks.

We had a brief lunch at a sandwich bar in the Strand and plunged under the arch into Middle Temple Lane to deliver briefs and papers to sets of Chambers favoured by JK. I had attended at nearby LSE for three years but had not even been aware of the existence of the Temple and was fascinated by the ancient buildings and the sight of gowned and bewigged barristers hurrying about the narrow lanes and hidden little squares. I marvelled at the Chambers clerks' rooms cluttered and piled high with pink-ribboned briefs, some, I thought, dating back to the beginning of the century. I later learnt that the genre of work we had been engaged in was called 'outdoor work' to distinguish it from the management and handling of cases and legal matters in the office. There was a whole sub-category of employee known as outdoor clerk. Now all these processes, including the completion of property sales and purchases, are dealt with online.

Back at Bunhill Row, Mr Wright took me up to his top floor office which I was to share with him. It was in essence an attic, low ceilinged with uneven, creaky floors. My workstation consisted of a small desk facing the wall and a telephone. The bedrock of JK's practice was defending claims for personal injuries and damage to vehicles arising out of road traffic accidents which poured out of a number of large insurance companies for whom JK acted. Mr Wright had a huge caseload: a mixed bag of claims of all sizes and defending drivers charged with a variety of driving offences. There was a pile of files on my desk waiting to be handled by me. With help from Mr Wright, I very quickly got the hang of the steps to take and the procedures to follow. I was allocated a drawer in one of Mr Wright's three full-to-the-brim filing cabinets for my files. I began to read my way through these while Mr Wright made phone calls and dictated correspondence and instructions to counsel with a fluency and assurance which I despaired of ever possessing. His work completed, he sat back in his chair and lit a cigarette.

"Well, Mr Rumney how have you enjoyed your first week in this madhouse?"

"Confusing. So different from what I imagined."

"What did you imagine?"

"Something more orderly, streamlined. Less chaotic. Less Dickensian."

"Oh, somehow it works."

"Well, I'm full of admiration for the way you work."

"I've been at it for long enough haven't I? Too long maybe. Roll on death, demob's a washout!"

Mr Wright was in his mid-thirties, fleshy without being fat, round and merry faced with dark, slicked back hair. He had served in the Far East during World War II and the constant *cri de coeur* of conscripts was 'Roll on demob'. Disillusionment with civilian life had led him to adapt the wartime phrase. I later gathered that his discontent had something to do with his marriage to a woman he found so unlovely that he likened her to a board with two drawing pins stuck in it. He described marital relations with her like going to bed with a piece of meat.

Two or three times a week JK called me down to his office. I felt as if I was in the Army again, hauled before my Commanding Officer to be reprimanded for my general slackness.

"Well Rumney, how are you getting on?"

"Fine, sir."

"Got enough work, have you?"

"Keeps me busy sir."

"Good. Well, here's four new cases I think you'll find interesting. Exercise your brain cells."

They weren't interesting and all they exercised were my stress levels at the mounting number of cases I was handling, virtually unsupervised. As well as doing the bulk of the outdoor work, I attended conferences with

Counsel, sat through cases in court, dictated correspondence, obtained statements from witnesses, drafted court documents and prepared cases for trial. It was not long before I had so many files that I needed a filing cabinet of my own.

Roy Hallel, JK's other articled clerk was financially far better off than I and drove to work in his own Ford *Pilot*, a streamlined, prestigious car of its day. Not having gone to University he was in the last year of his mandatory five-year articles, law graduates being required to complete only three. In his well-cut, double-breasted suits, he looked every inch the young, modern solicitor, not the bowler-hatted, black-jacketed, pinstripe-trousered version I believed I had to ape in order to conform. He was an amiable man but sharp and quick-witted. By the time I met him he was experienced and competent, a formidable negotiator and without doubt the best all-round lawyer in the firm. He was generous with his time and expertise and it was he to whom I went to for help with knotty problems. He wasn't a stuffed shirt either; one afternoon having completed our work for the day by lunchtime, we bunked off and went up West to see *Doctor in The House,* well worth the bollocking JK gave us next day. He, Mr Wright and I regularly had lunch together in a cafe just by Moorgate station. Much to their embarrassment and reproving looks, I reenacted my old Whitechapel Road trick: ordering Scotch broth and accompanying it with my own made at home sandwiches.

Roy and I mainly talked shop but one day we got onto the subject of girls. We were on our way to the Law Courts when he suddenly exclaimed, "My word, she's a smashing piece of work, isn't she?" pointing to a tall, willowy blonde. I was more of a bosomy, brunette man myself.

"Yes, very pretty."

A slight pause and then I asked, "Have you got a girlfriend, Roy?"

"Who's got the time?"

"Come on Roy, what's time got to do with it? You're a good-looking bloke, you've got a car and money. You'd have no difficulty getting a girl."

"I've got Law Society Finals next year. There's a huge amount of work and seven papers to pass. You wait, you will be facing it in a couple of years."

"Well, I refuse to take a vow of celibacy just because of the stupid exam."

We were approaching the Courts. Roy asked,

"What about you, Boris. Have you got a girlfriend?"

"Yes, Beryl. We've been going out for about eighteen months."

"Is marriage on the stocks?"

"No, I'm not really in love with her. I wish I were. She's a nice girl but there's something missing. I've been out with other girls but what I really want is to canalise all my feelings into one person."

"I'm not sure what you mean by canalise."

I had been very pleased with myself for the use of that word.

"Nothing particularly original; I mean putting all your energies and desire into loving one person and one person only for the whole of your life. It's about fidelity, you know, forsaking all others, sharing and keeping the ship afloat, come what may."

"Hmm. Sounds like the C of E marriage vows to me."

C of E or no C of E, I realised that I had articulated my true desire, and that my obsessive chasing of girls was in the service of my search for one true love, a devoted monogamy.

All was not well between me and Beryl. She was in her second year at the LSE, I, wrapped up in my work, family life and a busy social life with old friends. I was no longer even nearly-in-love with her. We still went out together and marked occasions such as birthdays by special outings. We arranged to celebrate my twenty-fourth birthday by having dinner out, followed by *The Mousetrap*, then in the second year of its run. There was a drinking culture at the firm in which I took no part but which was most enthusiastically partaken of by JK and John Dee; the latter was often discovered in the afternoon after pub closing time, slumped over his desk. At lunchtime on my birthday all the male members of the firm took me to the office local where I had two packets of salted peanuts, three gins and orange, a large whisky and, after all that, a pint of shandy to assuage a raging thirst. Mr Wright and Roy then supported me to our usual cafe where I downed my Scotch broth followed by two *Penguins*. I was very ill for the rest of the afternoon. By the evening I had recovered sufficiently to make my way to the LSE to meet Beryl. When she saw the state I was in her face showed her disgust. Jews drink but don't get drunk. Everything in moderation. I said, "Look Beryl. I don't feel very well. The chaps in the office took me to the pub. Could we skip dinner?"

No longer the compliant girl I was used to, her face tight with anger, she said, "No, Boris, I'm hungry."

So we went to The Kerb, an inexpensive restaurant, just off the Strand where I toyed with a plaice with parsley sauce. An oppressive silence hung in the air between us throughout the meal. At the Ambassadors Theatre, feeling increasingly nauseous, I somehow managed to bear the inanities of *The Mousetrap* until the final curtain.

And it was the final curtain for Beryl too as far as I was concerned. I could only see it from my point of view. My hangover was a one-off. I wasn't a drinker. It wasn't my fault. Nothing like this had ever happened before. I didn't get into that state to spite her. If she really loved me, felt for me as the reliable, sober person I usually was, she would have found it in her heart to forgive me, let me off the hook. No, she insisted on her pound of flesh, ha, had that all right, fillet steak, the most expensive dish on the menu. After this incident we saw less and less of each other and Beryl, because of its effect on her or because she despaired of any future with me, cooled perceptibly and our affair, such as it was, crept to its conclusion, without a word, a row or a letter.

She had started going to a Jewish undergraduate club where she met a man to whom she became engaged within a year. I met her for coffee to congratulate her. Afterwards I accompanied her to her bus stop and as we crossed Oxford Street, purely out of courtesy, I took her arm. Viciously she snatched it away.

In the summer of 2011, my wife, Rona and I, by chance met Beryl and her husband while we were having coffee in the Pump Room, Bath and asked them to join us. I was shocked to see her. Instead of an older version of the dark haired, rosy cheeked girl I had known and nearly-loved, she was in a wheelchair, slow in speech but unimpaired in mind. We caught up on half a century's news, neither of us alluding to or even hinting at our previous relationship. I was conscious of this throughout our conversation; surely she must have been. My last sight of her was in her chair, as her husband wheeled her across Abbey Churchyard on their way to visit the Abbey.

38. ARTICLES – PART 2

It was Iris Dean, a woman I knew from the LSE, who alerted me. I had become increasingly dissatisfied with my training at JK's. It wasn't just the money but the limited range of the legal work on offer. I wanted all-round experience in the major areas of a solicitor's practice. As far as conveyancing and probate were concerned, John Dee was for at least half of each day incapable of handling his own work, let alone initiating me into their mysteries. The litigation was overwhelmingly weighted in cases relating to road traffic accidents; there was no divorce or criminal work to speak of.

So when Iris told me that her articles at a Jewish firm in the West End had come to an end and that consequently there was a vacancy, I lost no time in getting her to arrange for me to meet the principal, Alan Rubenstein. On the basis of the number of cases I had handled at JK's, he offered me articles on the spot at a starting salary of £2.50 per week to rise to £4 during my second and final year. The formalities of transferring articles from JK to Alan Rubenstein were soon completed and I left JK's at the end of 1954 and presented myself at my new firm Alan, Edmunds and Phillips' second-floor offices at the corner of Oxford Street and Duke Street, immediately opposite Selfridge's. Alan himself was busy and delegated Dolores Cohen to show me around and introduce me to members of the firm.

Dolores was tall, big boned but shapely, not pretty but attractive, with her large cruelly curved mouth, shrewd eyes and direct, slightly abrasive manner.

"What's your job here?" I asked.

"Same as you. I'm Alan's other articled clerk."

"Are you three or five years?"

"Five. I started here as Lionel Phillips' secretary. He's the conveyancing partner so I've kind of slipped into handling mainly property sales and purchases."

I felt a pang of disquiet. Was I going to be again sidelined into the subject I knew most about, litigation? My anxiety was quickly dispelled by the animated atmosphere which pervaded the office. When I commented on this, Dolores said, "Yes, we are a lively lot. I suppose it's because we're such a young firm. Everyone's under thirty except Alan and he'll only be forty in a month or two. We are all on first name terms. It's very informal here"

So far she'd introduced me to Lionel and the secretaries, Mr Prag, deaf and mute and aged uncle of Alan, dogsbody, messenger and postal clerk, more an act of nepotism or compassion on Alan's part then an employee. Dolores pointed to an empty room.

"That's Rex Cowan's room. He's in court this morning."

I had come across Rex at a law seminar series we had both attended. I explained this but that we had never spoken and added, "What does he do?"

"He was articled here. Qualified a couple of months ago. Assistant solicitor now."

"What's he like?"

"Oh, he's really something. You'll see."

We reached Tom Nelson's room. Tom was at court. There was a second desk against the back wall. This was to be mine. A large pile of files were neatly stacked on the desk for me to deal with. I had scarcely opened the first of these when Tom entered.

"I'm Tom Nelson," he announced, extending his hand. "You must be the new articled clerk."

Tom was the only non-Jew in the firm. Tall, handsome and dapper in his navy-blue double-breasted suit.

I picked up the weightiest of the files on my desk and started to read. The first thing I noticed was that AE&P had been instructed in the matter three years ago. It was one of those cases that nobody wants to handle, complex and meatier than anything I had ever seen. First netted by Alan, the senior partner who brought in work rather than did any, passed down to Tom Nelson who was soon out of his depth, transferred to Rex who brought it up to date and then disappeared to spend his obligatory six-month period of study for solicitors' finals, during which time it languished unattended. Rex now had a full caseload, so the file was handed over to me.

I had not even begun to understand what the case was about when Tom piped up, "Come and join us for lunch, Boris."

A small party consisting of Tom, Dolores, two secretaries and me, made its way to Gino's, a small, Italian trattoria in James Street which served minestrone soup, spaghetti Bolognese and coffee for 20p. What impressed me was the high spirits of our group, the banter, office gossip and scurrilous anecdotes about clients and staff alike. I liked the friendliness with which I was admitted to their indiscretions, as if a long established member of the firm.

After lunch, Rex strode into my office. He scrutinised me intently for several seconds with an unwavering stare and said, "You're the new articled clerk, aren't you? I'm Rex Cowan. Come and have coffee."

His voice was husky, nasal, clear, cultured, imperious and authoritative.

I accompanied him out of the office to the other side of Duke Street to what became our habitual coffee break bar, the Montparnasse. Rex quickly took me under his wing on the unspoken understanding that I became his acolyte, confidante, second fiddle, Leporello to his Don Giovanni, Boswell to his Johnson. We, or rather Rex, with his greater authority and chutzpah, established a routine of vanishing to the Montparnasse each mid-morning. We found that we had much in common, music, psychoanalysis and girls, especially girls. In summer, when they appeared in Oxford Street, in their revealing dresses, from the eyrie of his second floor office, we would peer down at them as they passed in their dozens, Rex keeping up a running commentary on their finer points: hair, face, bust, legs, he took them all in. He was immeasurably better off financially than I. His father was managing director of and a major shareholder in a public company, Cowan de Groot Ltd. Rex lived with his parents in a large mansion flat overlooking the north side of Regents Park. He owned a convertible Hillman car and a large collection of classical records which I greatly envied.

He was not a conventionally good-looking man. Below average height he was stocky, bull-necked, with flat planes to his face, accentuated by the flattened bridge of his nose and his penetrating blue eyes. At various times he reminded me of Ernest Hemingway, Humphrey Bogart and Napoleon. He could be cruelly mocking. Once driving from Whitestone Ponds down the hill towards South Hampstead, I said, "This is so rural. Who would think we're just a few miles from central London?"

A banal comment, admittedly, but I don't think it deserved Rex's sarcastic response.

"Who would think? I would think? He would think? They would think?"

Perhaps at some level, this remark and others of a similar nature, were salutary. They came as a shock, brought me down a peg, crumpled my omnipotence, made me realise that I was nothing special or extraordinary but was as mundane as the vast majority of humankind.

Once I had completed my articles and left Alan, Edmunds & Phillips, our day to day contact ended and our paths diverged. But converged again in a dramatic fashion several years later when Rex, Bryan Lipson and I went into legal partnership as Cowan, Lipson and Rumney.

39. CONTEMPORANEOUS EVIDENCE
Diary Interlude Jan-Apr 1955

While writing this memoir, I discovered a pocket sized, day-to-a-page diary in which I chronicled the main events of my life. It was full of surprises. I had a general memory of this period as being almost completely work orientated with clear and vivid memories of my work colleagues at AE&P, Rex, Dolores and Tom in particular. In fact, what dominated my life was a hectic social and cultural life involving dozens of friends and acquaintances with a continuous subtext of meeting, getting to know and taking out girls. That is why in my categorisation of the subject matter of my diaries, entries describing social and cultural events frequently blur into those subtexts. Numerically, social entries topped the list at 51, an almost daily description of meetings, lunches, parties and get-togethers with friends, singly or in groups, most now beyond recall or with whom I have long since lost touch. Those I have referred to most frequently have remained friends throughout my life: Jack Fox, Michael Goldman, Rex Cowen, Gerald and Ida de Groot, Warren and Beth Robin. Michael and Eve Honey also formed part of this group but both died some years ago.

Gerald held Sunday morning open house for his friends which I often attended, meeting there many LSE and local friends such as Martin Shaw, Len Gatty and Warren. Occasionally I took my own friends along: Jack, Don Roodyn and both Michaels. We first heard the news of Beth's first pregnancy there. Sometimes Gerald's parents sat in with us; an entry dated 20th February records that *Mrs De Groot told me long stories about Gerald when three.* Marriage was in the air. Warren and Beth were already married and on 6th March my diary tells me that Michael Honey planned to marry Eve in Israel in summer. The entry continues: *As Mike always used to say "Man always pays for it in the end but he figures it different."* On 13th March I was again at *the de Groots and saw Martin and Len. Mr and Mrs de Groot went off to book the shul* [synagogue] *for the wedding – the boys thought up a joke or two about that.* This refers to Gerald's engagement to Ida; that much I know, but I wish I could recall the jokes.

The diary opens on New Year's Day with an account of a New Year's Eve party with Jessie *who would have been a consolation had she not fallen asleep.* Later we all went to the West End to mingle with the thronging crowds there and then *home with Don at 4am.* Jessie was an extremely attractive Trinidadian with whom I had a flingette until she returned home later that month. *What a charming girl she is!* I exclaim in that first entry but the girl I was a little in love with during these months was Theola Barnes. I took her to Covent Garden to see *The Marriage of Figaro* and though enamoured of her as I was, understated my feelings in a brief sentence: *It was a delightful performance and Theola is a delightful girl.* I phoned her a couple of weeks later: *she does not seem awfully enthusiastic to come out with me – gave me a long spiel about illness, tiredness, housework. A tentative invitation to come round for coffee next week at her place.* Ten days later I was round there; no coffee but off we went to the Hampstead Everyman to see Jean Cocteau's *Les Enfants Terribles.* Nothing more that day about Theola but a few words from my inner film critic. *Gripping but unhealthy – about incestuous relationship between brother and sister.* There are no more references to Theola after this and I express no sadness or regrets but throw myself into other activities and interest in other girls who appear on the social scene.

On the 2nd January *I went to Paul's social evening. Imagining us all to be suffering agonies of spiritual torment he provided us with a rabbi to answer our questions.* Our host, Paul Roodyn, was Don's brother, and because I was a frequent visitor to Don's house and Paul was always at home I knew him quite well. He was older than Don, timid, inward looking and lacking any social or sexual life; he had never been out with a girl and we all, including Don, looked on him as an oddball and misfit and much to my shame, teased and sometimes cruelly mocked him. Only a few weeks before his social I asked him how he was celebrating Christmas and before he could reply, Don chimed in, "No, he's celibating it!" Paul was furious, uncharacteristically swore at us and rushed out of the room.

Although I felt profoundly Jewish, lived in a Jewish neighbourhood and most of my friends were Jewish, we were all militantly secular atheists, left-wing in our politics and strong supporters of Israel. None of this prevented us from going out with non-Jewish girls but the issue of marrying out was very live. John Webber and Warren Robin married out, Gerald de Groot and Michael Honey in. I always assumed that I too would marry in and think this was 80% a question of cultural, or even racial, identity. But what is revealing about the diary is the paucity of reference to Jews or Jewishness apart from Paul's social, Gerald's parents going off to shul and the odd Jewish word thrown in here and there.

What I do regret is having no recall of what actually happened at Paul's social. Did we ask the rabbi any questions and if so what was their tenor? Did we listen to the answers or plunge into fruitless theological argument? Did we proudly proclaim our secular stances? Or did the Rabbi, as is the wont of clerics generally, assail us with a lengthy harangue, describing the joys of adopting a Judaic regime according to the strict laws of the Torah? Now that would have been interesting. Shortly after this event, Paul joined the ultraorthodox Jewish community in Gateshead. I assume that they speedily found him a wife because the present Rabbi of one of the North London synagogues is Jonathan Roodyn who is the right age to be Paul's son.

On the cultural front, I record numerous films, concerts, operas, plays and ballets. I was going through a ballet phase and for a time believed it to be the most exciting and integrated of all art forms. I saw Margo Fonteyn at Covent Garden in *Daphnis and Chloe*, and shortly after, Fonteyn again, Michael Somes and Beriosova in *Swan Lake*. This time it was my inner ballet critic that kicked in and I opined that *the principals' performances were excellent but the corps de ballet was ragged*. Lastly, Beriosova in *Coppelia – whole performance very good*.

There is much about finding a buyer for my old gramophone and buying a Pye Black Box on hire purchase. *It plays like a dream.* I recorded an eclectic list of music. Operas seen: *Marriage of Figaro, La Traviata* and *Prince Igor*. Concerts and music listened to and vinyl records borrowed from the record libraries of which I was a member: Hackney, Westminster and the American Embassy in Grosvenor Square.

I even seem to have squeezed in a few books, mainly middle of the road in taste: Ring Lardner, Ernest Hemingway, Christopher Isherwood, James Thurber. For deeper reading I had a go at *Human Society in Ethics and Politics* by Bertrand Russell. I obviously had an appetite for humorous books involving ballet and two books by Caryl Brahms and SJ Simon appear in my list, one of which, I found so funny that I re-read it two days later.

I already was showing signs of the avid TV watcher I was later to become, mainly films, plays and documentaries. I judged the Arthur Askey Show *the funniest thing I have ever seen; otherwise could life be duller?* which suggests that TV was the last resort when nothing more desirable was on offer. Films include several classics: *Les Enfants Terribles* (already mentioned), *How to Marry a Millionaire* (Marilyn Monroe, Betty Grable and Loren Bacall), *The Seven Samurai* (*Magnificent, a film classic* – great perspicacity on my part), *Vera Cruz* (Gary Cooper – *not bad, rip-roaring, fast-shooting*) and *Bad Day at Black Rock* (Spencer Tracy – *fine film*)

Two visits only to the theatre: The Arts, Ted Allen in *The Ghost Writer* – *shouted rather* and Ben Jonson's *Volpone* in modern dress at the Theatre Royal, Stratford – *excellent production on the whole*.

With all what now seems frenetic activity, I am amazed that I had time or energy to work and learn my craft. References to work include a farewell to JK – *the bugger didn't even shake my hand* and joining AE&P a few days later. Dolores soon became a social friend as did Rex and it is with Rex that my diary is spattered with outings and meeting girls.

Family rates far fewer mentions. My grandparents, living with us in Clapton do not even merit one. I took my mother to the cinema on one occasion. Alf and Rosa pay several visits, bringing a little life into our dullish household. I had *an awful row with mum arising out of its usual obscure origins.* When I recently read that, I thought, "So what had changed?" For as long as I can remember, I had a tempestuous relationship with my mother; she had a quick temper, the origins were always obscure and the rows always awful, within hours the content forgotten but Mum's silent punishment could go on for days. What is remarkable is that not more than *one awful row* is recorded over the period of the diary.

I suspect that all this manic activity betrays a more depressed or dissatisfied self. I can't get back to my twenty-five-year-old self and the diary, not being self-analytical or introspective does not help. As soon as the carousel stops the stationary me has time to reflect and that must have been painful. The most significant clue is to be found in the entry of 19th February. *A bad attack of 'phlegm'... Got up at 11.30 and did not move out of the house into the snowy wastes all day. Read the New Statesman and Times from cover to cover – watched television, spoke to two friends on the phone... Watched more TV. My God! What degeneration is eating at my soul.*

I cannot know what ailed me on the day of that entry, but guess that it was the same old sickness of the soul that propelled me nightly to the copse, tried to force myself to love Beryl and was sick at heart at my failure to secure Theola as a girlfriend. With my usual resilience and energy, I sprang back into action the next day – *Could not face the prospect of staying in another day in spite of appalling weather so phoned a friend* and went to Hampstead for tea. I think the truth was that I could not face myself alone, without the protection of company, an outing or visit. The diary begins to peter out at the end of March. There's a gap of one month from 4th April and the last short entry appears on the 5th May: *Had lunch with Michael. Very tired so went to bed early.* I cannot remember in any detail what happened after that. Perhaps at some level in those simple words I realised that the game was up and I needed a period of rest, recuperation and reflection before plunging back into the world of action, but in a less frenetic fashion.

One event not recorded in the diary stands out where I behaved so badly, so un-feelingly, that it has left me with an indelible sense of shame; sixty years on I still squirm whenever I recall it.

40. A VERY BAD THING

Sometime in April 1955, I went to a party in Bayswater given by an old prommer friend of mine, Ralph Levy, who had been part of the Door 11 gang. I hadn't seen much of him during the intervening years as he too had been in the Army, but in Germany, and then away at Bristol University. At the party I met his sister Doreen, a history teacher at a comprehensive school in Manor House. She had a flat in Finsbury Park and as this was on the Piccadilly Line on the way to Clapton it was natural for me to do the gentlemanly thing and take her home. She invited me for coffee. We talked and found we had a lot in common: Jewish background, secular left-wing convictions, youthful membership of *Habonim* and a passion for music. A passionate lover too and although I liked her and we had a great deal of fun together, I was not in love with her. But she was an oasis, offering much-needed refreshment in the arid sexual desert through which I had been trudging for more than a year. She was a lively companion and we became something of an item, going to concerts and other entertainments together. Without anything being said, I gained the impression that her feelings for me were stronger than mine for her.

One evening we were in Doreen's flat, chatting and listening to records when the phone rang. Doreen took the call and when it had ended she was in a state of irritation.

"That was Ralph. He's having another bloody party. You're invited of course. What the hell is up with him?"

"What the hell is up with you?" I asked.

"Boring, boring, boring! It's a kind of showing off. All those dull people he collects. What's it all for?"

Doreen didn't get on with her brother. She had spent much time talking about this, complaining that he was controlling, was her big brother and acted like one, disapproved of her teaching in a deprived area, living in Finsbury Park and her lifestyle generally. I had listened sympathetically but without offering much in the way of useful advice; as an only child the ways of siblings were a closed book to me.

"And there's another thing", she added. "He's bloody gone and invited Kay."

"Who's Kay?"

"Our cousin."

"What's wrong with her?"

"Oh, there's nothing wrong with her. Well there is, but it's only me being bitchy."

After a short pause I said, "Go on, be bitchy!"

"I'm sure it's only because I'm jealous of her. I really shouldn't be; she's only nineteen. Very beautiful. Talk about silver spoon. Dad's rich and spoils her rotten. Best clothes money can buy. Finishing school in Tring. She's there now so I suppose she'll stay at Ralph's – I think he's a bit sweet on her."

"I can't wait to meet her"

"Oh you!" she exclaimed, hurling a cushion at me, jumping onto my lap and pummelling my chest.

Doreen and I arrived at the party. I immediately spotted Kay. She was indeed beautiful. Stunningly so. Tall, slim hipped, full breasted, long black hair tied at the nape by a small scarf and with the dusky, olive skinned complexion of a biblical Israelite maiden, not surprising as she was Jewish. She had a slight awkwardness in her movements as though she was determined to persevere in her stilettos but was not completely at home in them. We danced and I was lost and so was she. I ignored Doreen for the rest of the evening and left with Kay. My parents were on holiday so we went back to their vacant bedroom.

In the morning I was preparing breakfast for the two of us when my grandmother came into the kitchen to get something from the fridge she shared with my mother. I grabbed her arm, pointed to the bedroom and said urgently and sotto voce, "There's a girl in there, I brought her home last night."

My diminutive grandma looked up at me, her face wreathed in a beatific smile and said "Did you slipp mit her?"

I popped out to the shops to buy a few things for lunch and the Sunday papers, my mind in a whirl of Darwinian derived thoughts. What a wonderful wife she would make, what wonderful children she would bear. I was in a state of awe at her beauty and tenderness and having chosen me. After lunch we spent the rest of the day together, walking in Regent's Park and I saw her off to Tring from Marylebone station.

The next day, all hell broke loose. Ralph was on the phone to me before I left the house for work.

"How could you do such a thing? How could you treat Doreen like that? She was distraught and inconsolable. You humiliated her. You betrayed our friendship. Apart from being a babysnatcher. Didn't you know she's only nineteen? She's just an innocent. You took advantage. I was responsible for her and I've let her and my uncle and aunt down. The whole family is up in arms. What are *you* going to do about it?"

What indeed? Thoughts of Doreen had been driven out of my mind while I was with Kay but once we had parted, while I had no regrets for what I had done, I did feel a great sense of guilt. I had treated her despicably. I was nothing but a cad to cause another human being such pain and even though that was not my intention, if I had stopped to think for a moment, I could have foreseen the outcome for her. But I did not think. I was incapable of thinking in the face of the intensity of the attraction which Kay and I instantly felt for each other. As soon as I got home that evening, I wrote a long letter to Doreen full of *meae culpae* and 'I don't know what came over me' and posted it the next morning – for all the good it did. Now an old man, I do regret my actions that weekend; in fact, they are up there with the three or four major regrets of my life, one of the worst things I have ever done.

None of the furore and distress stopped me from pursuing a relationship with Kay during the remainder of her summer term in Tring. I visited her there one brilliant July day, a charming ancient town. We had tea in an olde worlde tea shoppe and then visited the Rothschild Natural History Museum, with its extraordinary collection of stuffed animals. I would never have known of Tring or its museum had I not met Kay. She came up to London several times and we wandered the London parks and I introduced her to Hampstead and Hampstead Heath. The sun never ceased shining during that summer which matched perfectly the heat and blinding brightness of my infatuation with her.

Our little Eden was not to last; enter the serpent in the form of Kay's mother who came to London to spy out the lie of the land and in particular to meet and quiz the, no doubt, demonised beau of her daughter. It was all put quite delicately as an invitation to tea but in effect I was summoned for scrutiny to the hotel where she was staying and subjected to a lengthy interrogation about my family, their jobs and backgrounds and my own, at that time, very uncertain prospects. I was no doubt adjudged unworthy to associate with her daughter and although I thought I had acquitted myself quite well and courteously in the circumstances, I could not help but feel a smidgeon of disapproval towards me on Mrs Levy's part. Kay was present but said not a word. It was my turn to feel humiliated; that I was not good enough in myself but had to pass socially and financially before I could be admitted as a suitor. Although my mother and father were now together, this interview opened old wounds and felt very much like Beryl questioning me about my father.

There were other ways in which Kay reminded me of Beryl. I loved being with Kay. I had never had such a gorgeous girlfriend before and was proud to be with her and to be seen with her. But as the summer wore on I began to realise that she was not the one. There was no commonality of cultural interests. At her school her strong suit was dance, particularly ballroom dancing. I actually attended an event in which she was judged on her dancing as part of a diploma she was working for. This was such a strange world to me and the people involved felt so alien that I began to see that we could never be a couple – our interests and aspirations were too far apart.

Towards the end of July, the academic year came to an end and Kay returned to the parental home in Leeds. We kept up a sporadic correspondence which soon petered out and I never saw her again. I resumed a friendship with Ralph from whom I learned later that year that Kay had married a Dr Paul Greenberg. My uncharitable thought was that her parents, rattled by her affair with me, had determined to put her out of harm's way by getting her respectably married without delay.

41. LAST LAP TO QUALIFICATION

I cannot say I was heartbroken. Kay was not the girl in the copse made flesh, beautifully put together though that flesh was. I became busier and more experienced at AE&P and I even had a room of my own there. After a holiday in the South of France, I took the customary six months off to prepare for Law Society finals and joined the crammer course run by Gibson & Weldon in Chancery Lane. *Crammer* described the course precisely; they not only crammed huge quantities of law into us – there were seven three-hour papers to take – but also crammed forty or so of us into an overheated basement room, bare of everything but rows of long tables at which we sat for three hours on end, copying notes dictated to us by our lecturers. The combination of heat and the monotony induced by this method of teaching – effective though it was in getting us through the exams – frequently caused me to nod off and my normally legible handwriting rapidly became an unreadable scrawl and finally flatlined completely.

We had two principal teachers: Mr Passingham, toothbrush moustache, brisk, very much the Major, who enunciated the law in the barking, clipped manner of an officer issuing orders or reprimanding a particularly stupid rookie. Although this was long before the advent of *Dads' Army* on our television screens, Mr Passingham reminds me now of a more peppery Captain Mainwaring. The other teacher, Mr Darnell, was tall, thin, dark haired, with a sombre face, aquiline nose and deep resonant voice. If an actor, he would have made a very passable Sherlock Holmes. In lecturing/dictating he had a clear delivery and a habit of dramatically lowering his voice half an octave and extending the final digraph when speaking the word *death*. This was a common occurrence as the subjects he taught included Wills and Probate.

At the end of these afternoon sessions a group of us would make for the Lyons cafe opposite for tea and toast and to let off steam, criticise the course and mock the teachers and then make for home to mug up on the day's lectures in readiness for the frequent tests designed to keep us on our toes.

I had made a vow to renounce all fleshly and other temptations for the whole of this study period and succeeded in keeping to a rigorously monastic regime but not without some resentment. On a beautiful Whit Monday – then a bank holiday – I took my notes to Springfield Park. The park was packed with people, playing putting, tennis, picnicking, reading or just sitting in the sun while I was struggling to memorise the provisions of the Law of Property Act 1925. I envied them their carefree enjoyment and was filled with longing for the time, which then seemed so far off, when I could join them.

The course ended, leaving me eight weeks to revise on my own. I worked very hard and on the day before the first exam, Bryan popped in to wish me luck, adding that I would never again know so much law as at that moment. And so I was on the last but exhausting stretch of the road to qualification. There were seven papers in the first week and five honours papers in the second, that is thirty-six hours of exams spread over ten days. Honours were optional but I thought I'd have a go.

42. PARIS 1956

Results were not due until October, as was the expiration of my articles at AE&P. Bryan had been spending time in Paris with his cousin Arnold Wesker who was living and working there with his wife-to-be, Dusty. I wangled an invitation for myself for six weeks from mid-August.

Arnold and Dusty were living in a single room in the *l'Hotel Windsor*, rue de l'Ancienne Comedie, just off Boulevard St Germain with Odeon Metro station at the corner and were both working at le Rallye restaurant, Arnold as a chef, Dusty in a more menial position in the kitchen.

Arnold met me off the airport bus and on the taxi to the hotel told me that he had organised a party for me in their room. Some years ago, browsing through the remaindered section of my local bookshop, I came across a copy of Arnold's autobiography, *As Much as I Dare*. Much to my surprise the book contained a lengthy account of that party:

Cousin Bryan had by this time spent his holiday with us in Paris, sleeping on a spare mattress on the floor of our room in Rue de L'Ancienne Comedie. We'd given him a good time, shown him the sights, partnered him off with Dusty's friend, Marianne. Boris, Bryan's friend from college, had just finished law exams and was soon to become a lawyer in partnership with him. He had heard from Bryan about his exotic days in Paris and asked could he too share our room for exotic days in Paris – the rent sounded most reasonable. We extended an invitation to the city about which we were becoming proprietarily proud, and he wrote back heady with expectations: would we not only reveal the world's most exciting city but also – find him 'a woman'? We promised him hospitality, exotic days and – a woman.

Boris was an affable young man in the tradition of Jewish humanism, declaring his love of the Sunday Observer and the weekend Statesman and Nation. With a degree of self-serving self-deprecation, he claimed that we – he included us in his 'we' – belonged to that new group of ineffectual young intellectuals characterised in books we'd not yet heard of like Lucky Jim by a new novelist called Kingsley Amis, and plays like – he'd named another we'd not yet caught up with – Look Back in Anger by a young playwright called somebody Osborne. Boris's view of human behaviour in those days was that there was a reason for all things whether that reason was known or not – not a view with which I had sympathy. Art and music, he said, meant a lot to him, but although I could see he was alive to them I was never certain he was alive through them. Widely read, intelligent, witty – I felt he worked at himself too much. He must be a very different person today, but in his eager days – well, the lad wanted a woman? Then he should have one.

The plot involved our friends and neighbours in Hotel Windsor – Dolores and Jose, the fiery flamenco dancers. He was Mexican, she was from the States. A dark, handsome couple, looking their parts. As soon as Boris arrived, we were agog with news of a beautiful Spanish woman, married to a Spanish man of violence who fortunately was never there since he travelled the world conducting nefarious deals, leaving his wife to seek tenderness and kindness where she could, when she could, from whomsoever she could during his long absences. Which agogged Boris! His gullible, handsome eyes shone with masculine protectiveness and tumescent promise.

With our black-haired, dark eyed bohemian friends, we arranged that shortly after introducing Dolores to Boris – a tryst planned for our room - 'the husband' would burst through the door, utter bloodcurdling summonses and threats, Dolores would scream, swoon away upon our bed, leaving Dusty and me to freeze with horror.

Boris couldn't wait for rendezvous hour. During the minutes leading up to it we stirred his blood and expectations with a mixture of Latin promise and descriptions of her Latin lover's uncontrollably jealous rages which, fortunately, were many miles away. The appointed moment ticked into place, Dolores entered. She was breathtakingly bizarre. She had put together a personality we had never seen, theatrical and stereotypical beyond our imaginings. High heels, black stockings, flamenco-style black dress, mantilla complete with the veil, the longest eyelashes in the world and a cigarette plunged into a cigarette holder you could play billiards with. Dusty and I gaped and swallowed our laughter, but Boris fluttered and shook with excitement like a small puppy about to be fed, or stroked or shown a playmate. He barely knew what to do with himself, what to say, where to place his limbs, how to address her. Nothing so exotic had ever entered his life. Nor ours, come to that. Dolores played her role a touch over the par of subtlety, talking to him about God knows what while we tiptoed around making tea or coffee or something. I seem to remember that she spoke to him pathetically, seeking his sympathy, his pity for her plight of abandoned, brutalised wife. Boris was all sympathy and Anglo-Jewish gallantry until, on cue, came a loud and frightening banging on our door and the voice of violent Spanish spousedom thundered through the thin wood.

Dolores screamed and assumed a look of fear and terror. I said something like 'Oh my God, it's him!' and urged Boris to flee in danger of his life. Poor Boris, flee to where? His murderer was the other side of the only exit available. All that was left were the windows. Even if he could get to them in time he'd break his legs from the drop. Sliced jugular or splintered limbs – a harsh choice for a young man who had psyched himself up to experience life's darker passions rather than it's bloody ones, to clutch breasts not drainpipes. The only place he could think to hide was along the wall against which the door would almost certainly be crashed open by the jealous husband with no regard for what might stand behind it. Boris might be bruised by the slam but – briefly he'd be hidden. Or was it me who grabbed and thrust him there? The door was catapulted open and the most ferocious looking Jose strode three paces into the room brandishing a long knife. Dolores swooned. Boris, seeing the two Spaniards engrossed by one another, sidled around the door and fled. I rushed to close it after him and we all waited, with breath held, before collapsing into uncontrollable laughter. I found him some time later hiding in the lavatory under the staircase. He was hurt and very angry when told the truth.

His protestations of injustice were, I have to confess, justified: he had not been given the opportunity to be so brave since I had told him to flee for his life. Besides, he didn't see the point in dying for a pleasure he'd not achieved. And what, he asked, would we have done in the circumstances? What would anyone else have done? I suggested that even though I might not have thrown myself in front of the woman to defend her, others, braver than either of us, might have done. Or attempted to disarm the assailant. Or at least cried 'Help!' Boris was not persuaded. Though he was finally amused. Sheepishly.

© Copyright Arnold Wesker 2016.

In mitigation of his mockery at my request that *he find me a woman*, I would plead my renunciation of all distractions whilst studying for the Law Society finals and had scarcely spoken to a girl, let alone take on one out, for more than six months. At that time, I still nursed the fantasy that Paris was a city of louche bohemianism, love and easy-going morals and that Arnold with his love of poetry and dreams of literary fame would be bound to mix in a circle containing interesting, attractive young women.

There are other brief references to me in his book [pages 237, 419 and 451]. His description of me as having taken a degree in psychiatry is forgivable but wrong. In fact, I had met him at a party and in catching up with each other, I mentioned that I had qualified as a psychoanalytic psychotherapist and that led to an interesting discussion in which Arnold maintained that under no circumstances would he undergo any kind of analysis for fear of taming his creative daemon.

Also mentioned on pages 419 and 426 is Marianne who was introduced to me by Arnold and Dusty (perhaps as reparation for the trick they perpetrated on me) and who became my girlfriend during the whole of my stay. She was Finnish, fair with large blue eyes and full lips, warm and open; staying in Paris as an au pair girl with a family who lived in a palatial flat in Avenue des Ternes, a short walk from l'Etoile. We saw much of each other, visiting Montmartre, art galleries, going to the cinema and sitting for hours listening to the guitar playing, folk song singing students on Pont Neuf. On nights when she was babysitting I would keep her company in her flat.

Sleeping in the same room as Arnold and Dusty caused no embarrassment; they left the hotel while I was still asleep and went to bed long before me. Often they would bring back prime steak, duck or other items pilfered from their restaurant. I for my part shopped most days for the three of us at the local market from lists of food prepared by Dusty. This together with a third of the rent was my contribution to communal expenses.

Most mornings I spent having coffee at Le Relais, a cafe on Boulevard St Germain. Mysteriously, through the freemasonry of youth, I gradually built up a number of cafe acquaintances of whom I remember two artists, John and Mary Clarke and Raoul, a guitarist, whom I met while he was busking outside the Relais and with whom I remained friends both during and after my stay in Paris. Raoul's parents who were political refugees from Franco's Spain, lived just up the road from the *Windsor* and I was a frequent visitor to their flat where we discussed music and international politics.

On the day before I left I bought thank you presents for my hosts: *The Brothers Karamazov*, Arnold's choice, from Shakespeare & Company and for Dusty, *Je Reviens* perfume from la Samaritaine. I said my goodbyes to Marianne, we vowed to write and we did but our correspondence – as with so many holiday romances – petered out after a few months. She returned to Finland and we both resumed our day-to-day lives. I had had discussions with Arnold about his future; at that time, he was keen to develop his creative life within the cinema and I promised that once back in London I would find out about film courses and send him details. I kept my word and at the end of the year he returned to London with Dusty and embarked on a six-month course at the London School of Film Technique.

43. FIRST JOB

For my part, I was quickly thrust back into the life I had chosen for myself as a way of steadying myself down and ensuring that I would not end up rudderless like my father. While I waited for my results and went off to job interviews, I went back to AE&P to bring up-to-date and hand over my, by then, heavy caseload. The day of the Final results arrived; they were to be notified at 2pm at the Law Society's Hall in Chancery Lane. Many of my friends from the LSE were there. At 2pm sharp, lists of the successful candidates were pinned to the noticeboard. We had all passed and I had also gained third class honours although I had done nothing in the way of additional study to achieve this.

Cyril Goldberg, although a barrister had come along for support and joined Brian Cookson, Harry Futerman, Stan Jones and me for a celebratory drink at the Seven Stars just round the corner in Carey Street. For me it was the end of six long years of hardship and heartache and the beginning of a thirty-year career as a solicitor.

I secured a job right away as litigation solicitor at Tatton, Gaskell and Tatton, a High Street firm, but what a high street, Kensington High Street, within a stone's throw of Kensington Palace and Barkers and Derry and Toms department stores, now both closed and housing other retailers. No sooner had I fixed a starting date than I went down with a bad flu which took me to my bed for several days. This was October 1956 and though ill I was completely swept up by the dramas which were being played out on the international stage. Nasser, president of Egypt, had declared the nationalisation of the Suez Canal, so exappropriating it from Britain and France. Anthony Eden, the British Prime Minister, colluded with his counterparts in France and Israel to mount an invasion of Egypt to prevent this. Meanwhile, Hungary, a vassal state of the Soviet Union, in a bloodless coup, overthrew the Communist government and installed a democratic one. The Soviet Union, not prepared to relinquish its domination of Hungary, sent in its army to squash the infant democracy. With the invasion of Egypt taking up Britain's full attention, it was difficult for it and its French ally to exercise any restraint over Russia, particularly in the face of the argument that if they were entitled to use armed force to protect its vital interests, so was Russia. Even though I was a devoted supporter of Israel, from my sick bed and reading the Times and the Daily Mirror from cover to cover, I was far better informed than usual and condemned the government for its reversion to imperialistic ways of solving international problems, rather than through the United Nations. I was so indignant with the Eden-led Conservative government that for the first (and only) time I wrote to my MP, David Weizmann along these lines. The American president, Eisenhower, was also furious with Britain for invading a sovereign country and threatened to withdraw all financial support. Britain was so dependent on American economic help that Eden had no alternative but to withdraw our troops from Egypt. Russia unopposed by the West resumed its control of Hungary.

The crisis passed as did my flu and I joined the firm of Tatton, Gaskell and Tatton. It was a small firm, the senior partner, an elderly bachelor, Mr Lewis, was remote and gentlemanly and dealt with most of the firm's conveyancing. Leonard Darke, in his early 40s, was the junior partner. I think he too was a conveyancer but I never did understand precisely what he did or what part he played in the power structure of the firm in so far as there was one. What I did know about, because he told me frequently and at great length, were his musical connections. He was a keen amateur pianist, an indefatigable concertgoer and shared a love of classical music with me, though there was no sharing of conversation as he cornered me almost daily to boast of those connections: his uncle, the organist Harold Darke, his client, the singer Joan Sutherland and his distinguished piano teachers.

On my first day I was invited to lunch by the probate managing clerk, Mr Fairclough and the firm's cashier, Mr Dawson, at the dining room of a large institutional building catering for the elderly, just off Kensington Church Street. Mr Fairclough's entrée to this facility was through his frequent visits to old people who wanted to make a will. For a few pence we tucked into mince and mash and spotted dick, plain fare but tasty enough and filling. On the way back to the office we popped into The Windsor Castle, a pub I have always loved for its secluded garden in the heart of London. The secretary allocated to me was a plain middle-aged woman, Miss Worne, pleasant, very professional and efficient.

The work was not heavy, consisting mainly of divorce and landlord and tenant disputes. I was bored; the practice lacked the dynamism and youth of AE&P and I missed it. The firm was genteel and formal, bordering on the fuddy-duddy and I lacked the fun and energy of colleagues of my own age. My room overlooked Kensington High Street and when I wasn't busy, I looked out of my window at the people passing by and I wished that I was one of them as I fantasised the exciting lives they led. I dreamed of action, running my own practice, free from the constraints of my old-fashioned, stuck-in-the mud firm. Still a socialist, I despised the affluent and stuffy middle-class clientele we served. There were occasional enlivening moments such as the arrival of a beautiful young woman from Iceland who was seeking a divorce from her English husband, or anxiety provoking ones, as when a client was involved in a planning dispute with Kensington Council and I was completely ignorant of planning law.

What I claimed I wanted was a working-class practice in the East End of London, but what I really wanted was a practice like that of AE&P, with offices in the West End, successful and stuffed full of Jewish clients.

Sometimes I went to lunch on my own, visiting the roof garden at Derry and Toms, 100 feet above Kensington High Street, a haven of peace and beauty where I would eat a sandwich and read a book, often pausing to carry on dreaming of a better life. Mr Lewis, old woman-ish though he was, lived well. He had a flat in Dolphin Square and owned an Armstrong Siddeley Sapphire, a luxury car of its day, in which he took all the executive members of his firm to the Law Society's refresher lectures in Chancery Lane. On one occasion he invited me to dinner at the Dolphin Square restaurant and I reciprocated by asking him to join me to see John Osborne's *Look Back In Anger* at the Royal Court Theatre. The truth was that I had bought two tickets hoping to lure one of my many women friends to accompany me to the play, but not one was willing or available. I found the play funny, groundbreaking and thrilling. It chimed in precisely with my own feelings of frustration with the dead hands of tradition, formality and stiff–upper–lipness which characterised Britain then. After the play ended Mr Lewis and I went for a drink.

"Well Mr Lewis, how did you enjoy it?" I asked.

"It was very well acted. I just didn't understand it."

"What was it you didn't understand?"

"The character of Jimmy Porter. Spoilt, rude young man. What has he got to be angry about?"

I embarked on an analysis of what I saw in the play as a critique of our old, deadbeat, backward looking society but Mr Lewis was not convinced.

"I can't see what the young man had to complain about. The country's never been so prosperous."

With these words Mr Lewis predated by several months, Prime Minister Harold Macmillan's famous assertion that we had never had it so good.

44. MAIDA VALE

One of my many women friends was Stella Isaacs, a pleasant young woman with a slight but becoming lisp. Her family was affluent; her father owned a successful chandler's shop in Lower Road, Rotherhithe in the heart of the London Docklands. Stella went to the progressive co-educational Bedales School, followed by a spell at St Martin's School of Art and when I first knew her, she worked as a window dresser at Liberty's in Regent Street. We were friends for a number of years and amongst the many people she introduced me to, was Ivor Viner, four years older than me, tall and slim with a long broody face, luminous dark eyes and jet black hair, slicked back in the fashion of the day. He worked in the family fake fur manufacturing business but was deeply dissatisfied with his lot, was a convinced socialist and yearned for a more creative life. We became good friends and through me he got to know Michael Goldman. In January 1957 he phoned me with a startling proposition: an uncle of his owned a property in Maida Vale, the ground floor had become vacant and his uncle wanted it occupied by a family member. The rent was £5 per week, there was room enough for three, so my share would be £1.50, Ivor bearing the larger share as he would appropriate the best room for himself. Was I on? Subject to seeing the place, with great enthusiasm, I said yes.

"Would Michael like to join us?" he asked.

"I'll find out," I replied.

Michael was interested, so we both arranged to see the flat. Number 20, Maida Avenue was just off the Edgware Road in Little Venice and Maida Avenue itself ran alongside the Regents Canal. The flat was large; Ivor's room faced on to the canal as did the one I opted for. Michael preferred the larger bedroom overlooking the extensive and pretty rear garden, the main disadvantage of which was that an *en suite* bathroom, to be used by us all, was within it. There was a kitchen and dining/living room to be shared by the three of us. We were to establish a once a week rota for communal shopping, splitting the cost three ways. We both agreed to join in the venture on the spot, Michael was to move in in two weeks, I a few weeks later at the beginning of March.

That very evening I broached the subject of my move to my mother. She was aghast.

"Boris, why are you doing this?"

"Getting to the office will be much easier: tube from Warwick Avenue to Paddington, then..."

"Yes, but why are you doing it?".

"Well there are other reasons of course: Little Venice is lovely and with Ivor and Michael, social life..."

"Aren't you happy here?"

"Of course I am but I'm coming up twenty-seven and..."

"So you're not happy here?"

"Mum, I am but I want to..."

"People will think there something wrong between us."

So that was it. People would think. Even a financially independent Jewish male didn't leave home unless it was to get married. If you did, people would think the worst.

I moved in on an early spring morning. London was fresh and sparkling. I bought a bunch of daffodils at the flower shop on the bridge at the corner of Edgware Road and Maida Avenue before strolling down Maida Avenue itself to my new home, feeling alive and excited at the prospect of the new independent life ahead of me, one I had not led since St. Asaph, seven years before.

Independence, to freedom, to liberty, to taking liberties, to libertine. The lack of parental surveillance, disapproval, judgmentalism and frequent rows, particularly with my mother, as I struggled against her familial expectations of me, was intoxicating and I took full advantage of it. I went through a period of serial pursuit: Malika, a French au pair I met at a dance, Anne Muggeridge leader of the Royal Festival Ballet's corps de ballet. Even a short fling with Dolores. All brief affairs.

But I also loved the flat, the area, the way of life. The three of us got on well, sometimes we ate and socialised together, sometimes separately. When I ate alone, I bought fillet steak from Barkers food department. At weekends we shopped locally for the week ahead and pottered and read in our garden or by the pool at the confluence of the Regents Canal and Paddington Basin.

In August Michael and I set off in his little blue Austin 30 along the A1 to the north. We made a brief stop at Durham to visit the great Norman cathedral. As we stood in the nave marvelling at the size and solidity of the ancient building.

Michael said, "All that driving. I'm really tired."

Without a beat I replied, "Take a pew!", pointing to the seating to our left.

That was one of the high points of our holiday as far as I was concerned although Edinburgh in Festival time came pretty close. We stayed the two days taking in the Monet exhibition and the Monte Carlo ballet before pushing on to Skye and Portree. On the second day we set off on a hike to the Cuillins Mountains but rain of increasing intensity drove us back and it continued day after day. We had a shot at redeeming the holiday by holing up in Oban but the rain followed us and we left the morning after going to a dance in a hall which was so misty and murky that we couldn't even make out the attractiveness or otherwise of the girls lining the walls, waiting to be asked to dance. Two days later we were back in sunny London, and for me, the reality of some fundamental changes to my professional and personal life.

45. SOLE PRACTITIONER

The deal was unspoken but clear. I had completed a number of routine tasks at the High Court and was in the Temple delivering papers to Counsel's Chambers when I bumped into Cyril.

"Boris, long time no see. How's life treating you?"

"Can't grumble. Life's good but I'm bored out of my mind at Tatton, Gaskell & Tatton."

"What's boring? The work?"

"No, the work's fine. It's the people. They're so old and stuffy. My boss is so terrified of losing papers that we are not allowed files; everything has to go into large brown envelopes. It wasn't like that at Alan, Edmunds and Phillips. Anyway, how's your job?"

Cyril had opted to become a Civil Service lawyer.

"Comfortable but boring. Both the work and the people. The only thing that keeps me going is the free legal advice service I run at the Canning Town Women's Settlement."

"Interesting. What sort of cases do you get?"

"Oh, all sorts. Work accidents, mainly dockers. Lots of divorce and matrimonial. Tenancy disputes. A bit of crime. I can only give them advice; if they need a solicitor I refer them on. You know, if you had a practice nearby I could send you two or three cases a week."

We parted and as I made my way back to Kensington my mind was whirling. A practice of my own! It was something I yearned for. Files instead of envelopes! It seemed out of the question until my chance meeting with Cyril. But I knew there was a subtext. Cyril's partner, Valerie, had recently been called to the Bar. She was trying to build up a practice but in those male dominated days, work for a newly qualified woman barrister was thin on the ground. The quid pro quo for Cyril's referrals was that I would instruct Valerie whenever the stage of instructing a barrister was reached in one of his cases. This caused me some misgivings which I quickly stilled. Valerie was a bright girl, she had done well in her law degree and I could always give her a try. What was friendship for? Anyway I would always be in control and could discontinue giving her work if she proved incompetent. So I argued myself through and out of the moral maze.

The next few months were a frenzy of activity. Ambition and desire brought out untried aspects of myself: planner, opportunist, negotiator, man of action. First I had to find premises, preferably in Canning Town. I was very lucky, the only bank in Canning Town, Barclays, had three first-floor rooms available at the rent of £150 p.a.

Money was the next problem as I did not have the resources to finance the project myself. I approached my old principal, Alan Rubenstein. His firm already had branch offices in North and South London, so I thought he might be interested in investing in one in East London. I was right and I negotiated very generous terms. They would pay for the setting up costs, to be repaid once the practice was up and running and I would be paid a guaranteed £600 p.a plus 60% of the new firm's profits, the remaining 40% to be theirs. Just as important to my status-conscious self, I would become a partner of Alan Edmunds & Phillips. The fact that my income would be limited to the Canning Town practice did not matter to me; I was to be a partner in a well-known and successful West End firm. And there was in me a residual socialist idealism which motivated my move from affluent, middle-class Kensington to Canning Town. I had always had the dream of running a neighbourhood law firm in a deprived area and until I arrived, there are was no other solicitor practising in Canning Town.

The office suite I had found was ideal for a one-man practice. The large corner room I appropriated as mine. The middle sized room was perfect for a secretary, or two if pushed, and the smallest would serve as a waiting room. Alan had a client who owned a second-hand office furniture shop. I selected an imposing desk and a swivel chair for myself, two ordinary chairs for clients and other essential items for operating an office. My parents were in the process of re-furnishing their sitting room and for my waiting-room, I took over their dilapidated, gingery-brown, leather three-piece suite which they had bought new in 1927, the year they married. The Oxford Street office donated a large Olivetti typewriter, surplus to their requirements. I was starting my new professional life on a shoestring, but I was used to living on a shoestring and in any event the austere furnishing of my office was more than compensated for by the arrival from our printers of the firm's stationery with *Boris Rumney LLB (Hons)* appearing on the list of partners. Once the offices were adequately furnished, I opened the doors for business early in November 1957.

Cyril was as good as his word and referred two clients in the first week: an industrial accident and a divorce. By the end of the month I had about twenty cases, but even though I was my own typist, twenty cases did not constitute a caseload and I had plenty of spare time to explore and familiarise myself with my new environment.

The Bank at 103 Barking Road had been recently rebuilt on a bomb site. The ground floor was occupied by the Bank and for the sake of convenience and in the hope that they would recommend their customers to me, I opened the firm's accounts, as well as my own, with them. I shared the first floor with Mr Bennett, an elderly dentist, whose National Health patients thronged the shared entrance hall all day long. Mr Bennett's dental technician, Mr French, had his own small room, crammed with the tools, materials and products of his craft. Dozens of sets of false teeth, gleaming white, grinned ghoulishly at you from their shelves as they waited for their owners to be fitted with them. This macabre sight suggested that Mr Bennett's professional preference was for extraction rather than conservation.

The second floor was a flat occupied by Ted and Marion Day, former bank employees, now spending their retirement as grace and favour tenants and housekeepers, responsible for keeping the building secure and cleaning the bank premises. On the day of my arrival, unasked, they provided me with drinks and sandwiches and within days I arranged for them to take on the cleaning of my offices.

Barking Road was a bustling shopping street with wide pavements, a Woolworth, a large municipal library (which I immediately joined) and several shops owned by the Granditer family, including a gents' outfitters and a furniture shop, displaying cheap, flashy goods (including one item that caught my eye: a giant cabinet radiogram at 39 guineas) and advertising them all on easy terms.

I spent much of my empty time during these early days looking out of the picture windows in my office. Opposite was the busy Ordnance Road street market as well as a large bomb site always crowded with people trawling through the piles of second-hand clothing, bedding, kitchenware and electrical goods on sale there. It resembled the poverty-stricken Third World markets you see on television today.

London districts were greatly more class-stratified than now and Canning Town was overwhelmingly working-class. Its inhabitants lived in the row upon row of identical nineteenth century, two-storey terraced houses. There were numerous factories, including the Tate & Lyle sugar refinery. The Royal Group of docks was packed with commercial shipping and employed thousands of dockers. It was from this huge pool of workers that I hoped to build a busy industrial injury practice.

As a matter of economic and geographical convenience I had moved back to my parents' home in Clapton. Canning Town was not the easiest place for me to get to from there but I still retained some of my boyish love of trains and my preferred route was the steam train from South Tottenham to Canning Town passing through the massive marshalling yards and industrial wasteland north of Stratford, now transformed into the Olympic Park.

My move from Maida Vale to Clapton coincided with a big row with

Ivor over our tripartite arrangement to share the shopping for communal food and other staples every Saturday. As soon as the Canning Town project was mooted, I became very busy looking for premises, attending meetings and generally preparing the ground for opening the practice, so I excused myself from taking my turn in the shopping rota. This understandably caused some resentment but there was another factor. Ivor wanted to install his new girlfriend, Joan, in the flat and was looking for a pretext to free up some accommodation. I provided that pretext.

"These apples are really sour", I grumbled

"That's the thanks I get from doing your shopping."

"I am not criticising you, Ivor. It's the apples."

"I don't care. It's your ingratitude I can't bear."

"Look I'm sorry. I am grateful. But that doesn't alter the objective fact that the apples are sour."

"See! You're still on about the apples. You just don't get it do you?"

"Get what?"

"That you're a selfish, insensitive sod. I can't stand you. I want you to leave. By the end of next week."

"That's fine by me. I was going to leave anyway."

True, but it felt a little lame as I was being thrown out and not going in my own time.

I advertised for a secretary and Nadine Ellis appeared while I was two-finger-typing a long letter. I think she was very impressed by this. I was certainly impressed by her. She was a strikingly pretty blonde of nineteen, and I immediately took to her lively and open manner. After a brief interview, I offered her the job and she accepted. She was still with my firm when I retired in 1987. We became and still are good friends.

In fact, I phoned her to record her memories of our first few months together:

"You were very nice and patient and explained things because I didn't have a clue about legal work. You taught me how to organise briefs and legal documents. You also taught me how to play chess in our lunch hours. I just loved meeting all the clients. The first Christmas there were just the two of us, too few for a party, so you took me out to dinner at a posh restaurant in Stratford, I think it was. The waiter came round with an *hors d'oeuvres* trolley. I was a real greener then and had no idea what to choose, so you stepped in and said, 'The lady will have a little of everything'."

She assumed gallant gentlemanliness on my part but I suspect that I was preparing the way to ask for a little of everything myself

Within months I was frantically busy. Work poured in from all quarters. Cyril sent me two or three cases a week, a mixture of personal injury and divorce cases. I became friendly with Mr Thomas, the bank manager. We often lunched together at The Royal Oak, a pub a few yards down the Barking Road and he began to refer bank customers, usually in a small way of business, who needed a solicitor for a whole range of services: making wills, buying houses, taking or granting leases, collecting debts and commercial disputes. Walk-in clients began to walk in. Recent immigrants from the Indian subcontinent, usually called Singh, appeared whose first words to me were: "You get me mortgage?" or, thinking more suspiciously about it now: "You get me passport?"

My biggest haul was Popular Garages (opposite the bank). I was also building up my own personal connection – family and friends and their recommendations.

In those days it was common for sole practitioners to be generalists and the rapid build-up of the variety of work, typical of a High Street practice, was valuable experience. Very soon I needed help and AE&P posted Barry Spencer, one of their articled clerks, to give me a hand. Another visit to the furniture shop. My room was large enough to accommodate another desk (obviously smaller than mine) and before long Barry was handling a caseload of his own under my supervision.

Being the boss of my own practice triggered in me an insatiable appetite for new work. All my energies and efforts went into the work and expanding the practice. I began to go into the office on Saturday mornings, to see clients who could only manage that day. I socialised with one eye on potential clients. My ambition to create a large practice bordered on the obsessional. I took on any work that came my way, big or small. Even though I had no experience of advocacy, I appeared in cases for clients in Bow County Court and in minor criminal and driving offences at West Ham and Stratford Magistrate Courts.

They were not my proudest professional moments; I was not a very good advocate and had a tendency to get tied up in laborious, fruitless cross-examinations which irritated the judge or magistrates and probably worked to my clients' detriment. The outcome of my criminal cases became a standing joke among my friends. I would regale them with accounts of these.

"So what was the verdict?"

"Guilty."

"And the sentence?"

"Prison. Three months."

I dined out on these stories of forensic failure. My friends were so amused it was surprising that they didn't nickname me 'Grief Brief'. Perhaps unknown to me, my incarcerated clients did. Fortunately, the influx of work and pressures on my time became so great that I soon gave up court appearances and instructed a barrister, mainly Valerie, instead.

I suppose that I must have continued to enjoy a personal life but work and the development of the practice was so all-consuming that I have very little recollection of it. I went on a few dates but had no steady girlfriend during this period.

I embarked on a novel on the theme of two lawyers' lives, drawn on me and my own experiences, but ran out of steam (or time) by the end of Chapter 2. The foolscap Counsel's notebook containing these fragments remained forgotten in the bottom drawer of my desk and remained there long after I left Canning Town in 1961 to join my old friend Bryan Lipson in partnership in Central London. I brought my arrangements with Alan, Edmunds and Phillips to an end, bought out their share of the practice and we renamed the new firm Lipson Rumney and Co.

Over the years Bryan and I gave temporary employment and work experience to members of our families and children of friends and clients. One of these was Geoffrey Romney, my second cousin, who worked for us during long vacations whilst studying law at Oxford. We gave him a spell at Canning Town and during his time there, presumably riffling through my desk drawers, he came across my two aborted novels (written in 1958) and took it on himself to edit it. The hitherto blank cover of the notebook now bears Geoffrey's title page:

> *Two short stories by Boris Rumney*
> *Edited by Geoffrey Romney*
> *Probably Written in 1959*
> AS YET UNPUBLISHED

He also entitled the two sections '*The Assistant*' and '*A Long Way Off*'. In the latter I described the experience of Andrew, one of my two principal characters on the top deck of a bus in East London in the rush hour. I think there is much of me in Andrew as well as Tony Harper at that time.

> *The other passengers were manual workers, tired and spiritless after a day of heavy and repetitive work. Wearing grubby fawn raincoats, government surplus greatcoats or navy blue, thigh length 'shorties', almost invariably cloth capped, they sat slumped, huddled, withdrawn into themselves, smoking skinny, own rolled cigarettes, reading battered copies of the Daily Mirror or the Star. The heads of some were shrunk into their chests as they nodded and jerked in fitful doze. The bus was enveloped in a murky mist of damp and cigarette smoke as its main constituents. There was very little conversation but a constant chorus of rich bronchial coughing and hawking gave the bus a 'lived in' atmosphere.*

Andrew is also very conscious of the class gulf which exists between him and his fellow passengers.

> ...the truth was that Andrew feared physical contact with these men because he felt inadequate to their hardness, their grime, their roughness and their unlubricated speech; these were feelings and attitudes which had been inculcated in him since childhood and he had never been able to eradicate them in spite of his fervent left-wing views.

Smoke was everywhere in 1957 and 1958. The Clean Air Acts were not then yet fully in force. Smog and fog, smoke billowing from factory chimneys, power stations and steam trains. And cigarettes, pipes and cigars smoked on buses, trains (both steam and underground) and in restaurants, offices, theatres, cinemas and homes. You couldn't escape it. You took it for granted that everyone smoked. I didn't until I was twenty when I was seduced by one of Joy Barnett's un-tipped *Piccadilly* brand, as I rowed her by Hackney Marsh along the River Lea. Becoming a confirmed smoker was a gradual process but by the time I was working at Canning Town, I had become a twenty-a-day man. I described one of its helpful functions in *The Assistant*.

> *Tony Harper dictated his morning's work with great fluency, smoking all the time to provide a smokescreen for the occasions when he had to pause for the word that eluded him.*

46. BETTER LUCK NEXT TIME

Everyone deserves a second chance and, by chance, I was given one. It was New Year's Eve 1957 and I had been invited to two parties, one by Gay Nash, a friend of Michael, in Wimbledon and the other by Charlie Conway, an old LSE friend, in Camden Town. At that time, New Year's Day was an ordinary working day. New Year's Eve that year fell on a Tuesday. Camden Town was much nearer my home then Wimbledon and directly on the 653 trolleybus route and as I did not fancy getting home late and working the next day, I opted for Charlie's.

There was, I am sure, a darker motive at work in making that choice. Charlie was a modern man, ahead of his time sexually and the envy of all the men who knew him at the LSE. The story was that Charlie was living with a Swedish girl who was fitted up with a Dutch cap. Our fantasy of him enjoying anxiety-free sex-on-demand was almost too much for us to bear. I cannot recall if he was with the same girl by the end of 1957, but the thought must have been at the back of my mind that perhaps there would be at Charlie's party a girl similarly accoutred for me. In fact, the party was one of the dullest I have ever been to; only ten or so guests turned up and I left to catch the night bus home as soon after midnight as I could.

I met Michael a few days later. He, of course, had gone to Gay's party: great fun, lots of guests, plenty of girls, great food, limitless drink, dancing. Everyone stayed on until two or three in the morning. I did not know it at the time but Rona was at that party, and it was not until the following June that I had the great good fortune to redeem my lust-led error of judgment.

EPILOGUE

13th June 1958

Friday the 13th. Unlucky for some, lucky for me. This was the date on which I had gone to a party with Michael Goldman, just another party, so I wasn't expecting very much. Rona was there. We talked and danced. On the way home, I told Michael that we had made a date and added "This could be important". We were engaged by the end of the year and married the following September. This year, 2016, we celebrate our 57th anniversary. I had been yearning for the other, the missing bits in me, ever since, at the age of seventeen, on summer evenings I would wander off to the nearby copse in the hope of meeting the girl of my dreams. Rona of course was, and has remained, that girl. It was helpful that she turned out to be Jewish; her Anglican mother converted to Judaism in order to marry her father.

'This could be important'.

I had never said or even thought such a thing about the numerous girls I had met and been attracted to.

I think now that at some unconscious level I must have understood that with her I could heal my Jewish/English split and reject the horrifying yet seductive fleshpots of Jewish north-west London, with what I then experienced as its materialism and obsession with success, by making our home in south-east London.

For the first time in my life I felt a complete and ordinary member of the human race. Of course marriage was not a cure but it went a long way to healing the worst ravages of the splits. Sigmund Freud believed that a successful psychoanalytic treatment transformed *hysterical misery* into *ordinary unhappiness*. And post Rona, my transformation was from feelings of anomie and absence to being grounded in the normal ups and downs of life.

I am now in my late eighties. I retired from paid work ten years ago and for the first three, busied myself on professional and other committees, drafting codes of ethics, organising symposia and giving papers at conferences. That is in the past. I am now fully retired and like many of my contemporaries, experience myself as invisible, but more than that, irrelevant, in the sense that I have no power and make no impact on, or contribution to the world outside. Does that feel like a loss? On reflection, no. There is great freedom in irrelevance. Nothing is required or expected of you and you neither require nor expect anything from the world or anyone in it.

The writing of this memoir has faut de mieux led me to reappraise my life as I have called up and given words to the past and reacquainted myself with the boy and young man I was. There is much to dislike; my narcissism and self-absorption, possibly brought about by the loneliness and disruptions of my life. And to my own detriment, I was endlessly argumentative, cocky, bumptious, stubborn and tactless. But I also had some positive qualities; steadiness of purpose, loyalty and a resilience, demonstrated by my capacity to recover from setbacks and relaunch myself.

My life has been a long recovery from the malaise caused by the splits and nearly sixty years on, I am no longer the person of my memoir. Now I can greet that person and all the others who, often unwittingly, pierced my heart and mind, with feelings of love and sadness.

Printed in Great Britain
by Amazon